Fixing Bad UX Designs

Master proven approaches, tools, and techniques to make your user experience great again

Lisandra Maioli

BIRMINGHAM - MUMBAI

Fixing Bad UX Designs

Commissioning Editor: Merint Mathew
Acquisition Editor: Siddharth Mandal
Content Development Editor: Mohammed Yusuf Imaratwale
Technical Editor: Sushmeeta Jena
Copy Editor: Safis Editing
Project Coordinator: Hardik Bhinde
Proofreader: Safis Editing
Indexer: Rekha Nair
Graphics: Jason Monterio
Production Coordinator: Nilesh Mohite

First published: February 2018

Production reference: 1260218

Published by Packt Publishing Ltd.
Livery Place
35 Livery Street
Birmingham
B3 2PB, UK.

ISBN 978-1-78712-055-6

www.packtpub.com

To my father Waldemir Luis Maioli, who always encouraged me to write a book; to two of my favorite designers and friends, Leandro Varanda and Euler Araujo Silveira, who I love to work with; to Jill DaSilva, James Stables, and Marcelo Morais, who are my inspiration in UX; and to Dave Kearny, who introduced me as a UX blogger and who kindly accepted the mission to write the Foreword.

I dedicate this book to all these wonderful people and many others who support, help, inspire, and believe in me.

– Lisandra Maioli

`mapt.io`

Mapt is an online digital library that gives you full access to over 5,000 books and videos, as well as industry leading tools to help you plan your personal development and advance your career. For more information, please visit our website.

Why subscribe?

- Spend less time learning and more time coding with practical eBooks and Videos from over 4,000 industry professionals

- Improve your learning with Skill Plans built especially for you

- Get a free eBook or video every month

- Mapt is fully searchable

- Copy and paste, print, and bookmark content

PacktPub.com

Did you know that Packt offers eBook versions of every book published, with PDF and ePub files available? You can upgrade to the eBook version at `www.PacktPub.com` and as a print book customer, you are entitled to a discount on the eBook copy. Get in touch with us at `service@packtpub.com` for more details.

At `www.PacktPub.com`, you can also read a collection of free technical articles, sign up for a range of free newsletters, and receive exclusive discounts and offers on Packt books and eBooks.

Foreword

Many books talk about how user experience work can be done—assuming that there are no barriers, blockers, or stakeholders who prefer to hear their own voices over those of their users.

Not so this book.

Instead, Lisandra Maioli takes this challenge head on, introducing hundreds of tried-and-trusted tactics for designing great user experiences, along with the strategies needed to ensure that your users are heard in your organization. Implementing the ideas contained in these pages will allow you to affect real change.

It's no surprise that the wisdom contained in this book is so broad.

A decade of Lisandra's experience as a journalist and UX researcher includes working with start-ups and multinationals across three continents. Her real-world examples cover every area of UX—from user research to prototyping, data and analytics, marketing, team balance, and communication. Her experience means no topic of importance to a modern UX professional has been left untouched.

What this book leaves out is a single proscribed methodology for success. Instead, it gives you a powerful suite of processes and tools, explains their benefits in simple, accessible language, and combines them with practical real-world examples. It talks about when and how to use each process, but ultimately leaves you with control over which methodologies to use to solve the unique user problems your organization faces.

No work like this can be created without a passion for creating and improving remarkable user experiences. That passion has taken Lisandra from Brazil to Silicon Valley to Ireland, where I was fortunate enough to work with her, and onward to the Netherlands. It has taken her from journalism to marketing, and from marketing to her eventual home of UX—the only place where Lisandra's unique ability to connect users with meaningful solutions shines through.

If you care about making your customers' voices the most powerful voice in your organization, then there is no doubt that you should study the words contained herein. It has everything you need to ensure that your customers are heard, appreciated, and understood.

Study well, grow wise, and challenge yourself to be better.

Dave Kearney
Founder / CEO of FluidUI.com

Contributors

About the author

Lisandra Maioli is an Italian-Brazilian journalist with certification in UX (General Assembly LA), post-graduate Diploma in Marketing (UC Berkeley), in Digital Marketing (UCLA), in Interactive Digital Medias (Senac SP), and in Digital-Cultural Journalism (PUC SP). She has about 2 decades of international and multidisciplinary experience in Digital Communications in different roles, working for different companies and clients based in Brazil, the US, Italy, Ireland, China, Germany, and the Netherlands.

Many thanks to all those who agreed to have their images used in this book. Thanks to Brian Sheridan, Peter W. Szabo, and Basil Miller for the great and honest feedback. Thanks to Packt Pub and to the whole team involved, especially Siddharth Mandal, Mohammed Yusuf, and Sushmeeta Jena for the patience and partnership. To you all, my deep gratitude!

About the reviewers

Basil Miller is the cofounder of Devlight and an Ivano-Frankivsk based leading Android developer. Since 2014, Android developers all over the world keep spectating his progress and using free products developed in the role of an open source Android UI widgets provider. Those libraries have reached the top of the popular trend charts kept for a long time. Being a cofounder and developer, Basil is able and willing to collaborate in work on the new business projects and start-ups. Also, it is easy to contact Basil in order to involve him into the projects as a mobile development consultant.

> *Thank you to Packt Publishing and Sheejal Shah for involving me in this project. The second time you have given me a chance to use my skills in the correct source and boost myself in different directions.*

> *Thank you, author, for deciding to write this book. I hope everyone will read it and it will improve their daily UX.*

Brian Sheridan is an expert in UX research. He is an associate editor of UXPA and writes on UX among other things for the Fluid UI blog. He is a lecturer at Maynooth University where he was a supervisor on major research projects for over 10 years. He is part of the team at Fluid UI which helps users to create wireframes and prototypes in minutes and unlock their creativity.

Peter is a passionate user experience designer, researcher, frequent conference speaker, and best-selling author. As the principal of far Zenith, he has over nine years of success in UX, having worked for big brands, such as Amazon, Tesco, Virgin Atlantic, HSBC, or British Gas. He was also leading the UX team at the world's biggest online gambling company—The Stars Group Inc. If you want to learn more, visit his UX blog—the Kaizen-UX.com. Oh, and before we forget, he loves cats!

Packt is searching for authors like you

If you're interested in becoming an author for Packt, please visit `authors.packtpub.com` and apply today. We have worked with thousands of developers and tech professionals, just like you, to help them share their insight with the global tech community. You can make a general application, apply for a specific hot topic that we are recruiting an author for, or submit your own idea.

Table of Contents

Preface

The challenge that most UX designers and product owners face is to ensure that the UX of products and services is user friendly. Some common issues are simplicity, navigation, appearance, maintenance, and so on. In this book, we will address all these issues through real examples and main overall problems and solutions on accessibility, conversion, content, and UI, just to name a few. You will learn to simplify, fix, and enhance some common, real-world application designs.

As you progress through the book, you will learn about the information architecture, usability testing, iteration, UX refactoring, and other similar concepts. You will also learn about UX design tools with the projects covered in the book. By the end of the book, you will be armed with the knowledge to fix bad designs and ensure great customer satisfaction for their applications.

By understanding business and user needs, you will be able to focus on what exactly should be fixed. It is important to have a clear idea of what the problems are that your UX efforts aim to solve and understand what are the solutions the company provides. With the UX issues identified and project challenges defined and agreed, you will need to turn these findings from user research into potential solutions, listing assumptions and presenting the ideas to the stakeholders in a clear and effective way.

In the second part of the book, you will see specific UX issues, mostly common, and how to fix them through different methodologies and using a variety of tools. You will learn how to increase conversion with UX, how to use UI elements and content for better communication, improving IA for better navigation, besides considering accessibility as part of the UX and also thinking about user experience in public environments.

By the end of the book, you will know how to create better documentation that communicates well with other teams, and also, you will know how to test and validate the potential design solutions before the implementation. Closing the full UX circle, you will be confident to measure the results of the UX fixes and prove to the stakeholders how the focus on UX impacts the success of the product/service and how important it is to keep investing in fixing bad UX Designs.

Who this book is for

This book is mainly for UX professionals, but also for product owners, project managers, entrepreneurs, and even designers and developers who would like to learn how to solve problems with the existing UX design.

What this book covers

Chapter 1, *Understanding UX and Its Importance*, introduces you to the importance of UX for the success of services and products. You also understood why UX matters for your product or service, what ROI, Metrics, and KPIs of UX are, and what is the importance of getting stakeholders involved. Once it is clear to the company and stakeholders the importance of applying UX to the services and/or products offered by the company and how it can impact business in itself, it is time to further understand what the needs of stakeholders and users are. This next phase of the project will help you define the MVP of the project better and focus on what really matters to the user and understand how to fix bad UX designs.

Chapter 2, *Identifying UX Issues – UX Methodologies*, shows how to identify UX issues and understand the project challenges by interviewing stakeholders, using different user research methodologies, doing comparative competitor analysis, and designing user journeys and writing problem statements. For each project, you might use a combination of different methodologies in order to find the UX issues. Although it can be interesting to plan which methods will be used to ensure that they will be accommodated into the budget, it is common to feel like you need to use other methods after each test.

Chapter 3, *Exploring Potential UX Solutions*, presents the importance of putting the findings together in order to analyze them and start thinking about the potential solutions. By having these findings organized, it is easier to work on design potential solutions, starting with paper sketches, moving to wireframes (low, mid, and hi-fi) and to clickable prototypes, which will be tested, validated, and iterated.

Chapter 4, *Increasing Conversion with UX*, focuses on how to fix UX issues that are dropping the conversion of a website or app, impacting the business results. You will learn how to identify conversion issues by doing a UX Analysis, such as quantitative/data analysis and deeply understanding the users by performing research, interview, and usability tests. Besides testing solutions to fix the issues you have identified, you will also see practical examples of how to fix UX issues by considering to build responsive and accessible websites, improving loading time, saving time for your user, and following design trends.

Chapter 5, *Using UI and Content for Better Communication*, presents the importance of content and UI for a great user experience and how these elements, when badly designed, can create big issues for a clear communication between your website, app, product, or service with your user. I hope you could notice how all these aspects and elements, such as hierarchy, typography, iconography, color, copy, and such, are interconnected and influence each other. Although content strategy and text creation can be the job of copywriter or the choice of color scheme, typography, iconography can be the job of a UI designer, as a UXer, you should influence those decisions and ensure that all of them will allow great user experience. Understanding these aspects in depth will help you identify UX issues impacted by these elements and be able to make wise suggestions on how to fix them.

Chapter 6, *Considering Accessibility As Part of the UX*, focuses on Accessibility and its importance and presents how to consider people with any kind of disability also as part of your target groups. You will learn how to evaluate and analyze apps and websites to find whether they follow the W3C standards for accessibility and how to fix UX issues related to it. You will also see a few cases not only from the digital and online universe but also examples from the physical world and can understand that accessibility is an important topic for not only designers but for everyone who creates products and services for real people in the real world.

Chapter 7, *Improving the Physical Experiences*, presents that it's also possible to improve the user experience or fix UX issues in any service or environment where we have user interaction, although it is more common to think about websites and mobile apps when we talk about UX. You will find that there are *Norman Doors* issues everywhere waiting for great design solutions, keeping the user in the center of the project, from ATMs, elevator panel, boarding passes, bus stops, and car panels to public toilets.

Chapter 8, *Improving IA for Better Navigation*, explains what is IA and how to improve navigability and findability using IA methodologies such as Card sorting, tree testing, taxonomy, and such. You will see how important it is to label and categorize the content in order to help the users find what they need and accomplish their task with no problem, in an easy and intuitive way based on their mental models, besides considering the context and the content. In this chapter, you will find IA tools and deliverables such as task flow, navigation schema, content inventory, navigation flow, flowchart, sitemaps, and content tree.

Chapter 9, *Prototyping and Validating UX Solutions*, presents the process of testing, validating, and refining UX solutions through wireframes, paper sketches, and different level of prototypes (conceptual, lo-fi, mid-fi, and hi-fi) before delivering the final wireframes and maps to the dev and design teams as a good practice. You will also saw a few options for tools to help you prototype and run tests (online, in person, moderated, and unmoderated), as well as how to run Tree-Testing to validate the IA improvements.

Chapter 10, *Implementing UX Solutions*, presents a few examples of how to create documentation to a great communication with other teams that are involved in the project and will be responsible for the implementation. You will learn how to create clear and digestible documentation and be able to communicate well with the teams responsible for the UI design and develop/implement the UX fixes.

Chapter 11, *Measuring UX Solutions*, goes deeper into UX metrics, KPIs, and ROI. You will learn how to verify that all your efforts were made in the right direction; it is important to measure the impact of these changes. By understanding what you are measuring in order to validate the changes you made to fix UX issues, you can demonstrate to the stakeholders the value of investing in UX. Besides deciding which metrics and KPIs really matter for your project, we will also look at different methodologies for qualitative and quantitative approaches.

Appendix, *Keeping Up to Date*, Working with UX requires you to keep yourselves constantly updated, find and try new tools, discuss with other professionals, and so on. In this appendix, you will find a few links to great references, sources, and discussion groups to help you in this mission.

To get the most out of this book

In order to get the most out of this book, it's preferable that you have some experience developing products or services, besides knowing the basics of UX. It might be good as well if you have some knowledge in using designing tools. Although this book will show you a few great tools to be used, this is not a book focused on tool or software tutorials. Be prepared to use not only online tools, but papers, sticky notes, pens, paper templates, canvas, whiteboards, and drawable walls. Last but not least, be open for a more business approach of getting the best results of fixing bad UX centered on your user.

Download the color images

We also provide a PDF file that has color images of the screenshots/diagrams used in this book. You can download it here: `http://www.packtpub.com/sites/default/files/downloads/FixingbadUXDesigns_ColorImages.pdf`.

Conventions used

There are a number of text conventions used throughout this book.

`CodeInText`: Indicates code words in text, database table names, folder names, filenames, file extensions, pathnames, dummy URLs, user input, and Twitter handles. Here is an example: "Mount the downloaded `WebStorm-10*.dmg` disk image file as another disk in your system."

Bold: Indicates a new term, an important word, or words that you see onscreen. For example, words in menus or dialog boxes appear in the text like this. Here is an example: "Select **System info** from the **Administration** panel."

 Warnings or important notes appear like this.

 Tips and tricks appear like this.

Get in touch

Feedback from our readers is always welcome.

General feedback: Email `feedback@packtpub.com` and mention the book title in the subject of your message. If you have questions about any aspect of this book, please email us at `questions@packtpub.com`.

Errata: Although we have taken every care to ensure the accuracy of our content, mistakes do happen. If you have found a mistake in this book, we would be grateful if you would report this to us. Please visit `www.packtpub.com/submit-errata`, selecting your book, clicking on the Errata Submission Form link, and entering the details.

Piracy: If you come across any illegal copies of our works in any form on the Internet, we would be grateful if you would provide us with the location address or website name. Please contact us at `copyright@packtpub.com` with a link to the material.

If you are interested in becoming an author: If there is a topic that you have expertise in and you are interested in either writing or contributing to a book, please visit `authors.packtpub.com`.

Reviews

Please leave a review. Once you have read and used this book, why not leave a review on the site that you purchased it from? Potential readers can then see and use your unbiased opinion to make purchase decisions, we at Packt can understand what you think about our products, and our authors can see your feedback on their book. Thank you!

For more information about Packt, please visit `packtpub.com`.

1
Understanding UX and its Importance

The challenge that most UX designers and product owners face is ensuring that the UX products and services are user friendly. Some common issues are simplicity, navigation, appearance, and maintenance, and so on. In this book, we will address all these issues using real examples, and examine the main overall problems and solutions regarding accessibility, conversion, content, and the UI, just to name a few issues. You will learn to simplify, fix, and enhance some common, real-world application designs.

As you progress through the book, you will learn about the information architecture, usability testing, iteration, UX refactoring, and other similar concepts. You will also learn some interesting UX design tools with the projects covered in the book. By the end of the book, you will be armed with the knowledge to fix bad designs and to ensure great customer satisfaction with your applications.

In this chapter, you will learn the following:

- UX is present everywhere
- Bad UX is bad for your business
- The ROI of fixing bad UX design
- Getting stakeholders involved
- Metrics and KPIs

UX is present everywhere

In his book, *The Design of Everyday Things*, Donald A. Norman tells us about his constant trouble with opening doors:

> *"I push doors that are meant to be pulled, pull doors that should be pushed, and walk into doors that neither pull nor push, but slide. "*

He says, explaining his frustration. This is one of the examples that he presents in his book to illustrate how a poor design can have a negative effect on user experience:

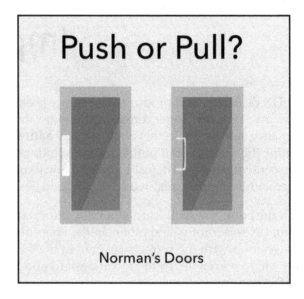

Known as **Norman's Doors**, we can see examples of these misleading designs everywhere: remote controls, sink taps, buttons, elevator panels, utensils, home appliances, and a number of other examples of how poor design has been causing day-to-day confusion.

We are constantly playing our role as users, having positive or negative experiences, not only when using products, but also offline or brick and mortar services such as navigating in a supermarket, using ATM machines, searching for our gate at the airport, even using toilets can be challenging. And every experience online or offline can be designed or redesigned to be positive. It doesn't matter if it is an app, a website, or a Norman Door.

Just to give an idea of how a poor design can impact different aspects and environments of our day-to-day life, a recent survey by the Japan Restroom Industry Association showed that foreign tourists often have a hard time of understanding the many and different controls of Japanese toilets, making the experience of using the toilet more complicated than they thought: 25% of them confirmed that they did not know how to use a Japanese-style toilet. Alarmingly, *I pressed the emergency button was a similarly common*, expressed by 8.8% of foreigners. Concerned about being more tourist-friendly for the 2020 Tokyo Olympic Games, Japan's Restroom Industry Association (a group of 10 companies that include Panasonic and Toshiba) has agreed to create a set of standardized pictograms:

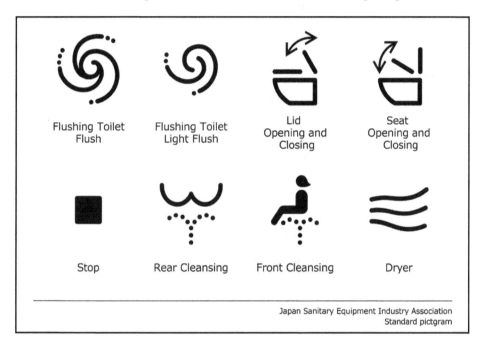

Image source: http://www.sanitary-net.com/global/pictgram/

As you can see, user experience does not only apply to digital applications, but it can also be seen in simple, everyday activities. It is the main job of a UX designer to turn all these negative experiences, as results of a poor design, into positive experiences.

Bad UX is bad for your business

A badly designed experience can not only be frustrating to the user, but can also highly impact a business, especially when we talk about online businesses. To give you an idea and statistical evidence to demonstrate this statement to your clients or boss, a report by the Baymard Insititute shows that a better design and checkout flow experience could have improved about 35% of ecommerce conversion, in other words, by fixing small UX issues, companies could saved billions of dollars.

It is interesting to closely analyze the study by Baymard (2016) and note that most of the reasons for the abandonment of a business are related somehow to the whole user/client experience:

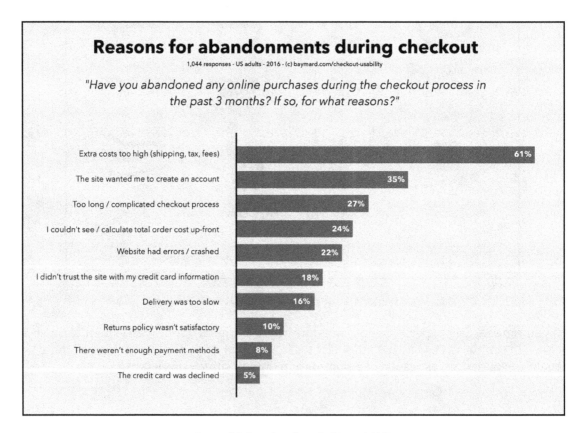

From a study by Baymard.com (Last updated: January 9, 2017)

The study *The App Attention Span* (2014)—by AppDynamics in partnership with the **Institute of Management Studies** (**IMS**) at Goldsmiths, University of London—demonstrates that 90% of users confirmed that they stopped using an app because of poor performance, and 86% of them deleted or uninstalled an app because they found problems with its functionality or design. According to the *Customer Experience Report* (2010) by RightNow, 82% of customers have left a company because of a bad customer experience.

Other studies show the negative impact of a bad experience: About 40% of users might abandon a website if it takes more than three seconds to load, while 79% will search for another website in order to be able to complete their task.

Going beyond these figures, a bad user experience can impact not only on the customer's relationship with the companies, but also on the employee's performance. In 2013, the Avon Products company reported that it had discontinued a $125 million mobile software development project after running a pilot in Canada, which showed that the iPad version was too hard to use, resulting in many sales reps quitting the company.

The ROI of fixing bad UX design

Fixing a bad design can have an incredibly positive impact on businesses, as reported by Jim Ross, Senior User Experience Architect at D3 Infragistics Services on the study *The Business Value of User Experience*; it doesn't matter whether the users are employees or customers, a good user experience can help companies not only increase revenue and save money, but also, a bad user experience can seriously impact satisfaction, costs, and sales.

The software development agency On3 agrees with this fact when it points out that companies were able to increase their revenue by 37% thanks to their highly positive user experience:

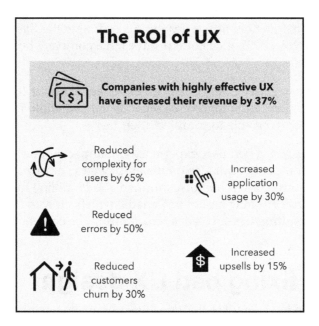

The business value of user experience study by On3

According to an article by Steve Olenski, published in Forbes, if you design a better user experience, you can boost your user retention. The author reminds us of research by Harvard Business School, which says that it is possible to increase profit by at least 25% by using UX design techniques to satisfy users and boost customer retention. It has a really significant impact on a retention strategy.

This Harvard Business study also shows that a subscription-based business client who ranks the experience as *poorest* will only have a 43% chance of continuing to be a member a year or so later. On the other hand, members who scored their experiences in the top two tiers would definitely have a 74% chance of remaining a member for at least another year, as you can see in the following chart:

The better the user experience, the greater the chance of remaining a member for at least another year

In the same study, researchers found that, among thousands of customers studied, the ones who had the best experiences in the past might spend about 140% more in comparison to those who had the poorest experience previously:

Customer who had a good previous experience are willing to spend more

Also in the study *Business Value of User Experience* (2014), we see that a positive customer experience will increase by over 14% the customers' willingness to pay for what you are offering online by over 14%. It also might reduce their likelihood of their of switching brands by over 15% and increase by over 16% the likelihood of their recommending your products.

The Baymard Institute has reported that a better checkout design can increase the conversion of the average large-sized ecommerce site by over 35%, which means that about $260 billion worth of lost orders in the US and EU could be retain with a better design and checkout-flow experience.

That a positive experience can impact the business was also reported by other companies, studies: the study *Customer Experience Impact Report* by Oracle (2011), for example, shows that 86% of customers will pay more for a better customer experience. American Express has found a similar result in their customer service survey in 2011, which says that 70% of Americans were willing to spend an average of 13% more with companies that they feel provide excellent customer service.

This direction, there is a famous case known as *the $300 million button*, in which a major ecommerce company has increased their revenue by 45% by just changing a button on their checkout process, as suggested by UX specialist Jared Spool. He helped the company make more than $300 million by making a small UX fix.

In order to find a proper solution, Spool and his team conducted usability tests that showed that the issue was not exactly in the design itself or even not the form of how it was designed, but the representation of it to the users: New customers were feeling suspicious about the registration form and felt that it was a way to add their contact details to the ecommerce email marketing scheme. Also, a great number of the returning customers couldn't remember their login and/or password, and so they either abandoned the cart or created a new account, which made 45% of users create multiple accounts.

The solution found by Spoll was simple: Just replace the **Register** button with a **Continue** button, along with a simple message: *You do not need to create an account to make purchases on our site. Simply click* **Continue** *to proceed to checkout. To make your future purchases even faster, you can create an account during checkout*. With this change, they helped the company generate $15 million-worth of extra purchases in the first month, and $300 million in one year, representing a 45% increase in purchases. It is definitely one of the best illustrative cases that you can use to convince sceptical clients that UX can highly improve conversion. You can be inspired and create variations of the Spool version focused on your user experience:

Have a profile?

Sign in to enjoy faster, easier checkout

E-mail

Password

Password is case sensitive

Forgot your password?

Checkout

No profile yet?

No problem! You'll be able to create a profile during checkout

Checkout as a guest

Adding a button, based on user feedback, increased sales by millions

Getting stakeholders involved

The cost of investing in a great UX should be clear to your company, and, as we saw before, there are many different studies to show it. By not focusing on UX, your company can decrease sales, increase the number of dissatisfied customers, and disengage employees. As we saw before, there are loads of studies to demonstrate the importance of UX and they should be used to not only convince your company about that, but also to get stakeholders involved.

As explained by Smartsheet.com in their article *What Is Stakeholder Analysis and Mapping and How Do You Do It Effectively?*, you should consider all the interested parties in a project as stakeholders, which means not only everyone who might affect and also influence the project itself, but also everyone who might be influenced by it.

In the book, *Articulating Design Decisions: Communicate with Stakeholders, Keep Your Sanity, and Deliver the Best User Experience*, the author Tom Greever explains the stakeholder needs and the importance of gaining their support. The summary of his book is that, as in any project, designers will need the stakeholder recognition of the value of fixing UX issues and the importance of investing in these tasks. By not having such support, the project might risk losing funding or even never going beyond the prototyping stage.

To ensure that stakeholders are involved can be one of the major success factors in integrating UX practices into services or product development processes and organizations, as pointed out in the paper *Stakeholder Involvement: A Success Factor for Achieving Better UX Integration*. One example of how important it is to get the stakeholders involved was mentioned by Adaptive Path in the study, *Leveraging Business Value: How ROI Changes User Experience*: After falling behind their competition online, Bank of America, a design team, in collaboration with a product manager, identified that customers were having a hard time completing the online enrollment process. *The design team led a collaborative process that included stakeholders from IT, legal, product, and other departments, and was able to increase the yield by 45%.*

It is important to know that the top three reasons projects get derailed are poor communication, lack of clarity, and expectation management amongst stakeholders, as pointed out by NNGroup. However, although it is easy to understand the importance of building stakeholder buy-in, it is something hard to do well, because of lack of knowledge, politics, time, poverty, or even lack of interest. The good news is that there are ways to build strong, mutually supportive relationships with your stakeholders that are tried and tested, before and we will talk about these in this book.

But when exactly should we get them involved? A panel of UX experts, organized by UXmatters, has discussed in one of their editions ways of involving stakeholders at different stages of a project in one of their books. One of the panellists, Dana Chisnell—principal consultant at UsabilityWorks and co-author of *Handbook of Usability Testing*—pointed out that we should bring in stakeholders as soon as you know who they are.

In an article published on the Xwerx blog, the company's senior UX analyst Murray Nolan reminds us that there's often a misunderstanding at the start of a UX project. In the article, Nolan mentions Xwerx's Head of UX, John Mooney, who reminds us that some stakeholders may believe that they already know what their users want and need, besides having no clue of what UX is and how UX can help their business. Nolan also mentions the author of Lean UX, Jeff Gothelf, statement:

> *"By creating interactions between product managers, developers, QA engineers, designers, and marketers, you put everybody on the same page and on the same level."*

Metrics and KPI's

The interesting thing is that having all the stakeholders' support and collaboration can also accelerate the UX process, and consequently determine the success of the project. To be able to measure it, you will need to define the metrics and KPIs with the stakeholders in order to demonstrate the results, bringing us back to the matter of how we show the ROI of the UX.

The **KPI's** (**key performance indicators**), or ways to measure performance, will help you to demonstrate the success of all the UX issues that were fixed or changed. They can be different indicators and come from different sources, such as user research (usability testing, surveys, structured interviews, heuristic evaluations, card sorting, heat maps, A/B tests, and so on) and/or analytics, as soon as task success rate, time on task, page views, clicks, taps, and so on:

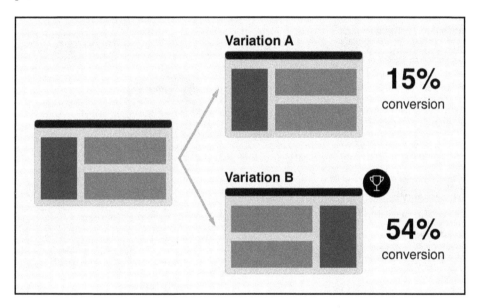

An example of an A/B test result

You should also consider more *business*-focused goals and indicators, which means any user touchpoint, such as customer acquisition cost, which is a growth MKT metric; average ticket, which can be impacted by increasing the conversion rate; and also sales data, churn rate, lead generation stats, active users, support calls, basket abandonment, subscribers, returning visitors, and so on:

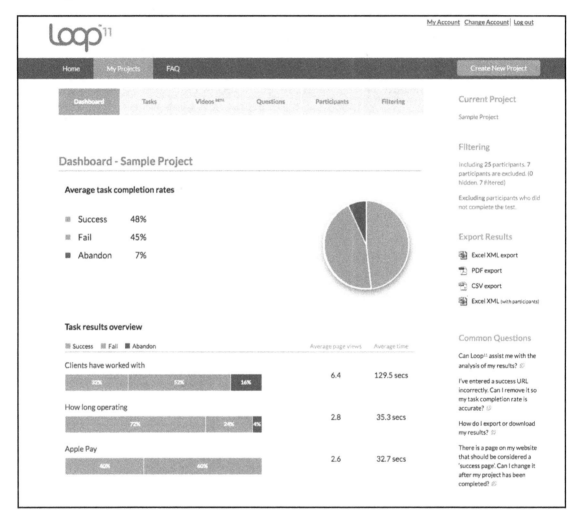

The online tool Loop11.com lets you make remote and unmoderated user testing

Besides it being important to define KPI's that you will be able to measure, you should also create a framework to track all these metrics. For example, you can create a framework for defining tasks, users, and metrics, and then measure before and after making changes:

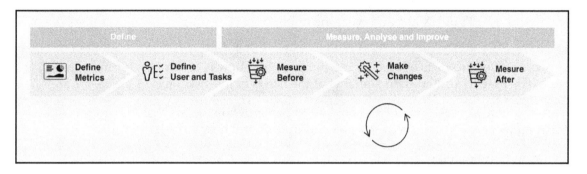

Framework to evaluate and improve the user experience presented by Jeff Sauro on his blog post for MeasuringU

To be able to define these metrics, you will need to understand the company's business goals, direction, and objectives. Having these definitions will help you to align the project objectives to the UX strategy and focus on what you should fix to help the company reach these goals.

It is important to keep in mind that designing an effective user experience requires an understanding of the needs of both the business and users in order to designing a solution that meets them. By understanding the business goals and user needs, it will help you to find exactly what you should fix on the bad UX design (which is what we will see in the following chapters):

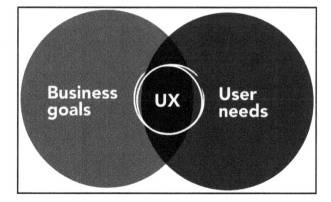

Summary

In this chapter, you were introduced to the importance of UX for the success of services and products. You were also shown why UX matters for your product or service, what the ROI, metrics, and KPI's of UX are, and what the importance of getting stakeholders involved is.

Once it is clear to the company and stakeholders as to the importance of applying UX to the services and/or products offered by the company and how it can impact business in and of itself, it is time to further understand what the needs of the stakeholders and users are.

This next phase of the project will help you to better define the MVP of the project, and focus on what really matters to the user and understand how to fix bad UX designs.

In the next few chapters, you will learn how to identify UX issues, explore, validate, implement, and measure UX solutions, as well as learn how to overcome UX challenges, such as increase conversion, improve UI and content, consider accessibility, improve the user experience in public environments, and reorganize IA for better navigation. Enjoy the journey!

2
Identifying UX Issues – UX Methodologies

By understanding business and user needs, it will be possible to focus on what exactly should be fixed. It is important to have a clear idea of what the problems are that your UX efforts aim to solve and understand what the solutions are that the company provides.

Keep in mind that anything that is preventing your users from accomplishing the task on your site, app, service, or product will result in a poor experience and will make it difficult for your business to deliver the solutions to your customer.

As we saw in `Chapter 1`, *Understanding UX and Its Importance*, a bad user experience can result in serious problems for your business. In this chapter, you will learn how to identify UX issues and understand the project challenges by:

- Identifying who are your stakeholders and their needs
- Identifying who are your users are, and their needs
- Doing competitive comparative analysis
- Understanding the user journey and finding touchpoints
- Defining what are the problems and the project goals/challenges
- Using UX researching/discovering methodologies

Identifying stakeholders and their needs

Identifying the stakeholders and their needs should be one of your tasks. Even if you believe that you already know enough about it, either because you have been working for the company for a while, or because you have already gathered this information in another way, it is always worth revalidating it. The company's strategy may change from time to time, as well as the stakeholders' view of the product or service, which will necessarily impact your design decisions.

> *"Empathy is a big buzzword in UX right now. There are books and blog posts espousing the idea that if designers can develop true empathy for users, then they'll build better applications. That's true, but what about stakeholders? Designers need to empathise with product owners, business analysts, and even executives too, if they hope to get the support they need for their projects to succeed."*

Prioritization map

Another way to identify the stakeholders is to add them in a prioritization map. On the website servicedesigntoolkit.org, you can find a template to help you to organize the stakeholders from the most to the least directly involved:

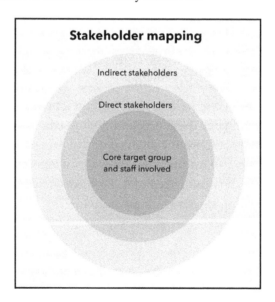

RACI matrix

The first step will be identifying the stakeholders. The larger the organization and project, the more stakeholders there may be, and the harder they may be to find. A great suggestion is starting from a responsibility assignment matrix, also known as an RACI chart, which is a project management tool to identify who should be responsible, accountable, consulted, and informed:

R **Responsible**
- Who is/will be doing this task?
- Who is assigned to work on this task?

A **Accountable**
- Who is going to approve/not approve it?
- Who has the authority to take decision?

C **Consulted**
- Anyone who can tell me more about it?
- Any stakeholders already identified?

I **Informed**
- Anyone whose work depends on this task?
- Who has to be kept updated about the progress?

You can use different formats to build your RACI chart, such as a spreadsheet (probably the easiest format). On the `racichart.org` page, you can download their template. This is an example of how this would be filled:

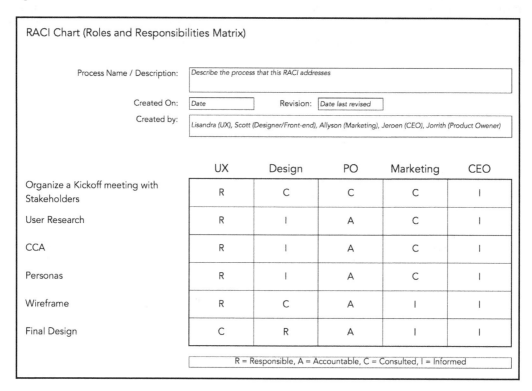

You can also add the tasks in detail or adapt the idea to other formats, such as a spreadsheet, for example:

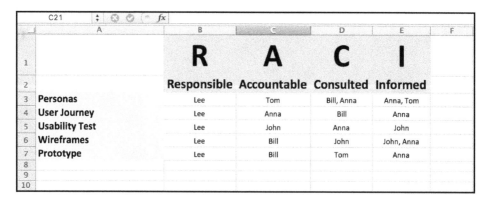

Stakeholder matrix

Another option suggested by the website `mindtools.com` is a matrix to classify the stakeholders regarding their power over the work that you are doing, and their interest in this work. In other words, it is a graphical tool used in this task is a map with two axes: power (vertical) and interest (horizontal). The purpose of this tool is to identify stakeholders to determine what strategies will be used to manage them. For example, imagine a project redesigning an e-commerce platform, who could be the stakeholders? Add the stakeholders to the map according to the parameters of the analysis that you already did, as in this diagram:

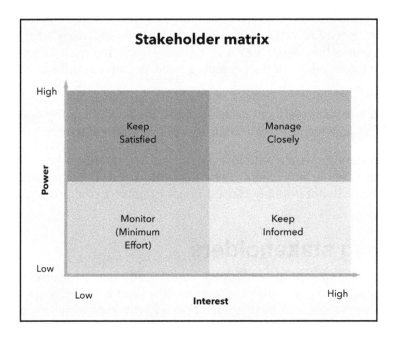

The first step is to look at the **Manage Closely** box and define who are the people who have high power and high interest in the project. These are the people we must manage closely and that usually involve sponsors, top management, directors, and so on. That is, people who need to be always talking, identifying resistances, and engaging, in order to keep ourselves on the same page regarding expectations and needs for the project's completion.

The second step is to look at the **Keep Satisfied** chart and identify who has high power and low interest. In this framework, we can include those people who will not participate so actively in the meetings, conversations, and definitions of the project, but must be engaged and satisfied with their definitions and progress, as they have the power to decide whether or not to go forward. We must take special care of them so that there are no unexpected obstacles in the future that might impact delivery.

The third step is to look at the **Keep Informed** chart, where people with high interest and low power will be. We include in this table the final clients, users, people who will use what is being *built* in their project and who have the power to influence the stakeholders of the preceding table (**Manage Closely**).

If something is not agreed and these people are not informed about what is being done in the project, the moment they use it they may be dissatisfied and may communicate this dissatisfication to the members of the preceding table, negatively influencing the future of the product.

Impacting this picture negatively can deconstruct all the good planning done with the **Manage Closely** table, which can lead to the loss of both frames at once.

The last step is to identify people with low power and low interest who will be in the **Monitor** box. These people may exhibit some discomfort and resistance and will need to be monitored, but they will not possibly cause a major problem to the project.

Interviewing stakeholders

Now that you have the stakeholders mapped, you should organize interviewing them. Keep in mind that stakeholders can reveal assumptions and knowledge gaps, technical requirements or restrictions, and tacit business/content requirements that can be essential for the project. A document by Oracle about stakeholders interviews focused on UX suggests that we should keep in mind that stakeholders are not substitutes for primary user research, but we should not rule out the importance of talking with them. These interviews will help us to frame our questions for users.

Besides previously knowing each of the stakeholders who will be interviewed, you should prepare a script to guide you. At the very least, have a list of topics to discuss and at the most, have a specific list of questions. It is important to keep in mind that you must be prepared, but it should still feel like a conversation. Consider sending questions or topics in advance. It is important to make the stakeholder more comfortable about the process and allow them to prepare a little. You can use the interview checklist suggested by Kim Goodwin, the author of designing for the Digital Age. The UXApprentice website also has prepared suggestions for questions to ask in the stakeholder interview, which you can find here: `uxapprentice.com/resources/stakeholder-interview-template/`.

Try to plan at least 45 minutes for each interview. A good suggestion from *Ten Guidelines for Stakeholder Interviews*, by the UXmatters website, is to leave at least 30 minutes between interviews and also limit an interview to just three or four major topics. It is crucial to listen carefully and not ask leading questions and be watchful about assumptions and bias. The interviews should help you to raise what would be the *Must Have, Nice to Have,* and *Not Sure* (or *Out of scope*) for the project. However, take care to not talk about solutions, features, implementation details, or other details such as colors and typefaces. You will want to understand the company culture, see what they know and think about the users's needs, identify problems, and set goals. Don't ask for solutions or take their ideas as final solutions, don't forget that you are designing for the *real users*, not for the stakeholders. Clarify answers you don't understand and be attentive to inconsistent information between different stakeholders. It might be a good idea to organize workshops to bring them together in order to have everyone on the same page.

You can also take advantage of all these meetings with the stakeholders to explain to them what UX is and what the purpose of the project is. This will make not only what you are trying to accomplish and solve clear to them, but also it will make them feel part of the process and also responsible for the solution. You might find suspicious or sceptical stakeholders. The more you educate them about the UX work, the more they will work in partnership with you and help the whole process be much smoother. It is also crucial to get them involved during the process as much as you can.

By the end of all these interviews, you might have a list of a few main issues that the company has been facing that might be affected by a bad user experience, such as high bounce rate, low conversion, low registration, lack of engagement, low number of subscriptions, high cart abandonment rate, and so on. Frequently, the issues raised by the stakeholders can be only symptoms that you will understand more deeply when you start doing user research. Make sure to organize and document all these takeaways.

Understanding users and their needs

Remember that designing an effective user experience requires an understanding of the needs of both the business and users, and designing a solution that meets them. So far, you should understand what the business goals are for your UX project. Now, it's time to understand the project from the user's point of view.

Make sure to have listed all the problems (and symptoms) raised during your stakeholder interviews. I like to have them on post-it notes on my wall. In this way, I can group and regroup them in order to find the main issues and problems that I have to check out. You will probably notice that during the user research, you might find other problems or find out that problems listed before were actually symptoms of another problem. For example, the high cart abandonment rate might be a symptom of difficulty in finding the next steps for a checkout process. You will find this out during your investigation.

Investigation

There are many different tools and methodologies out there that will help you to find UX issues. The ones you will use depend on which problems you want to find or deeply understand, besides time and budget. You might need to use more than one methodology and combine them in order to validate or refute assumptions.

Heuristic evaluation

Although we cannot consider ourselves as the end-users, we can start with heuristic evaluation. Developed by usability consultant Jakob Nielsen in collaboration with Rolf Molich in 1990, this methodology has the main goal of identifying any problems associated with the design of user interfaces quickly. They are called *heuristics* because they are broad rules of thumb and not specific usability guidelines.

Here are the Jakob Nielsen's 10 general principles for interaction design:

- **Visibility of system status**
  This means that you need to make sure that the interface always tells the user what is going on, that is, all actions need instant feedback to guide you copy.
- **Relation between the system interface and the real world**
  Do not use system words, which do not make sense to the user. All system communication needs to be contextualized to the user, and be consistent with the so-called user mental model.

- **Freedom and control of the user**
Facilitate *emergency exits* to the user, allowing undo or redo actions on the system to return to the previous point, for when the user is lost or in unexpected situations.

- **Consistency**
Speak the same language all the time, and never identify the same action with different icons or words. Treat similar things in the same way, making it easier to identify for the user.

- **Prevention of errors**
In the free translation of Nielsen's own words, *Even better than a good error message is a careful design that can prevent such errors*. For example, definitive actions such as deletions or requests can be accompanied by a checkbox or a confirmation message.

- **Recognition instead of remembrance**
Avoid triggering user memory all the time, causing each action to be reviewed mentally before it is executed. Allow the interface to provide context-sensitive help, and information that can guide user actions-that is, the system dialogues with the user.

- **Flexibility and efficiency of use**
The system needs to be easy for lay users, yet flexible enough to become agile for power users. This flexibility can be achieved with the permission of shortcut keys, for example. In the case of websites, use of masks and tabbed browsing in forms are other examples.

- **Aesthetics and minimalist design**
Avoid texts and design talk that are more than the user needs to know. The *dialogues* of the system need to be simple, direct, and natural, only present at the times when they are needed.

- **Help users recognize, diagnose, and fix errors**
The system error messages should have a clear and simple wording that, instead of intimidating the user with the error, indicate a constructive output or possible solution.

- **Help and documentation**
Good design should avoid the need for help in using the system as much as possible. Still, a good set of documentation and help should be used to guide the user in case of doubt. It should be visible, easily accessed, and a search tool should be offered in the help.

It can be done iteratively, that, in several phases of the product, from its *paper phase* to the final product. However, it has much more value in the beginning and in the intermediate stages, raising many trivial problems, before testing with users and discovering the less trivial ones.

The *output/deliverable* is a simple list of problems identified. Each has a severity associated with it (for example, slight, serious, very serious), which allows the definition of implementation priorities.

Nielsen recommends that the analysis be done by three to five evaluators who are familiar with the concepts of usability, but people previously instructed on the evaluation criteria can also be evaluators.

The execution of the analysis takes place in three distinct phases:

- **Individual analysis**: In this phase, each expert analyzes the application interface individually, for a variable period of time (usually one-two hours), according to the set of heuristics chosen. A report is generated in this phase, showing each of the errors found, and indicating in each one the heuristic violated, the location of the error and the severity of the problem, besides the possible solutions imagined by the specialist.
- **Consolidation of the analysis**: In this phase, all experts, together with the team leader, meet to discuss the individual results found. In this consolidation, each specialist has access to all the individual reports generated in the first phase. At the end of this phase, a unified report must be generated, containing all the errors that were found (in the same way as in the first phase).
- **Final meeting**: In this phase, the experts meet with the client (or the project manager) to define which interface errors to correct. Of course, in an ideal situation, we should correct every one, but as we have to deal with the famous *budget constraints*, or with *depleted resources*, it is not always possible to correct a mistake, especially when we are talking about summative evaluation.

Another useful practice is for the evaluator to have an observer close by, as well as a usability test, to propose tasks, record reactions, and even record or transcribe the evaluator's report if better records are needed. It is important that evaluators do not have contact with each other in order to have no influence and, if they prefer, they can write an analysis report according to the criteria used.

The evaluator can freely explore the system and then report the problems encountered, preferentially relating them to the heuristic criteria and classifying them according to severity—between 0 (not considered a usability problem) and 4 (a very serious problem that does not allow the completion of a task). In other words, each stage is assigned the value of the severity of each problem found in the interfaces through the scale proposed in (*Nielsen and Mack, 1994:* `https://www.nngroup.com/articles/ten-usability-heuristics/`):

- 0: Not entirely considered a usability problem
- 1: Only an aesthetic problem: Does not need to be repaired unless you have extra time available in the project
- 2: Lesser usability problem: The concern of this problem should be low priority
- 3: Greater usability problem: It is important to fix this, and it should be given high priority
- 4: Usability catastrophe: It is mandatory to repair it before the product is released

You can use this chart to help you to prioritize the errors:

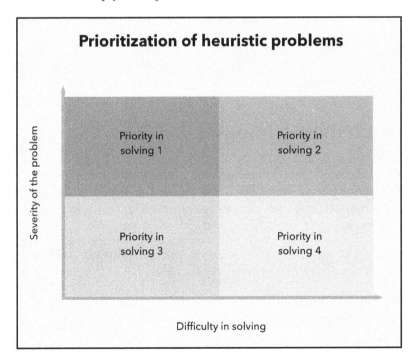

After tabulated errors are organized according to the importance of their correction, the heuristic analysis proposer proposes the necessary improvements and adjustments, so a new scale can be applied regarding the ease of correction —the points that must be attacked first are the more serious and simple solutions:

Violated heuristic	Error	Local	Gravity	Solution
Error recovery	The error messages are unclear	Error messages (JavaScript)	2	Place clearer error messages
Consistency and standardization	The terms *save* and *record* are used with the same	Recording warning messages	3	Uniformize the reference of (probably using) the word *save*

It is important to note that the UX professional must have some knowledge of frontend programming and/or have a programmer to turn to, to assess whether the proposed solutions are actually easier or whether there are other options to consider.

Make sure to have all your findings registered somewhere. In Chapter 3, *Exploring Potential UX Solutions,* we will talk about how to organize these findings and issues that were identified.

User research methodologies

There are different user research tools and methodologies to help you to better understand the users and their needs, such as quantitative and qualitative research, contextual inquiry, observation, netnography, user interview, surveys, card sorting, tree testing, A/B testing, diary studies, data analysis, eye tracking, and so on. Which one (or ones) you will you use depends on what you are trying to achieve and what you are looking for.

To help you to decide when to use which method, you can consider using a three-dimensional framework with the following axes:

- Qualitative versus quantitative
- Attitudinal versus behavioral
- Context of use

20 UX methods in brief

The UX expert Cristian has organized these different methodologies into a chart, *A Landscape of User Research Methods,* to help us to better understand them:

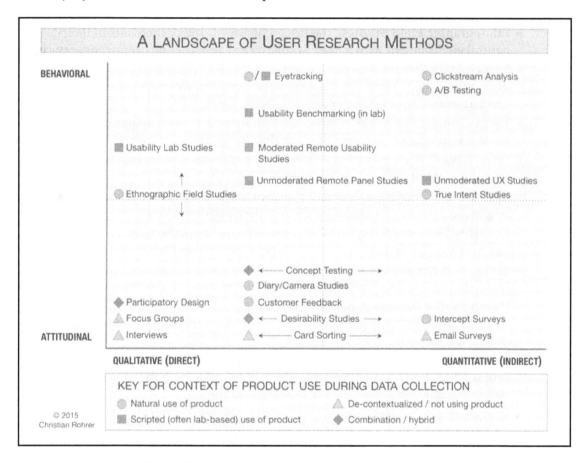

"When to Use Which User-Experience Research Methods" by Christian Rohrer on October 12, 2014
https://www.nngroup.com/articles/which-ux-research-methods/

Here's a short description of the user research methods shown in the preceding chart, described by NNGroup:

- **Usability Lab Studies**: The participants are invited to do a few specific tasks in a lab with the researcher in a one-on-one.
- **Ethnographic Field Studies**: The researcher meets the participants in their natural environment, where they would most likely use the product or service.
- **Participatory Design**: The participants are invited to enter the creative process in design workshops by designing their ideal experience in a concrete way. It is a good approach to get stakeholders involved, for example.
- **Focus Groups**: The research mediates a group of 3-12 participants to give feedback about a set of topics through discussion and exercises.
- **Interviews**: It is a one-on-one session with participants to discuss in depth what they think about the topic in question.
- **Eyetracking**: By using a device or specific computer, you can precisely measure where the participants are looking while they perform a task.
- **Usability Benchmarking (in lab)**: It doesn't care about the why, but focuses on just measuring a predetermined user's performance and satisfaction.
- **Moderated Remote Usability Studies**: By using screen-sharing tools, the researcher can conduct usability tests remotely.
- **Unmoderated Remote Panel Studies**: Participants are recorded while doing usability tests with a specific and strict set of tasks; they are asked to think aloud during the sessions.
- **Concept Testing**: It is an investigation of potential consumers' reactions to a proposed design, product, or service before introducing it to the market and validating if it meets the needs of the target audience.
- **Diary/Camera Studies**: In the Diary Studies, the participants keep a journal describing their activities, behavior, and attitudes over a period of time. They can be asked to record it.
- **Customer Feedback**: Information coming directly from customers about the satisfaction or dissatisfaction through a feedback link, button, form, email, and so on.
- **Desirability Studies**: You can use this methodology to analyze emotional response to a design by giving the participants a list of product reaction words and asking them to select those that best describe the design.

- **Card Sorting**: Participants are asked to organize items into groups and assign categories to each group. This is a good way to, for example, validate or refine information architecture.
- **Clickstream Analysis**: Also known as clickpaths, they are recordings of the route that visitors choose when clicking or navigating through a site.
- **A/B Testing**: The users are randomly exposed to two (A or B) different versions of the designs, a good way to measure the best solution between both. It is also possible to test more than two versions, which is called multivariate testing.
- **Unmoderated UX Studies**: Automated method to capture participant behaviors and attitudes while they need to accomplish specific goals or tasks.
- **True-Intent Studies**: Aims at understanding a user's objective and intentions while they are visiting the website or app, as well as to get actionable information about their experience.
- **Intercept Surveys**: While the users are on the site or application, a survey is triggered that they are invited to answer.
- **Email Surveys**: A group of participants receive a survey on their email to be answered.

If you are still not sure about which methods to use, you can consider:

- **Quantitative research**: Research generates numerical data to answer a question. Having such numbers helps prioritize resources, for example, to focus on issues with the biggest impact.
- **Qualitative research**: Research that generates non-numerical data, such as open-ended survey questions or interviews, helps to answer questions about why or how to fix a problem.
- **Attitudinal research**: Research aimed at determining how something is or will be perceived, focuses on understanding or measuring people's stated beliefs.
- **Behavioral research**: Research aimed at determining or predicting how people actually behave.

The following graph, by Christian Rohrer (twitter.com/christianrohrer), might help you better understand how to choose the best methodology when you consider **BEHAVIORAL** versus **ATTITUDINAL** and **QUALITATIVE** versus **QUANTITIVE**:

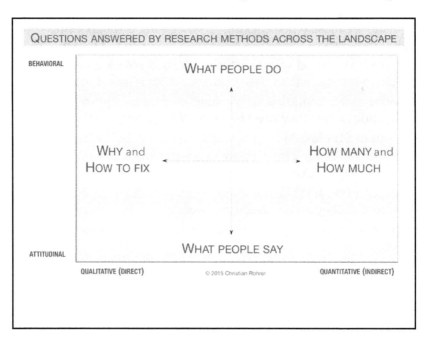

"When to Use Which User-Experience Research Methods" by Christian Rohrer on October 12, 2014
https://www.nngroup.com/articles/which-ux-research-methods/

There are many other methodologies, not listed by Rohrer, that can also be considered, such as the contextual inquiry, contextual inquiry interview, when the researcher will watch the users during their normal activities, which will be discussed in a one-on-one interaction lasting about two hours. Another option is tree testing, a type of card-based classification to evaluate the findability of topics on a website, a way to measure how easily users can find items in this hierarchy (Wikipedia); or is multivariate testing, a specialized type of A/B testing that generates multiple versions of a page based on more than one variable and determines which version performs best. There are also heatmaps (similar to eye tracking), using online tools that visually represent user clicks, taps, and scrolling behavior. You will probably hear about many other methodologies.

Screening and recruiting

Once you decide on your user research methodologies, you will want to define the users who will participate in the research, especially for the qualitative studies. It is crucial to recruit the right users to guarantee the quality of the results. For recruiting, it is important to understand who your target audience is, where they live, where they work, if they study or not, and so on. You probably have lots of information from the stakeholder interviews that will help you to define the users who you will recruit. Departments such as marketing, customer support, and sales might help you to find that information. Also think about recruiting users with different profiles and levels of engagement with your product or service, such as heavy users, light users, subscribers, nonsubscribers, returning customers, loyal customers, and so on. Besides recruiting actual users of your product or service, you might want to also recruit participants who are not currently users, but are potential ones. This will help you to find UX issues from different perspectives. For the more quantitative methodologies, you will also want to define the segments you will research.

Once you have defined the users' profiles that you need to do the research, it is important to have an effective participant screener to help the recruitment process. The screener is a list of questions that will qualify the user to be a participant or not, of the study and also to define which category of user the participant should be part of. There are a few online articles that can help you to define those questions, such as this one from UX Mastery (`uxmastery.com/how-to-write-screeners-for-better-ux-research-results`) or UserZoom (`userzoom.com/recruiting/importance-of-screeners-for-recruiting`). I would say that the most important thing to keep in mind is the purpose of the questions: qualify the participant.

For recruitment, you can consider using a specialized company in recruitment, or you can use the company user basis and, for example, send them the screener questions asking if they would be interested in participating in a user interview. To recruit actual users of a website, you can also use online plugins provided by online tools such as `Hotjar.com` or Intercom. On the other hand, you can go creative and use different places for it such as social media channels, for example, especially to find non-users.

You might be asked if you should disclose to the participant who the client is. You have probably heard before, especially from marketing researchers, that we not only shouldn't disclose the client, but also we should do interviews, for example, in a neutral environment. I would say that depends on a lot of the methodology you are using, the purpose of the research, and so on. You will need to consider different factors to be able to make this decision.

About the number of users to be researched: for qualitative research, such as user interviews and usability tests, Jakob Nielsen suggests five users, which will help you to find 85% of the UX issues, as you can see in the following chart:

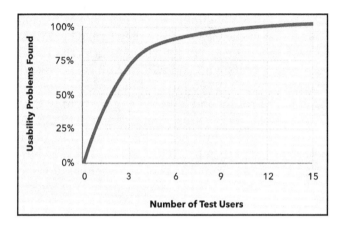

Also, as pointed out by NNGroup, you might need to test the new designs. A second study with five users will show you the remaining 15% of the original usability problems not found during the first round of testing. After that, if you want to check the 2% that might still remain from the first round, you will probably need to do a third round of studies.

Although most researchers still use these numbers suggested by Nielsen in 2000, other researchers might disagree on this topic. In the past 18 years (web) applications have become much more complex. For example, if you do eye tracking, the minimum number of users is 39, otherwise heatmapping is probably pointless, odd looking, very inaccurate, and probably not insightful. Besides that, it will also depend on complexity, and you might want to consider five users/platforms/journeys, and that would easily add up to more than 40 if you want to find 85% of the issues in the whole app, on all supported platforms.

Guerrilla research

If the project is too small, or if you don't have enough budget to spend on different methodologies or even to recruit participants for the research, consider doing guerilla research. According to UX Magazine, guerrilla research is a fast and low-cost way to gain sufficient insights to make informed decisions. The downside of this method is that the users you recruit are unlikely to perfectly represent your user base or even the potential users. So, it might be ideal for when you want quick results for timely issues and do not need a very specific public profile.

In this case, instead of recruiting the participants and setting a schedule, you go where they are. The first step is to look for a place with a high flow of people who have the *face* of your product. It could be a cafe, a mall food court, a park, a department store (ask permission!), or even a subway entrance (as long as you do not make people miss the train!).

It's good to choose a place with Wi-Fi. If it's not too noisy and you have a place to sit, better yet. On the spot, you approach people and invite them to take a quick quiz (it's fine to limit them to about 15 or 20 minutes). And, as a reward, you can give a shopping voucher for where you are or a voucher from a store nearby.

Although the guerrilla method might not be useful for in-depth usability testing, it is invaluable for quickly testing a general layout or interactive element and verifying the most glaring UX errors that have to be identified and fixed.

David Peter Simon, from UXBooth, suggests that you should plan your guerrilla research, considering the following:

- What shall you test?
- Where will you run the test?
- With whom will you test?
- How will you test?

Since usually the tests are conducted in public spaces where you can find people available to talk with you, the sessions shouldn't last as long as a formal usability test. This makes guerrilla testing extremely lean and agile and you can get insight quickly.

Markus Pirker, in a blog post for Userbrain.com, suggests following these steps:

1. Approach someone
2. Ask them if they would like to answer a few questions about your product or service
3. Give them a couple of simple tasks to do
4. Observe their interaction while they do the test
5. Ask about their experience

He also highlights that you might only need three to five people to spot the biggest usability issues, once you're collecting qualitative data during the tests:

Guerrilla research during VidCon in Orange County to validate video mobile app to millennials

Creating personas

Now that you know more about the users, it is pretty useful to create personas, which are archetypes representing your target or your client's customer, who is going to use your product or service, who we are designing for. As pointed out by UXBooth, a persona is a fictional character to remind us who our users are and it should have its own story. It is important that the story is good enough to make us believe it, so the more accurate this representation, the more likely our decisions will reflect the users' needs.

Although creating personas seems like a simple technique, you can be sure that it is a very powerful tool widely used not only by UXers, but also by marketers, designers, product developers, and other professionals who need to understand their users and customers. The idea here is to create a detailed user profile that might represent your target audience groups. Make sure to have the most information as you can about your users or customers, which can be collected from analytics tools or even surveys, interviews, usability tests, besides information from the sales team, support, and marketing departments.

The persona brings benefits not only for design, but also for the entire multidisciplinary team people:

- They make explicit assumptions about users by creating a common language with meaning.
- Data (largely qualitative) and information are indispensable, being the foundation of people.
- They allow you to focus on a set of specific users (who are not you!) Helping you make better decisions.
- By limiting our choices, personas help in making design decisions. Creating a product for a type of user will be more successful than for a wider audience.
- They generate empathy for users by involving their team in a way that other representations of user data can not.
- Personas are funny and come to life when team members accept them. Unlike wireframes and prototypes, personas are not used in a specific part of the process, on the contrary, they help the whole process.

The format and information that will make up the persona will depend mostly on your product or service. A good persona should consider personal aspects such as age, gender, and education level, besides professional aspects such as experience and background. Behaviors will be more related to motivations and needs such as reasons to use your service or product, when and from where they use it, frequency, and so on. Make it as personalized as possible: give a name for your persona, add a photo, set where they live, study, work, and so on.

It is important to understand here what persona will not represent:

- Statistical mean, since the variation is more important than the average
- Real people, because each person has its peculiarities and would not represent a large number of people—but personas are based on real data
- Market segments, because market segment is a group of people who respond to similar messages and not have similar goals and usage patterns
- Job description or functions, because functions are defined by the tasks that people do and not by the goals and behaviors

The fundamental insight of Alan Cooper, who developed this methodology, was that people had goals and behaviors that could be served by products through design to their behavior, thus ensuring greater likelihood of design to be successful. If personas provide the context for a set of observed behavior, goals are the drivers behind these behaviors. Designers can create scenarios and then ask themselves:

- Will this person perform this task?
- Will this person perform the task as planned?

A persona without goals can serve as a useful communication tool, but it has no use as a design tool. The goals you will want to list to the personas can be short notes that do not just point to specific usage patterns but also provide a reason for the existence of these behaviors. Understanding why a user performs certain tasks gives designers great power to improve or even eliminate tasks while still achieving the same goals.

The most important for the construction of a persona is the identification of the main patterns that end up jumping to the eyes when we begin to analyze the findings:

- How the identified behavioral and demographic variables group together to form patterns. Demographic variables only enter if they influence behavior such as age and technical ability
- If a group of interviewees appears in half a dozen of these variables, you can have the basis for one person
- When you find you have identified a pattern, look for others.

In order to set up a traditional persona, the information must be removed from effective searches on the users of the company or the project. But since every company knows at least a few of its users, they have some kind of relevant information about them, even if they have not been validated in some way, there is the possibility of creating a simpler variant of the person, the proto-person.

It is a contour solution for the common persona, that is, it is advisable not to be definitive and that your information be validated with real users later. Both traditional personas and proto-personas help guide the team in most of the decisions that involve the project. The proto-persona is interesting to start introducing the **User-Centered Design** (**UCD**) culture in the company, because it is something cheap and simpler to develop.

As content of the proto-persona, it is interesting that the proto-persona has the following information:

- Who is this user and how is he (personality)
- Some behaviors
- Demographic information such as age and occupation
- And the key point: your needs and/or goals

The layout of the proto-persona may vary depending on the team's creativity. A widely used template is where information is separated into four quadrants, as in the following example:

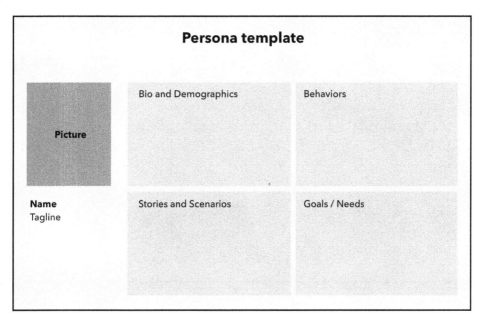

Keep in mind these characteristics:

- **Personal**: Age, gender, and highest level of education this persona has received
- **Professional**: Work experience, professional background, user needs, interests, goals, where they get information from about your issue or similar programs or services, and user environment, and context (when and where will users access the site)

- **Technical**: Technological devices used on a regular basis, software and/or applications used on a regular basis, the technological devices they primarily use to access the web for information, and time spent browsing the web every day
- **User motivation**: What is your persona motivated by, what are they looking for, what is your persona looking to do, and what are their needs

The leading product management expert who specializes in lean and agile practices, Roman Pichler, also made available a more simple template that you can use, as you can see here:

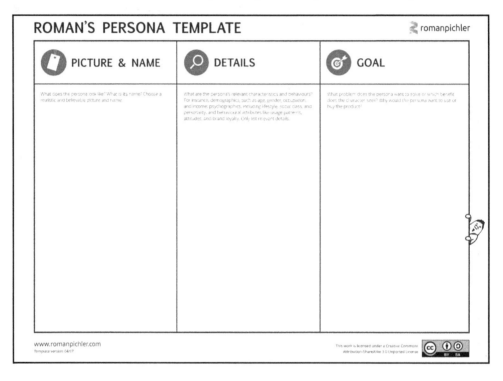

Author: Roman Pichler
Source: www.romanpichler.com
Licence: Creative Commons Attribution-ShareAlike 3.0 Unported (CC BY-SA 3.0),
https://creativecommons.org/licenses/by-sa/3.0/

Here is what Pichler suggests for each area, as it is on the template:

- **PICTURE and NAME**: What does the persona look like? What is its name? Choose a realistic and believable picture and name, that are appropriate and that help you develop sympathy for the persona.

- **DETAILS**: What are the persona's relevant characteristics and behaviors? For instance, demographics, such as age, gender, occupation, and income. psychographics, including lifestyle, social class, and personality; and behavioral attributes such as usage patterns, attitudes, and brand loyalty. Only list relevant details.
- **GOAL**: What problem does the persona want to solve or which benefit does the character seek? Why would the persona want to use or buy the product?

You can use different templates to create your personas or even come up with your own. If you prefer, you can find online tools such as Xtensio.com, makemypersona.com, or Userforge.com. If you want to do it by yourself, you can create something like this:

Or something like this:

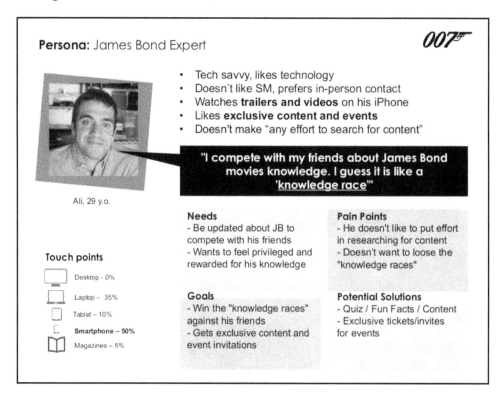

You can also find more examples of persona cards here: `https://www.pinterest.com/lisandramaioli/uxdi-personas/`

To create a persona, Alan Cooper in his book *About Face 3* describes seven main steps:

Step 1—Identify behavioral and demographic variables

List the distinct aspects of behavior observed in the research participants as a set of behavioral variables. Demographic variables are only worth being identified and considered if they in any way affect behavior (For example, product for children—age).

We usually identify distinct patterns of behavior if we focus on the following variables:

- **Activities**: What the user does, frequency, and volume
- **Attitudes**: How the user thinks about the business and technology associated with the product

- **Skills**: What education and training the user has; learning capabilities
- **Motivations**: Why the user is engaged in the product business
- Skills: user-related business capability and technology associated with the product

There is no exact number of how many variables should exist, but something around 20 to 30 variables is normal.

For corporate applications, behavioral variables are usually associated with job functions and it is suggested that variables be listed for each function separately (administrator, user, and so on.)

Step 2—map interviewees into variables

Once the variables have been identified, you should label the value extensions for each variable.

For some variables, this extension is continuous and we label two extreme and opposite values. For example, for an e-commerce application, the values of a variable called *reasons to buy* can range from *only when necessary* to *for pleasure*.

For other variables, continuous variation is impossible and we can use multiple choice options. An example would be the variable *payment preference* that could have the options *installment*, *cash only* or *cash* even without discount.

You now have to map each research participant within those value extensions of each variable. The best way is to see all participants for one variable and then move on to the next. The most important is to position each participant relative to the other participants. Absolute position accuracy is less significant.

Step 3—Identify key patterns of behavior

Once you have mapped the respondents into all the variables, look for the ones that usually appear together. If the same grouping of users appears in six to eight variables, it may already mean a pattern of behavior that will be the basis for one person. When you find you have identified a pattern, look for others.

But beware that some apparent relationships can induce false standards. Realize the relationships that really make sense. For example, there is logic if the standards show that people who buy often often buy in installments.

Identifying the main patterns, give them short, descriptive names, such as *the conscious shopper* or *the compulsive buyer*, and so on.

Step 4—List relevant characteristics and objectives

Identifying objectives and expressing them succinctly is one of the most critical tasks in modeling a persona, as these goals will guide design. Each objective must be inferred from the behavioral variables identified and expressed as a simple sentence.

User objectives serve as a lens through which designers must consider the functions of a product. The function and behavior of the product must meet objectives through tasks, a small number of absolutely necessary tasks. Remember, chores are only a means to an end; goals are this end.

For each pattern that you identified in the previous step, synthesize the details from the information you have from the searches, describing:

- Main tasks and day-to-day flow;
- Problems with current solutions;
- Environment of home or work;
- Behavioral and demographic characteristics;
- Goals.

Synthesizing the goals is the most important part of this step, since it is these goals that we want the application we are designing meets. One way of inferring the goals is to observe the actions people do - from each grouping that led to a pattern—do and for what reason: how are they acting and behaving today? What do they want to achieve with these actions?

The objectives, in a certain way, have to be related to the product to be developed. If it is not directly related, it is irrelevant to direct product design.

In his book *Emotional Design*, Donald (Don) Normam defines three cognitive processes: visceral (reaction to stimuli before action), behavioral (main focus of interaction designers) and reflexive (conscious reflection of past experiences).

Alan Cooper translates each of these cognitive processes respectively as goals of experience, end and life. Let's look at each one of them:

Experience goals describe how someone wants to feel using the product. Typically a persona has no more than one such goal, or even none, unless it is an entertainment product. Examples of experience objectives are:

- Feel smart
- Have fun
- Achieve a sense of fullness

The final goals describe what a person wants to accomplish; and the product may help directly or indirectly in this. They are most useful in determining the design of the product and usually a persona can have three to five final goals. Examples of final objectives are:

- Finish my work until 5 pm
- To be proactive rather than reactive
- Discover problems before they become critical

Life goals are more useful in consumer oriented products, but it is not appropriate to use them unless achieving that goal is the primary motivation for using the product. Usually identifying one or no life goal in a persona is considered common. Examples of life goals are:

- Retire at age 45
- To be the next Madonna
- To be promoted to art director

Responding to life goals makes the difference between a satisfied user and a loyal and fanatical user.

Step 5—Check the entire set of person to eliminate redundancies

From now on people are beginning to become more evident. Check all mappings, patterns identified with their characteristics and goals to see if anything is missing. To make sure you are not creating redundant people, see if they differ from one another in at least one meaningful behavior. If two or more personas are very similar and the only thing that differs them are demographic issues, try to eliminate one of the two or see if you can adjust the characteristics to be more distinct.

Step 6—Develop the narrative

Personas tell stories and thus become more convincing. A list of items do not convey what we want as well as narrative. Include a few personal details. They are small things that do not affect the product design: where did college, hobbies, and so on. One or two personal details are sufficient—many can divert their attention from the important behavioral data that the person must represent. Some tips on how to do the narrative:

- List items and group those that are related;
- Turn each group into one paragraph;
- Add the *personality* last;
- Quotes are also cool to use.

Step 7—Determine types of people

Once you have identified one or more personas, you must determine the type of each. The main ones are the primary and the secondary person, but there are several other types, such as negative, supplementary, served person.

The primary person is the one that needs to be catered for in every way by the product. She will not be satisfied if the design is done for anyone else. If we make the primary person happy, the others will not be sad.

The secondary is generally satisfied with the interface made to the primary, but has some additional specific needs. Make the design for the primary and then, as far as possible, accommodate the needs of the secondary.

The supplementary is neither primary nor secondary, but is satisfied with the solutions of the first or second. They are usually employed to materialize stakeholder assumptions.

The negative persona is the one for which the product was not made. It's another layer of data validation for the survey.

The served person does not use the product directly, but is affected by its use. For example, that person who waits for the clerk to make his room reservation.

One way to identify the type of personas is by elimination. Ask yourself who could not be primary. Ask the question—if you design this person, would the others be dissatisfied? If the answer is yes, this would not be the primary person. Are personas so different that they need totally different interfaces? Or could one of them meet most needs? If there are people with very different needs, we will probably have more than one primary person and each one will probably have its own interface.

Understanding the competitors

During the stakeholder and user interviews, they might mention a few competitors. The stakeholders probably will tell you the ones they consider as competitors from a business point of view. The users might mention the same competitors and likely other ones that they consider deliver the same or similar solutions. It is a good moment to also understand how they use the competitor and why they consider it as a substitute solution, what is best and worse if compared to your product or service. The users might mention competitors that the stakeholders didn't know exist or even don't consider as a competitor. During research you might find other ones too. It is important to analyze all of them.

Analyzing the competitors, especially those mentioned by the users, will help you to understand what they are used to. To start your **Comparative Competitive Analysis (CCA)**, you can first organize the competitors into two groups:

- **Direct competitors**: Which usually have the same core functions and similar user base
- **Indirect competitors**: Which might offer different functions, but might solve the same user' needs

The UX specialist, Jamie Levy, author of the book *UX Strategy*, has shared a template to do competitive analysis in a more business perspective. The idea is to analyze direct and indirect competitors according to these aspects:

- URL of website or app store location
- Usernames and password access
- Purpose of site
- Year founded
- Funding rounds
- Revenue streams
- Monthly traffic or app downloads
- Number of SKUs/listings (estimate)

- Primary categories
- Social networks
- Content types
- Personalization features
- Community/UGC features
- Competitive advantage
- Heuristic evaluation
- Customer reviews
- General notes
- Questions/notes to team
- Analysis

When you have the competitors listed, you can also use heuristics analysis or simply compare their weaknesses and strengths. One way to do this is adding notes on screenshots: red for weaknesses, and green for strengths, for example. You can also organize weaknesses and strengths in groups such as flow, design, communication, and so on:

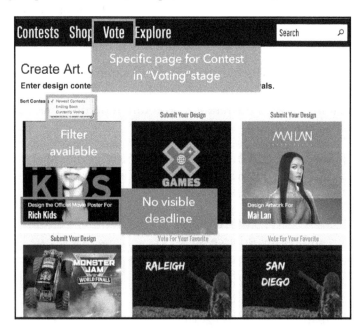

Competitive analysis highlighting weaknesses and strengths: https://www.slideshare.net/lmaioli/homework-11-lisandra-maioli1-pdf

You can also create a spreadsheet to analyze the competitors about navigation and content, for example:

You can also create more visual charts to analyze specific features or functionalities, as you can see in the following figure:

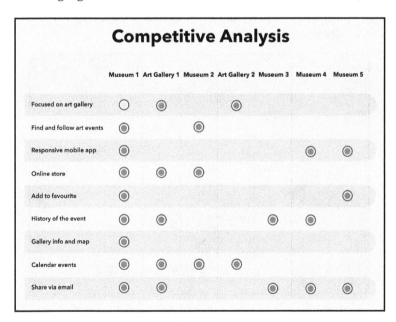

London-based interaction designer, Nacho, used the competitors' logos and organized them as *direct* and *indirect*, as you can see in the following chart:

		Chat feature?	Free tool?	Direct messaging?	How discuss topics?	Voice feature?	Video feature?
DIRECT	Trello	No	Yes	No	Cards	No	No
	asana	Yes	Yes	Yes	Create projects for meeting agendas	No	No
	slack	Yes	Free plan for small teams	Yes	Setting a channel topic or purpose	Scheduled	Scheduled
	Basecamp	Yes, adding extra (ClickDesk Live Chat)	No, only a free trial	Yes, adding extra (ClickDesk Live Chat)	With comments feature	No	No
INDIRECT	Skype	Yes	Yes	Yes	Creating meetings	Yes	Yes
	WhatsApp	Yes	Yes	Yes	Opening groups	Yes	Yes

You can find the full competitive analysis inspired by Nacho, the original can be found here: http://najux.com/trello-chat.html

Another very effective way to help you to find UX issues when you do competitive analysis is doing competitive comparative task analysis. In this case, you compare the same (or similar) tasks that the user would do on your website or app and on your competitors. When you compare the same tasks flows with different competitors you might find unnecessary steps, features and functionalities missing in the designed flow. You can use a wall with the printed screens from each step of the flow:

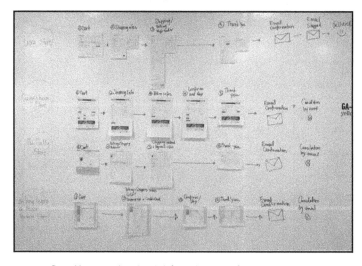

Competitive comparative task analysis for checkout process for museum online stores
https://www.slideshare.net/lmaioli/u-xproject-lacmaonlinestoreredesign

The best format to use on your CCA will depend on which UX issues you will need to identify. It is important to keep in mind that you don't need to only analyze your competitors, but also compare them, including the experience you are delivering to your user.

User journey and touch points

It is a fact that the more you understand the users, their needs and behavior, the easier it will be to find UX issues and know how to fix them. Understanding the user journey related to your services or products will help to better understand it, and it will help you to understand the context of users. You will gain a clear picture of where the user has come from and what they are trying to achieve. All the information you already gathered during the stakeholder and user interviews, and also CCA, will help you to come up with the user journey and its touch points. To draft the journey map, UX Mastery suggests you include:

- **Personas**: The main characters representing the user needs, goals, thoughts, feelings, opinions, expectations, and pain points of the user
- **Timeline**: A finite amount of time or variable phases
- **Emotion**: Frustration, anxiety, happiness, and so on
- **Touch points**: What customers are doing, their actions and interactions with the organization
- **Channels**: Where interaction takes place (the context of use)

The UX specialist Kate Kaplan, from NNGroup, suggests using this template:

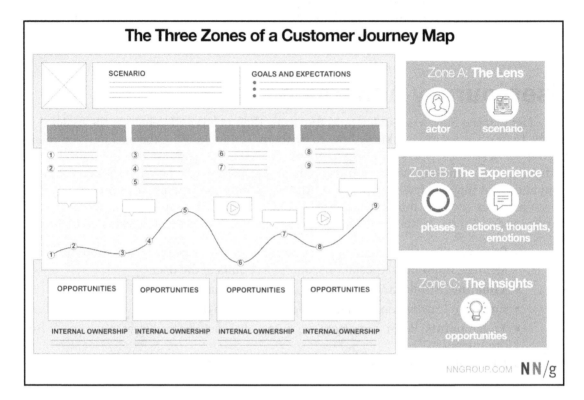

"When and how to create customer Jjourney maps" by Kate Kaplan on July 31, 2016;
https://www.nngroup.com/articles/journey-mapping-ux-practitioners

As regards the other UX tools, you can find many different templates, such as the following example, by designer Jonathan Lupo (`@userexperience`):

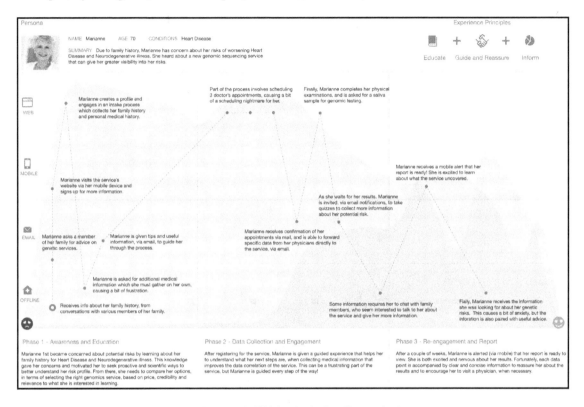

User journey map by UX designer Jonathan Lupo (@userexperience)

The following version by design agency, MadPow, is more detailed and a great example of a timelined journey map:

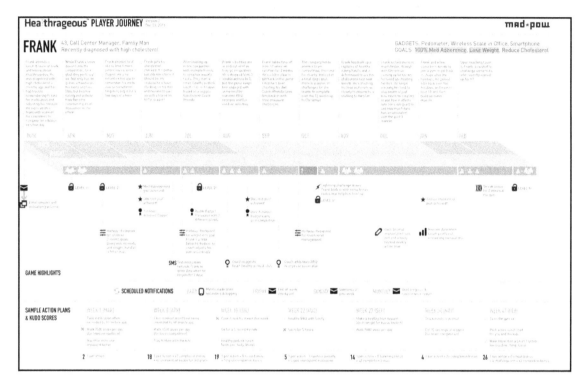

User journey map by design agency MadPow—http://www.madpow.com/

If you still don't feel confident enough to come up with your user journey map, I recommend the video *How To Create A Customer Journey Map*, by UX Mastery: `https://www.youtube.com/watch?v=mSxpVRo3BLg`.

Defining the challenges and project goals

At this point, you might have a great idea about the UX issues that you will need to fix. You should have a list of all the issues, which you can organize into groups to understand what the priorities are and the which are most urgent to be fixed. In this stage, you might not only know what the issues are, but also the consequences of them. By knowing the issues, you can come up with a problem statement.

To come up with this list of design problems, Evelina Tapia, from UXPin, suggests answering these questions:

- How do you know these are issues?
- Who is affected by these issues?
- When and how often do they occur?
- What benchmarks do you have?
- What change do you expect by fixing them?

It might be useful if you come up with a problem statement. To help you to write it, you can use the **Point Of View** (**POV**) tool, explained by Interaction Design Organization as "a meaningful and actionable problem statement, which will allow you to ideate in a goal-oriented manner". The idea is to define the right challenges of your project, capturing your design vision, and helping you to drive your design work efforts. You can use this template to write the POVs:

> [**User** . . . (descriptive)] **needs** [need . . . (verb)] **because** [insight. . . (compelling)]

You can also try these other templates to write the problem statement:

> _____ is a challenge for _____ because _____.

Or this longer one:

> We have observed that [**product/service/organization**] isn't meeting [**these goals/needs**], which is causing [**this adverse effect**]. How might we improve so that our product/service/team/organization is more successful based on [**these measurable criteria**]?

Or this one from the book *Lean UX* (`http://shop.oreilly.com/product/0636920021827.do`), by Jeff Gothelf:

> "**[Our service/product]** was designed to achieve **[goals]**. We have observed that the service/product isn't meeting **[these goals]**, which is causing **[this adverse effect]** to our business. How might we improve **[service/product]** so that our customers are more successful based on [these measurable criteria]?"

Summary

In this chapter, you learned how to identify UX issues and understand the project challenges by interviewing stakeholders, using different user research methodologies, doing comparative competitor analysis, and designing user journeys and writing problem statements.

For each project, you might use a combination of different methodologies in order to find the UX issues. Although it can be interesting to plan which methods will be used to make sure that they will be accommodated into the budget, it is common to feel like you need to use other methods after each test.

In Chapter 3, *Exploring Potential UX Solutions*, you will not only learn how to turn findings from research into potential solutions, but also how to present the ideas for them.

3
Exploring Potential UX Solutions

Now that you have identified the UX issues and understood the project challenges, it is time to turn those findings from user research into potential solutions, what we call assumptions, besides learning how to present the ideas. Creating visual graphs to illustrate your findings not only helps you to analyze them better, but also communicate them in a clear and effective way to the stakeholders.

In this chapter, you will learn how to:

- Analyze data and research/discovery findings
- Organize discovery/insights, exploring options
- Identify potential solutions (assumptions)

Organizing the reports

According to the Interaction Design Foundation, it is very hard to find a perfect format of a report that will suit every group of stakeholders or client. They suggest that you consider doing three kinds of reports for different stakeholders:

- A **brief high-level report** for the ones who would be interested in the research inputs, but who do not necessarily need to review the data or the method itself.
- A **mid-sized report** for those who are considered to be decision makers. For this audience, you should add the main explanation of what exactly needs to be done and what you did, being informative without becoming overwhelming.

- A **bigger report** for the ones who will be responsible for carrying out the work that the results describe on the report. You will want to detail what needs to be done and not much about what has been done.

One of the possible problems of the Interaction Design Foundation suggestions is that you can find is how much this can impact on the project timeline, as creating the reports might be time-consuming. In this stage, the stakeholders might be anxious and you have to manage different expectations. Taking so long to deliver a report can be painful for all people involved, including yourself. An idea to optimize your time is to come up with a bigger report (we are talking about 20 pages here) and have a presentation highlighting the main points of the report and indicating on which pages it is possible to find more details.

The UX specialist Danny Setiawan suggests that, after you have identified to whom you have to present your UX research findings, ask yourself these three questions:

1. **What?** Which part of the findings they'd find relevant and care about?
2. **So what?** Why would they care about it? Is there an opportunity or risk that this finding highlights?
3. **Now what?** What is the action item at the end of the meeting? What do you want from this stakeholder?

If you decide for the preceding Interaction Design Foundation suggestion, or even keep it simpler, keep in mind that your main goal when writing a UX research report is to communicate your findings to the stakeholders. Being visual and using graphs to illustrate it is usually very effective. It is highly recommended to present the findings in person, which can be a chance to let the stakeholders ask questions and also to engage with them.

Even if you decide to be very visual, your report might contain lots of text as well. Try to keep the language pleasurable to read, avoid academic language, keep it simple and straight. Use your UX knowledge to create this report, break it into clear, objective, and digestible sections.

Remember that this report might also help you to analyze the findings and insights to come up with potential solutions to be tested. Be honest with your analysis, don't be afraid of hurting feelings, but be nice and polite. Although you are looking for issues to fix, be sure to add positive feedback as well. This will also help the team to understand what they have been doing right.

Try to prioritize the findings, and organize them by using the **MoSCoW** method (**Must have, Should have, Could have, and Won't have**) or give them rates such as **Critical, High, Medium, Low** or **Critical, Serious, Minor**. An issue that is a block for a user to complete important tasks, for example, or an issue identified many times during the research, should be considered critical. Small cosmetic changes can be identified as low priority or minor, for example. Take both the severity and frequency of the issue into consideration when rating them. You might identify hundreds of usability issues in a typical usability test. Make yourself answer these three questions in order to classify these issues into low, medium, serious, or critical severity:

- Does the problem occur on a red route?
- Is the problem difficult for users to overcome?
- Is the problem persistent?

You can use this three-question process diagram to help you, created by Dr. David Travis, from userfocus.com:

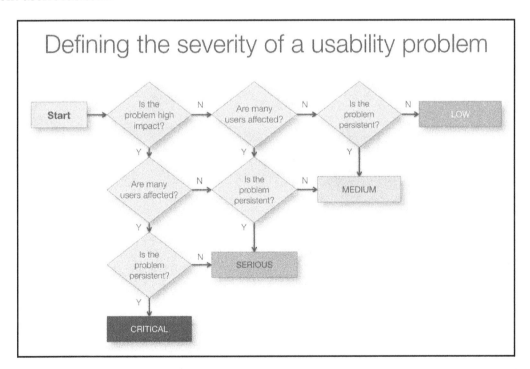

David Travis, Userfocus ltd – @userfocus

As soon as you identify the issues, you can organize them into groups or themes. You can now analyze how much design and development effort you have to put in to have them fixed. This will also help you and the product owner to define the roadmap. A good idea is to visualize, that is, adding the issues in a graph with the vertical axis showing how much of a problem it is for customers and the horizontal axis showing how much effort it would be to design or redesign it. You can use sticky notes or cards to represent it:

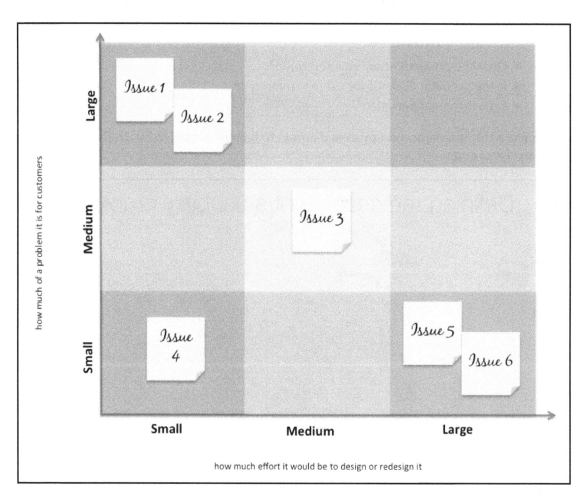

In this case, for example, you might want to start from issues number 1 and 2, as they represent a big problem for your customers, and you can expend small effort to solve it.

As a structure for your document, you can organize the report in four parts, as suggested by `Usability.gov`:

- **Background summary**: A brief summary of what was tested (website or web application), where and when the test was held, besides a brief description of the problems found, as well as what worked well, and so on.
- **Methodology**: An explanation about the test methodology used and how the test was conducted. You can also describe the participants and include summary tables of the background/demographic questionnaire responses, and so on.
- **Test results**: An analysis and description of the tasks, with a summary of the successful task completion rates. You can also add, for example, participant comments to be illustrative.
- **Findings and recommendations**: A list of findings and recommendations that can be organized by scenarios. You can add screenshots with callouts to show the findings and recommendations, as you can see in the following diagram:

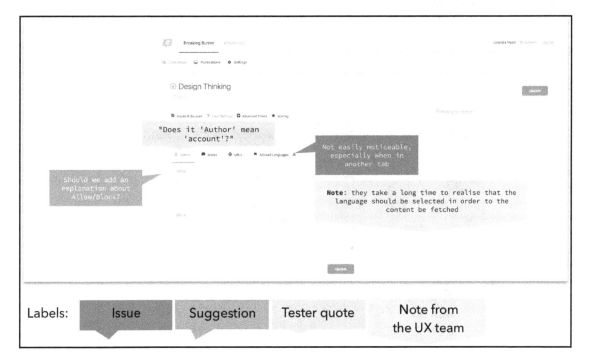

Template for the Structure of the document.

If you want, you can use a template by `Usability.org`, which you can find at: `https://www.usability.gov/how-to-and-tools/resources/templates/user-research-report-template-long.html`.

Be visual

Using graphs and making your report more visual helps the information become more digestible. We will now look at a few examples of how to present user research findings in a visual way.

Analytics

You might have gathered data from different analytic tools to better understand the user behavior. Organize this information, find patterns, and create graphs. Even information from surveys should be transformed into graphs and added to your report. And also add the results for A/B and multivariate tests. Usually, the tools you have chosen, such as Optimizely or VWO, might offer graphic results that you can add on your report. Make sure to add your analysis on the results, explaining the reasons that you decided to use those tools and what you were expecting. Try present result graphically:

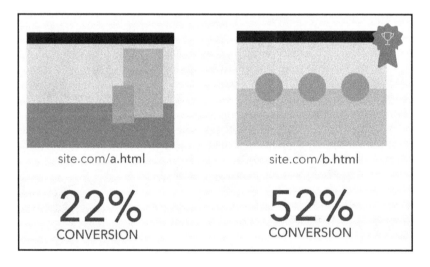

Or even using smiles to represent the sample size:

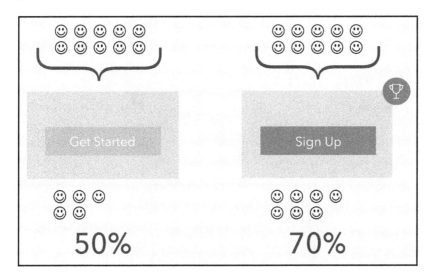

Or you can get inspired by CanvasClip.com graph by showing the heat maps:

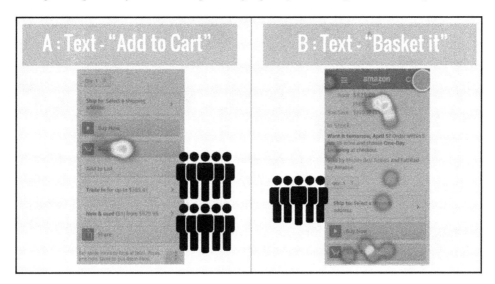

The thing here is, regardless of which format you find more suitable to illustrate your user research findings, the most important thing is to choose one that can make clear what versions you tested and the results of it.

Heuristic evaluation

In Chapter 2, *Identifying UX Issues – UX Methodologies,* you learned how to do heuristic analysis in order to identify UX issues. After this evaluation, you can come up with specific issues identified that you can point out on a screenshot. You can also use Microsoft Excel to create graphs:

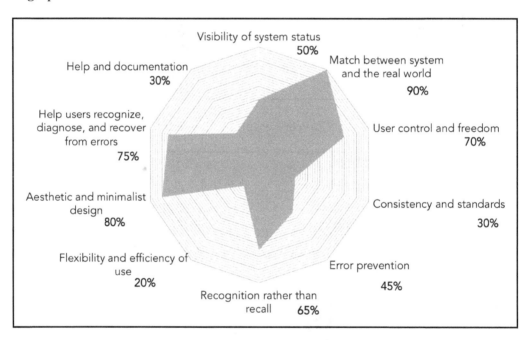

Another way to present the findings from your Heuristic Evaluation is the chart by The Understanding Group, using checklist and cards, which you can find here: http://understandinggroup.com/iaheuristics/

User feedback

UX specialist Raghav Haran presents, on his blog, a suggestion for a visualization of user feedback results for a study that he did for Airbnb, which can also be interesting. He ordered user feedback by the level of frequency of the following type of comments, and grouped the web usability issues by category and frequency in four distinct categories.

Then, he prioritized the issues based on how important he expected them to be to users and to Airbnb's bottom line:

Booking	Filters	Search	Navigation
"Seems like message host is optional with instantly book'	"I can't see below the first row on 'host language'"	"Will the 'Explore' links [on home page] still let me search for rentals?	"'Browse'button keeps fading on and off hover staete"
"What does instantly book mean?'	"Can I sort by quality of reviews?"	"Site automatically searched for rentals before I could enter a check in/out date"	"How can I go back to search results page?"
"Will clicking [intantly book] book the place immediately?"	"How can I sort by price?"		
"Not sure what the heart icon does"			

Frequency of Response (# of Users)

You can also use screenshots and add marks and notes to show user quotes, issues, and suggestions, as shown in the following example:

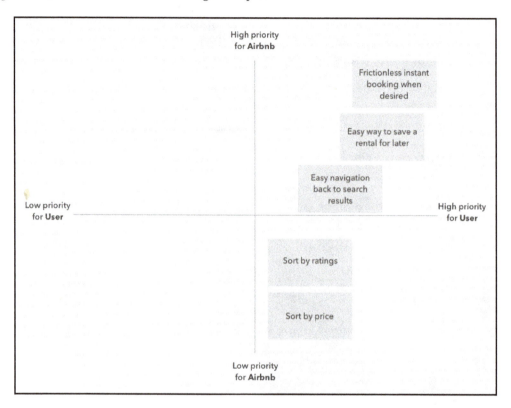

Using quotes from your reports is a really effective way to illustrate UX issues. This helps your stakeholders and team understand the user feelings and they verbalize the pain points when users struggle with the experience. It is nice as well to add positive quotes: again, it is important to the team to know what they have been doing right as well.

Finding solutions

The best thing of having all your user research findings documented and organized in a report is that now you can better analyze them and start thinking about the solutions on how to fix the main UX issues. It is important that you have on this same report the recommendations, potential solutions to explore, and suggestions for the next steps.

You now have a list of specific UX issues that you have identified and organized in priorities. Start drafting solutions for the highest priorities. It is common that the users interviewed during the research have given you hints for solutions. You might have heard from them "this feature could be like that tool". All these ideas raised during the user interviews and usability tests sessions should be sketched and tested.

For some issues, you might not have even had them verbalized by the users. In this case, you can do benchmarking to get inspired by other tools and solutions. You will want to start analyzing the tools and software mentioned by the users during the user interview or surveys. It is important to understand which other players your users are used to. Keep the solution simple and do not reinvent the wheel to help you to fix UX issues and improve the user experience.

If you already have practical design solutions to be tested you can draft the first ideas. If you still don't feel like you have the potential solutions to the issues you have identified, you can organize internal design workshops. The idea is to find different perspectives on potential solutions to the issues you have identified, based on the user needs (you should use the personas created before here).

For the workshops, it is important to have the problem statement very clear and the issues listed to be shared with the group. You will want to keep the focus on these issues; for this, you can have them visibly printed and pasted on the wall, for example, or on the screen. It is also nice to have copies of your report/findings, which you should present at the beginning of the session.

The workshop to address design problems could be handled in several ways – storyboarding solutions, drawing and discussing mock-ups, and brainstorming. But the goal is to agree on problems you're trying to solve and come up with possible solutions to solve them.

Another way to have some good ideas to design solutions is to do some good benchmarking. You can start focusing on one specific part of the design or functionality. For example, if you found issues with the forms or flow of it, you can focus your benchmarking on this. Try to find the best solutions for specific issues during your benchmarking and don't limit your research to the same field of your client, you can find good ideas from different kinds of website and/or apps; what is important here is: the more references of good practices you have, the easier it will be for you to come up with potential solutions. Also, it is a good idea to review your competitors and doing Competitive Task Analysis for the specific issues you have found.

Design, test, iterate, repeat

When you have a better idea of how you can design solutions for the UX issues that you have identified, it is time to sketch them using paper. Paper sketches help you to validate ideas in a fast and cheap way. In this stage, you shouldn't feel the pressure of sketching perfect lines and angles. Keep in mind that the idea here is to visualize the ideas and validate them:

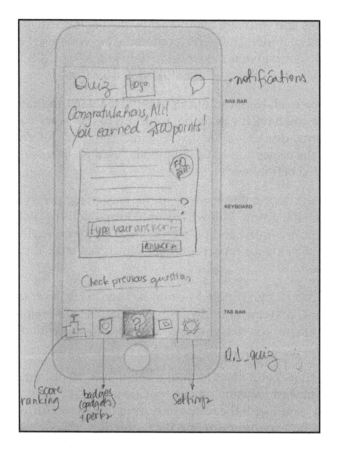

You can also start from a whiteboard before the paper, and if you prefer perfect lines, you can also use some tools, such as rules and pencils (like the ones by UI Stencil – `www.uistencils.com`). You can also use paper templates and different colors to represent different types of interaction:

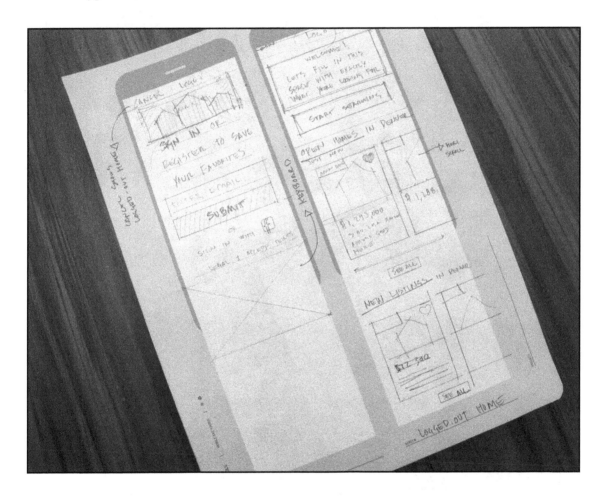

And use the tools by UI Stencil – `www.uistencils.com` like this one:

Use these sketches to validate your idea by doing quick guerrilla tests. Use this feedback to iterate and go to digital wireframes.

You can basically do three kinds of wireframes: lo-fi, mid-fi, and hi-fi (which means low, medium, and high fidelity). For lo-fi you will have a very plain wireframe, using only simple lines and a variety of grey colors. You can use, for example, `MarvelApp`, `FluidUI`, `Balsamiq`, or many others:

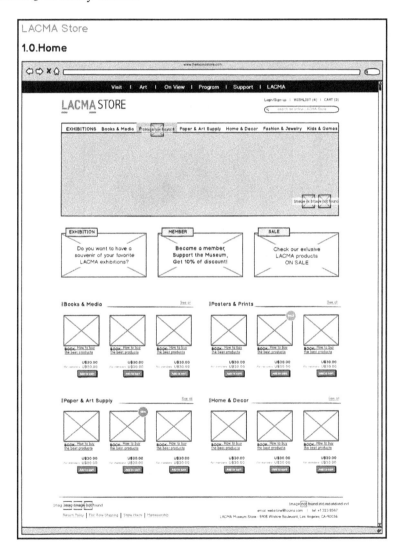

Lo-fi prototype using Balsamiq

The interesting thing about using these softwares is the possibility to create mockups and clickable prototypes, which you can test and validate. The app *Marvel POP*, for example, allows you to use your paper sketch for mobile versions to create navigatable prototypes very easily:

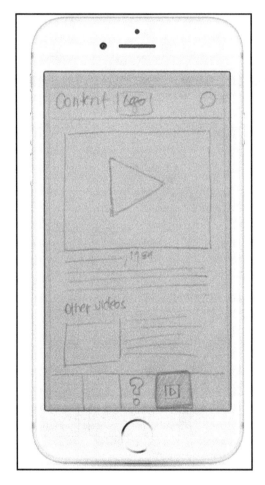

Navigatable prototype for mobile using Marvel Pop

It is important to do another round of tests, and again to validate the flow, the features, and then iterate again. You can either iterate your lo-fi wireframe, or do it by designing a mid-or hi-fi wireframe. These two levels of wireframes can be a little more elaborate and use elements that could close or be used in the final design. But don't feel the pressure to do so. The idea here is still to test and validate the idea before the final version is coded.

For mid or hi-fi wireframes, Sketch App and Axure can be good options. These are being more widely used by UXer more recently. The difference between them is that with Axure, you can also create clickable prototypes very close to a real website or app, with complex functionalities. With Axure you can also easily visualize and create the sitemap, which will be useful for the documentation that you might need to create to share with the Dev team and UI designers (they will need it to be able to work). We will talk more about it in Chapter 10, *Implementing UX Solutions*:

Mid-fi wireframe created by using Axure

Sketch App has been used by a large number of designers, and it is known for being a really flexible and easy software to use. You can easily create great mid, and hi-fi wireframes. Another great advantage of Sketch App is the great number of templates and source elements that you can find, such as on the Sketch App Source website. You can also find countless *plugins* and *extensions* available for Sketch App:

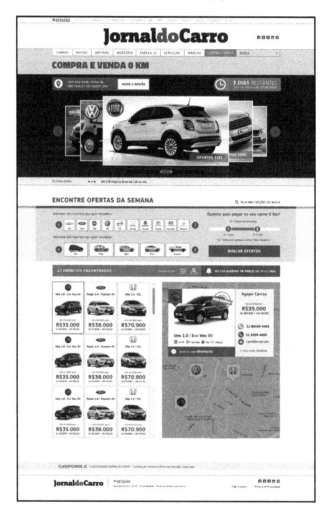

Wireframe created by Euler Araujo Silveira

The downside of Sketch App is that you will not have the option to create clickable prototypes. However, you can use prototype tools to do it, such as the Invision App, which is easily used together with the Sketch App:

Clickable prototype on Invision App with screens created by using Sketch App

A great online tool that allows not only wireframing and prototyping, but also runs remote tests, is FluidUI. Another interesting advantage of FluidUI is being able to see the flow and connections created between the screens. They offer their own library for elements, but you also can upload the screens designed by using different softwares:

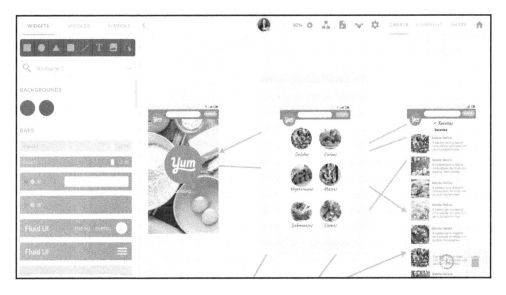

With FluidUI you can not only run online tests, but also see a high level of your project

Clickable prototypes are very useful to test and validate flows and functionalities. You don't need to have a full clickable, which would be really time-consuming, the suggestion here is contemplating specific and main task flows to be tested and iterated.

Keep in mind that the advantage of having a clickable prototype is not only to validate the flow and features, but you can also present the initial idea to your stakeholders, clients, and also use it as documentation to show to your Dev team, to let them understand the flow more easily.

After designing the potential solutions, testing and iterating a few times, you will feel confident about choosing the best ideas to be implemented. Just be careful to not keep this cycle running forever, it is OK to keep testing and iterating the solutions live.

Summary

In this chapter, you saw how important it is to put your findings together in order to analyze them and start thinking about the potential solutions. You also saw a few examples and templates to get inspired to organize and write your report in a visual way.

By having these findings organized and visual, you can work on a process to design potential solutions, starting with paper sketches, moving to wireframes (low, mid, and hi-fi) and to clickable prototypes, which will be tested, validated, and iterated, until you feel confident with the solution before it is developed.

In Chapter 4, *Increasing conversion with UX*, you will see a few practical examples on how to use UX methodologies to fix user experience issues.

4
Increasing Conversion with UX

When we talk about UX for conversion, some people would understand it as a way to trick the user to make them do what we want them to do. That is not the case at all! Remember that in UX, we should have the user at the center of our design; the goal here is to help them to be able to finish their tasks in the easiest way possible. If you let your user accomplish what *they* want to do and not what *you* want them to do, then you are going to have a successful user experience.

This chapter will show you how to do quick UX fixes in order to improve conversions. To help you understand how to do it, we will talk about:

- Identifying conversion issues
- Understanding user pain points
- Analyzing data and research
- The importance of responsiveness
- Responsive versus adaptive design
- Considering user journey and touchpoints
- Real examples or case studies
- Practical advice

Identifying conversion issues

According to user experience consulting firm Nielsen Norman Group, a well-designed interface in an e-commerce is able to increase the conversion rate by up to 83%. As you saw in, Chapter 1, *Understanding UX and Its Importance*, a simple change in a button can increase sales by up to $300 million, as proved by Jared Spool.

In another example, travel company Expedia managed to earn an additional $12m in profit thanks to a small UX change in one of its forms. The original version included an optional field that asked users to input their company name, which caused confusion for the users. Simply by removing the optional field, Expedia managed to increase conversions to the point that it achieved $12m in additional profit.

By using UX techniques, designers around the world have been facilitating user's steps in order to drive them to complete a specific task or even take them to a specific place on their websites or apps. In one of the articles for the User Testing Blog, the UX specialist Jennifer Winter highlighted that:

> *"conversion shouldn't be about making someone do something we want to, but it should be about providing an ideal environment that makes doing that thing irresistible."*

She uses a good analogy to highlight how important it is to consider the user perspective as we think about conversion. If you were a horse and there is a place to have water nearby, what exactly would drive your decision to go there and check it out? What would make you think that maybe there might be someplace better only two farms from there? As she suggests, we should think about the whole user experience when they are interacting with a company; if not, we cannot motivate them in the right way to make it possible that they will take the actions that we expect.

Through this analogy, she highlights that *you can lead a horse to water, but you can't make it drink.*

To create a great experience for the users, we should consider different aspects that will drive them to conversion. We can use Peter Morville's UX honeycomb to understand the aspects of an ideal user experience:

Peter Morville's UX honeycomb

The following is an explanation of each of the hive combs:

- **Useful**: We should not be content with coloring the design proposed by the client. As professionals, we need to have the courage and creativity to question the usefulness of the products we design and apply our knowledge to define innovative solutions.
- **Usable**: Ease of use is nevertheless essential, but an interface focused simply on good human-computer interaction does not address all users' needs. In short, usability is necessary, but not sufficient.
- **Desirable**: Our pursuit of efficiency must be balanced by appreciation of the power and value of an image, identity, brand, and other elements of emotional design.
- **Findable**: We must strive to create a good navigation, where the contents are easily located so that users can always find what they need.
- **Accessible**: Just as there are buildings with elevators and ramps, our sites should be accessible to people with disabilities or with some special needs (more than 10% of the population).
- **Credible**: Thanks to the web credibility project, we can better understand which elements of the design influence the credibility of our project in the eyes of the user.
- **Valuable**: Our sites should add value to stakeholders. For nonprofits, the user experience must advance the mission. For profit-oriented organizations, it must contribute to meeting needs and optimizing consumer satisfaction.

If we keep in mind the horse's needs as given as an example by Jennifer, the diagram made by Morville helps us to think from the horse's perspective, and these would be the questions that we should be able to answer:

- Can the horse find water?
- Does the horse actually need water, or even want it?
- Can the horse physically get to the water easily?

To answer those questions based on Morville's honeycomb, we can use a few UX techniques.

One of the first things that we should do, as we saw in Chapter 2, *Identifying UX Issues – UX Methodologies*, is definitely to understand our users and their motivations to be on our website or app, using our service or product. As we saw in the previous chapters, for this mission, we have different methodologies to be used. For each project, we can use a combination of them, as we discussed before. The idea here is not only to know about demographics from a marketing perspective, but deeply understand the whole user journey and their real needs and thoughts related to your service or product.

If we go back to Jennifer Winter's horse analogy, our goal should be understanding the horse's feelings:

- Is the horse thirsty?
- Does the horse feel safe?
- Does the water look drinkable to the horse?
- Is the water conveniently located and easy to reach?
- Is there another trough closer to the horse?
- Have the horse's friends tried this water?
- What did they think?

We will keep questions like that in mind, in order to help us to understand better the motivations behind the user's actions on your website/app or their use of your service/product. By understanding your user better, you will be able to understand what they need to do (and how easy it is to do it) in order to complete a task and accomplish their goal (buy something? Read an article? Engage with your brand? Download an app or a file? Complete a form? Subscribe a service?).

Previous analysis

Before understanding the user behavior on the website or app and finding the main pain points for the user to complete the tasks on your website, which results in conversion, take time to do some heuristic analysis (as we saw in Chapter 2, *Identifying UX Issues – UX Methodologies*). Don't forget to create personas and understand the user journey (also seen in Chapter 2, *Identifying UX Issues – UX Methodologies*).

In order to help us to better understand the main UX issues that avoid great conversion, the Brazilian agency Catarinas Design (`catarinasdesign.com.br`) prepared a kind of checklist with questions that are good to follow:

Are business/product objectives explained and understood quickly?

- The top of the website needs, in a nutshell, to explain the business:

Is the mark on top and visible?

- The brand must be at the top of the page (either the center or the left corner):

Are the benefits of the product featured on the homepage?

- The landing site must have an area that contains the benefits of the software and is easy to understand:

Is the main menu easily identifiable?

- If the menu is not visible, you should use icons known by all, such as the *burger icon*:

Are each country's currency, language, or delivery options changed based on the user's location?

- There are some plugins and libraries that modify the interface automatically based on the user's location; if this is not possible, at least translate the interface and inform the user that the site is not configured with your local currency, and indicate some converter:

In case of video presence, does the audio start only when the user requests?

- The user must have control of the actions, so audio and video should only be activated when the user clicks on them:

Does graphic design follow current design trends?

- Review the graphic design. As a suggestion, one can use flat design, large photos, parallax, interactive navigation, icons, and use of large fonts:

Are the product images good quality?

- Improve the quality of images and screenshots so the user can better identify how the product works:

    Does your site/landing *offer a trial or some material to capture leads?*

- If the software is saas, a good strategy is to attract potential customers through inbound marketing (materials of interest to your audience) and thus lead to a test of that solution—so-called trials, a way to prove value to potential customers:

    Do you use customer testimonials or videos to attract potential new buyers?

- Social validation is a great strategy for converting prospects who are in doubt about hiring the company. Confirmation of testimonials from anyone who has already purchased is something that can greatly increase sales:

    Does your site/landing have call-to-action buttons throughout the site/landing?

- Review your interface and include buttons to increase the chance of conversion:

    Is your site/landing *conducive to conversion?*

- On form screens, landing screens, or even conversion fields, it is important not to place links that will cause the user to exit the screen, not converting. Focus on the future lead!

Those questions can be a great start to analyze UX issues, but not the only way, as we will see further in this chapter.

Quantitative/data analysis

If you or your client already have an app or a website, hopefully you might be using an analytics tool. It will give you quantitative data that can help you to figure out the user behaviors on your product or service. If you are not using any tool yet, strategize a plan and select the right tools to help you with the analysis; keep in mind identifying and focusing on the data that aligns with your business goals.

Google Analytics

Google Analytics, for example, provides metrics and data that can help you to make better decisions about re-designing, design adjustment, or fixing UX issues that can impact on better conversion (even with a simple button, as we saw with the *$300 million button,* by Jared Spool). You can analyze information such as time on site, clicked links, pages accessing, and especially the conversion points and abandonment.

Mixpanel

To monitor events on your website or application, you can also use Mixpanel, which will help you to analyze, for example, user actions that do not generate page views. Another nice point of Mixpanel is the possibility of real-time analysis:

Image source: Mixpanel, Mixpanel Screen

Hotjar

Hotjar (`https://www.hotjar.com/`) is another nice tool to check a user's actions (clicks, page scrolling) through recorded video, heatmaps, and conversion funnels. You can better identify things that are getting clicked, but are not clickable; which parts of the page are getting the most attention; which of the links your visitors clicked on; and how far visitors scroll down your pages. Hotjar also allows you to create surveys and polls that you can target and use to get information about specific issues on your pages.

AppSee

To test mobile apps, you can use AppSee (`https://www.appsee.com/`) to track all the interactions performed, generating analytics that are displayed in a dashboard with touch heatmaps, conversion funnels, and crash-recordings:

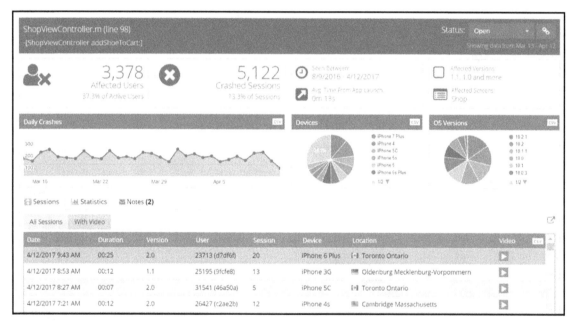

Image source: appsee.com, appsee screen

With AppSee, you can also check and analyze the heatmaps of your app:

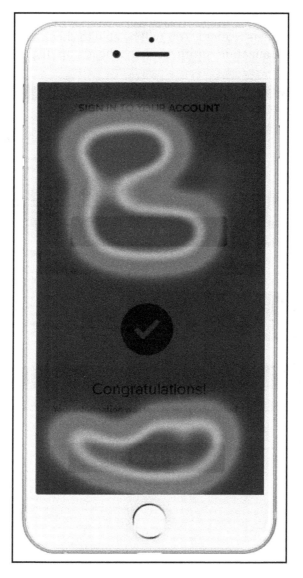

Image source: appsee.com, appsee screen mobile

Chartbeat

Considering content as a part of the user experience, you can use chartbeat, if you want to measure how content engages readers. You will be able to check data information on the website, but also data visualization information in a heads up display format:

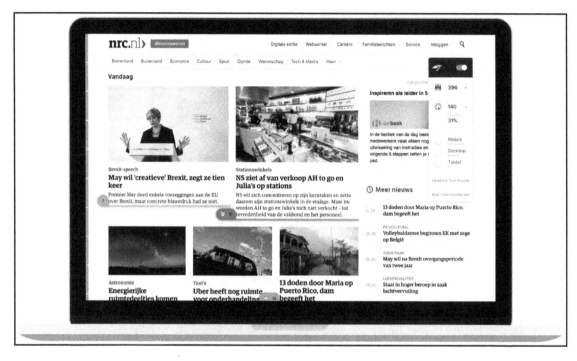

Image source: chartbeat.com, chartbeat screen

Chartbeat allows you to watch analytics in real time, and over time helps give you a better understanding of when people are using the website and how certain events or marketing efforts affect your site usage statistics. Here is an example of the historical analysis:

Image source: chartbeat.com, chartbeat screen

And here, how you will see the real-time analysis dashboard:

Image source: chartbeat.com, chartbeat screen

Inspectlet

To view analytics, study heatmaps, and watch video recordings of real user sessions, you can also use Inspectlet, which offers a powerful tool for recording user navigation. You can watch the browsing of your visitors as if you are physically behind them by viewing your computer screen. You can monitor each mouse movement, page scrolling, and any and all clicks. This data can provide you with valuable insights into what the users are noticing, what they are missing, and even what they are getting distracted by on your current website.

Woopra

You can also use Woopra, which lets you view the user activity in real time on the website. It shows a comprehensive profile of each user and tracks all their activity, even without them signing up. It also allows the customizable analysis of a set of data, such as segmentation, funnels, retention, and so on. With Woopra, you can even automate data-driven actions, such as displaying custom content or making real-time notifications or trends, as you can see as follows:

Image source: woopra.com, woopra screen

Woopra also lets you to check the user journey:

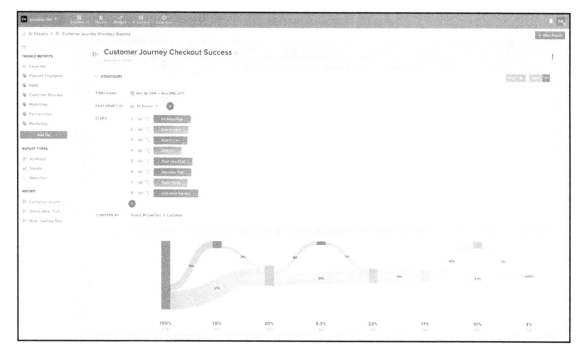

Woopra screen

Formisimo

Formisimo is a tool that specializes in monitoring the abandonment of checkout forms, which allows you to identify why customers do not complete the conversion process on a website. This issue may be related to the difficulty in interacting with the online store, the excess information required in the process, or the complexity associated with it, among other things. With this tool, less friendly interactions are identified and the organization can make the necessary changes to improve the user experience:

Formisimo to improve user experience

Lucky Orange

With Lucky Orange you can see exactly how many people are browsing the site in real time and how it compares to the past. It is possible to quickly compare historical statistics and see how keywords, sites, references, tweets, languages, and so on are sending traffic and behavior, and so on. This is in addition to being able to record the user navigation and their interactions:

Image source: luckyorange.com, luckyorange

Website Grader by HubSpot

Developed by HubSpot, Website Grader is a tool that evaluates your website in four categories: performance, mobile, SEO, and security. This tool also suggests actions to improve the performance of your website. Here, there are no configuration options, customizable parameters, or freemium versions, and the promotion of a good user experience reigns:

Image source: hubspot.com, hubspot screen

Other tools

These were just a few tools that can be used to collect data and information on user behavior. You can find other good options for analytics tools such as CrazyEgg (`https://www.crazyegg.com/`), SessionCam (`https://www.sessioncam.com/`), and KISSmetrics (`https://www.kissmetrics.com/`), among others. You can also find a few options here too: `https://www.conversioner.com/blog/6-practical-tools-improve-web-forms`). Make sure to choose ones that will help you to collect relevant information to support your decision-making to fix UX issues that are resulting in conversion problems.

Research and interviewing your users

Through analytic tools you might better understand and monitor the user navigation behavior and see *what* their main issues are, and now you want to understand *why* by listening to the user.

Doing a survey can be a starting point. According to FluidSurveys, 24.8% of people are willing to complete email surveys on average. Keep in mind that the survey questions should be quick, objective, and easy to understand. There are different nice online tools for surveys such as Survey Monkey (`https://www.surveymonkey.com/`), Typeform (`https://www.typeform.com/examples/surveys/`), SSI, former Instant.ly (`https://www.surveysampling.com/`), Polldaddy (`https://www.polldaddy.com/`), or even Google Forms (`https://www.google.com/forms/about`).

In addition to surveys, you can also do user interviews (we talked about this methodology in `Chapter 2`, *Identifying UX Issues – UX Methodologies*) and talk individually to the users and potential users who represent your target audience. Besides the *whys* behind the user behavior during navigation, which is to avoid conversion, doing surveys and running user interviews are great opportunities to better understand the context of using the website or app. You can check, for example, where the users are when accessing your app or website; at what times during the day or week they access it; and also what their motivations are to do so.

Interviews can take place online or in person. You can choose to do it in a laboratory, in a location chosen by the interviewees (such their own office, workplace, friend's place, co-work space, coffee shop, or wherever they can be found – a school, bookstore, shopping mall, pub, event, and so on). You can even consider running these tests in your company or office; although a few experts believe you can run the risk of getting biased answers, it should be fine if you conduct the interviews well.

There are a few interview methodologies that can be combined with usability tests, as described in `Chapter 2`, *Identifying UX Issues – UX Methodologies*, such as:

- **Ethnography**: When the researcher follows the day-to-day user. The ethnography originates from Social Anthropology, one of the four fields of anthropology, which arose from the need to understand the socio-cultural relations, behaviors, rites, techniques, knowledge, and practices of societies hitherto unknown, and which have been adapted by current problems. This observation study aims to understand it from the point of view of people. In the ethnographic method, the researcher immerses themselves in the researched community, observing and experiencing their habits, their habitat, their day-to-day life, their culture. Context is the most important element of ethnography.

- **Contextual Enquiry**: A user interview and observation session conducted wherever the user usually accesses your website, app, or uses your product or service (for example, in their home, school, or office).
(Make sure to ask for authorization if it's a commercial environment.) The idea is to observe them using your website, app, or product in their normal routine, as a regular activity. You can use the contextual inquiry to do a specific type of interview and gather field data from the users. Usually, it is done by one interviewer speaking to one interviewee (person being interviewed) at a time.
- **Diary Study**: When the user agrees to develop a diary that includes the use of the site, app, or product. You can prepare specific questions or tasks. The user will record activities, behaviors, feelings, perceptions, and so on for a period of time when using your website, app, or product and service. You can, for example, ask users to take photos to explain their activities and highlight what stood out during the day.

With the written consent of the interviewee (you can find templates on the `www.usability.gov/` website), you will want to record all interviews and take notes during the conversation. Please be aware that with any kind of methodology, if you interview children and teenagers, you must ask their parents' or guardian's permission. Also, compensate the respondent (and their parents' or guardian's, when they are underage) with some toast, a cash value voucher, or gift card

You can find good tools to let you do online interviews such as Silverback, Morea, or Appear.in (`https://appear.in/`). You can even use video chat tools also commonly used by your interviewees such as Skype, Google Hangouts, or even Facebook Messenger. Don't forget to record these sessions and ask them to consent to the recording, preferably by signing the consent form. At the end of the interview, check with the user about their availability in case you need them to provide additional information, or maybe to participate in a second round, testing the redesign.

The interesting thing here is that you may also find UX issues that your users are facing and mentioned during the interviews, which you will want to test.

Doing usability tests

As said before, you can combine usability testing user interviews and optimize time with the same user; the ideal time would be between 45 and 60 minutes.

Pro tip: test the script prepared in advance. Although you don't need to strictly follow the script, you will want to make sure you know the purpose of the test and what questions you want to have answered. Ask the users to give their first impressions on entering the site, app, or using a service or product. If they have already used or had previous experience with your site, app, product, or service, ask where they usually navigate and what they usually do. Let them be *the expert* by explaining to you how to do or use it.

Even before starting the test, remind the user that they are not being tested and that their participation aims to improve the navigation of the product, app, or product and service tested. This note will help the user feel more relaxed and confident during the test. They shouldn't feel like they are being tested at all. Take care to not interrupt the testers, let them feel free to speak and encourage them to *think out loud*, allowing some quiet moments so that they can think, as you analyze their navigation, use, and reactions.

When we are asked about the ideal number to obtain valid results for the usability test, we can highlight what expert Jakob Nielsen suggests: five test users should be enough, since the results begin to be repeated from the sixth user, according to him (as we saw in `Chapter 2`, *Identifying UX Issues – UX Methodologies*).

You can run the user interviews in person, in a laboratory, in your company, somewhere indicated by the user (home or office), or even use online platforms, as was said earlier. You can also do tests that don't involve an interviewer, or unmoderated tests, by using online tools such as `fivesecondtest.com`, `usertesting.com`, `usersthink.com`, `UserZoom.co.uk`, `userbrain.net`, `UsabiltyHub.com`, `userfeel.com`, `usertest.io`, `WhatUsersDo.com`, `trymyui.com`, among many others (you can see examples here: `remoteresear.ch/tools`). `Loop11.com` is a great tool for this purpose:

Image source: Loop11.com

In an unmoderated test, you can use the same test script, defining tasks that must be tested by the online user tester, who is encouraged to speak and explain aloud their actions while browsing the app or website. All of the test is recorded to be watched later.

There are other test methodologies that you can combine besides user interviews, such as card sorting, a technique used to find out how the user classifies certain information in their mind by doing activities with cards to test organizational areas or content of your website. You can also use tree testing to test the site navigation tree. Tree testing is a great validation technique for content structure, which allows you to validate users' performance by finding particular content or performing a certain action without any visual interference.

Doing A/B tests

A good way to test different options for design solutions is through A/B tests, which is a design test method through which random elements with two variants, A and B, are compared, where these are the control and the treatment of a controlled experiment, with the aim of improving the percentage of approval. The A/B test is used to identify changes in web pages that can cause positive or negative changes in the users' interests. As the name says, two versions are compared, which are identical except for one variant that can impact user behavior. Version A may be the version currently used (control), while Version B is the version that has been modified (treatment). Significant improvements can be seen through testing elements such as copying text, layouts, images, and colors, but not always.

The objective is to test two different versions in real time with current users: one group will see option A and the other group will see option B. After a period of time set by you (a few tools can help you to calculate it) with the two versions live, you will be able to identify which of the two versions performed better and which you should use as a final design. A/B tests are one of the most efficient ways of validating two different hypotheses and it helps to find and fix UX issues that are impacting conversion:

To run an A/B test, you can use online tools such as Optimizely (`https://www.optimizely.com/`), which can be used for both sites and mobile applications.

VWO (Visual Website Optimizer) is considered one of the top tools for A/B testing. The formula is simple. With VWO you can create multiple versions of a website or landing page to know which one brings the most results. This tool was created for those users who, having no specific computer knowledge or team of professionals available, intend to test and optimize their pages. HTML knowledge is not required.

In addition to the A/B tests, VWO also allows for more complex tests, which integrate several variables of your landing pages.

In addition to the test options, this tool offers other functionalities: visual editor, analysis, reports, and personalization, among others. In total, there are over 100 options that cover all the potential of your pages to ensure the conversion rate increases.

Besides A/B tests, you should also consider doing *multivariate tests* or bucket tests, which are similar to the A/B test—but these tests cover more than two different versions at the same time. These multivariate tests allow you to test multiple hypotheses and determine which combination of variations performs the best out of all of the possible combinations. For this kind of test, you usually can use the same tools mentioned before.

Google fans will like the Google Optimize 360: in addition to allowing work with A/B, multivariable, and redirection tests, the platform has a visual editor that allows the creation of new page variations without the need to recode the site for each test performed. Google Optimize 360 also enables the use of behavioral rules for content segmentation by integrating with Google Analytics 360, and it offers a number of built-in features to make it easier to manage the tests.

Building responsive and accessible websites

It is a fact that the number of people using mobile devices to access the internet has been increasing worldwide. More and more people are using their smartphones and tablets to consume content and make transactions, not to mention the adoption of wearables (such as watches, glasses, and so on). The Pew Research Center reported that 12% of adults rely on a mobile device to use the web exclusively. Some researching sources also estimate that 60% of internet searches are from mobile devices. In this new context, planning your website to be responsive is mandatory.

To give you an idea, 45% of transactions on Groupon came from mobile devices from the start of 2013 (compared to less than 15% two years earlier), according to Mary Meeker, in its report, *Internet Trends*. Etsy has reported that 50% of user traffic came from mobile devices from early 2014. Walmart (`https://www.walmart.ca/en`) had a conversion boost of 20% on all devices, by redesigning their website in a responsive way. On mobile, orders went up by 98%. There is no doubt that mobiles can be crucial for conversion and it is a big issue if this is not considered in your project.

Keep responsive web design, m-commerce, website development for smartphones, and mobile marketing intelligence in mind to optimize your site for mobile devices. Keep in mind that the way people use their desktop or laptop is different to when they use their phone, tablet, or even IoT devices. Take into account also the context and environment when they are using the device: is it an executive using it in his office? A doctor in a clinic or hospital? A teenager with their cell phone at the bus stop or shopping mall? Consider different and potential scenarios and contexts. To give you an idea, a study by Google (2012) showed that smartphones are used in the following contexts:

- When on the way home, to work, to school, and so on
- At home
- To communicate and connect with other people
- When they need information quickly and immediately
- For only short periods of time

While tablets are also used for entertainment and navigation, desktops are more used for serious tasks or when any intensive investigation is needed. Still, according to this study, smartphones are the most common starting point when the user wants to:

- Search for specific information online
- Navigate
- Do shopping
- Access social networking

There is also a big group of users who use mobile devices as the only platform to do online activities. Make sure all your design and content is responsive and adapted to it:

You can use the resizer tool from Google to analyze whether your site is responsive or not. As other options to perform this task, you can also use DesignModo, Responsinator, Semalt, browserstack, and WhatIsMyScreenResolution (http://whatismyscreenresolution.net/), just to name just a few.

You should also consider the accessibility to your site as we will see in Chapter 6, *Considering Accessibility As Part of the UX*. Keep in mind that among your audience, you might have users with low vision or hearing, blindness, and so on. They are also important customers and potential customers who you want for conversion.

To analyze your website you can use online tools such as Toomino, which adds voice navigation support to your site and the web accessibility checker. We will see more about this in Chapter 6, *Considering Accessibility As Part of the UX*.

Helping your users save time

Users have less patience to navigate on your site or application and have no time to waste thinking about what should be done on your site or app. A good design should be *simple and intuitive*. It is important to make navigation paths easy to let the user complete the tasks (such as complete a purchase). A well-organized site's information architecture can be crucial with appropriate prioritization and hierarchies (we will talk more about this in Chapter 8, *Reorganizing IA for Better Navigation*), with clear global navigation and navigation hints such as the well-known *Breadcrumbs* that outlines the user path on the website or app.

One way to help users to save time, for example, is to automate form fields. Each form field can be an opportunity to acquire your user information; if the form is too long or complex, you may end up losing a client. Some of the easiest places you can do this are the addresses (cities and states), which can be filled automatically by the system. Even though this might sound small, those five seconds you *save* for your user can make a difference to a conversion.

If you have an option in the form to fill the zip code, leave it above the address, so when filling in the zip code, the city and state fields can be filled automatically.

As soon as those fields are filled, the cursor can go to the next field automatically and *auto-complete* can also help your user to save time when filling out form fields or searches. Another tip is let the information be saved to optimize the user time when returning to your site. Also, keep in mind that shorter forms convert better than longer forms.

To avoid possible user errors, feedback should always be provided. For example: your city and states will be filled in automatically, or the fill will be so fast that the user does not have to wait. The cursor should also go directly to the next field by *jumping* what has already been populated automatically by the system.

It is also important to ensure that your user has easy access to the support contact or chat in case of help needed. In this way, the user will feel more comfortable knowing that they can ask for help if necessary.

Making your user think as little as possible and save as much information as possible

In the case of selection of dates as an airline and hotel website, the user should start searching for a city and there should already be options, and if you select the date of entry, leave a possible departure date for the same month selected and year, preventing you from selecting each new search for a new exit date. On the Ibis website, the information is quickly populated and some fields are already enabled to facilitate the search.

This is very important in e-commerce in many situations; for example, when possible, save the last option that the user has accessed on your site. In the case of an e-commerce, if the user visits several products, let them have access to the last visited; this facilitates a lot at the time of purchase. In a few e-commerce websites, for example, you can see last products visited, even if they were on different days and still separated by categories.

Leaving the main function of your site prominent

Sites that have clear goals, such as making the user sign up, make an appointment, or sell, should make it explicit to users. If the function of the site is, for example, to sell air tickets, highlight this function and if possible eliminate or give less emphasis to secondary functions.

On Virgin America's website, for example, the main functions is to search for flights.

Improving the loading time

Waiting too long for a page to load is not something well-accepted by users: according to a study by the University of Massachusetts, streaming video services such as YouTube and Netflix, for example, can get or lose users in seconds. *We found that people are patient within two seconds*, said an NPR News science teacher at the University Ramesh Sitaraman.

There are also other studies that demonstrate how risky the loading page time is for conversion:

- Amazon found that every 100 milliseconds a user has to wait represents a 1% decline in sales. Also, a page load slowdown of just one second could cost them $1.6 billion in sales each year.

- According to a survey by Kissmetrics, 40% of users abandon a website that takes more than three seconds to load.
- Two seconds is the time users expect a site to load. After the third second, up to 40% of users abandon the site, according to a study by Gomez.com/dynatrace (`https://www.dynatrace.com/capabilities/synthetic-monitoring/`).
- Regarding online buyer behavior, `Gomez.com` found that *in times of peak traffic, over 75% of online consumers left for the site of a competitor instead of waiting*. The same study points out that 88% of online consumers are less likely to return to a site after a bad experience.
- Lara Hogan published in her book, *Designing for Performance*, that 85% of mobile users expect loading to be as fast or faster than sites on a desktop.
- According to Akamai, experiencing a problem such as freezing, broken links, long time to load, or a complicated payment process will make 75% of online shoppers not buy from that site.
- An increase of half a second loading time of its results pages made Google lose 20% of profitability and user traffic, as reported by the company.

To find out how fast or slow a website is, you can use Pingdom to check the load time of each page or element. The Pingdom Website Speed Test allows you to intuitively test the speed of your site and, similarly to previous tests, receive a final grade, ranging from 0 to 100. The tool also shows graphs about the loading time of the site files, server responses, and file size. Alternatives to Pingdom are tools such as dareboost (`https://www.dareboost.com/en/home`) and GTmetrix (`https://gtmetrix.com/`).

Another cool site that can help in this task is Google's Pagespeed Insights. PageSpeed Insights, for example, analyzes the contents of a web page and then gives a score (from 0 to 100), called the PageSpeed score, as well as generating suggestions to make the page faster. Another positive point: you can check the site's optimization for mobile devices.

To improve the load time of a page, you can count on frontend specialist help. Consider using different font types and sizes, image size and weight, and reuse elements and other design decisions that can impact on loading time, as Lara Callender Hogan suggested in her book, *Design For Performance*. These decisions can (and should) be discussed with your developer.

You can also consider replacing icon images with icon fonts to have a measurable impact on the performance. This improvement happens for basically two reasons:

- While icon fonts use vectors, icon images use raster graphics, so the first is smaller in size (in terms of bytes)

- Icon fonts (such as `fontawesome.io`, `weloveiconfonts.com`, `fontello.com`, or `icomoon.io`) are included in a single file, which minimizes HTTP requests

According to the PicTonic blog, by using icon fonts instead of icon images it is possible to reduce page load time by 14%.

Following design trends

Websites and apps must not only be functional and easy to use and navigate, but also be pleasing to the eye. You can work together with a UI designer or art director to make these decisions.

Choose a suitable color palette to not only communicate the message brand, but also to impact users' emotions, draw their attention, and put them in the right frame of mind to make a purchase. According to the Kiss Metrics Color Psychology Study, 42% of users base their opinion about the website on overall design alone and 52% don't return because of overall aesthetics.

Keep in mind that colors communicate and provoke feelings. You can take advantage of marketing studies on it, such as this color emotion guide of brands:

- **Blue**: The meaning of the color blue is mainly associated with the sensation of peace, as well as white, but in a more subtle way. It reminds you of cleanliness, water, serenity, and productivity. In dark tones it conveys safety, confidence, success, and power. It is used a lot in technology companies.
- **Purple**: The meaning of the color purple refers to wisdom, fantasy, mystery, and spirituality. Purple is a color that calms and imparts well-being, so beauty products, body care ads, and alternative treatments are frequent applications of this shade.
- **Red**: The symbolism of the color red represents love, emotion, excitement, romance, and pleasure. It also expresses urgency, and so is commonly used in the advertising of stores in clearance.
  Combined with yellow, it is widely used in food segments, as in restaurants and fast food chains, as it stimulates the appetite.
- **Green**: The color green is directly associated with health, nature, hope, and life. It reminds us of balance, freshness, harmony, and health. Its use in science, medicine, ecology, tourism, and organic food companies is quite common.

- **Pink**: A light pink color expresses innocence, while in darker tones it inspires desire, affection, and femininity. It is commonly used in products aimed at the female audience.
- **Brown**: The symbolism of the color brown conveys a sense of tradition, conservatism, reliability, solidity, and security, and it is widely used by furniture and interior decoration companies, and architecture.
- **Yellow**: The color yellow encourages creation and communication, and awakens joy, animation, and entertainment. For attention, it is used in traffic signs and also in store windows.
- **Orange**: The color orange represents an energetic, stimulating, young shade. It encourages expansion, creativity, enthusiasm, and optimism. It promotes change and dynamism. It is used in food, sports, and leisure segments.
- **Black**: The color black, according to the context, can represent sadness and mourning, but if it is used well it conveys nobility, tradition, curiosity, superiority, power, and professionalism. Engineering companies, law firms, cosmetics, and luxury products often use this color.
- **White**: The color white in combination with other colors is harmonious, expressing peace, faith, light, and purity. It is commonly used by medicine and dentistry companies.
- **Gray**: Gray is a classic, neutral color that conveys elegance and respect. It is used by technology and automotive companies, as it also demonstrates responsibility and professionalism.

Also be mindful of the images that are used. Studies by IRCE show, for example, that 75% of users list the quality of the images of the products; in e-commerce, this is the most important feature of the buying process, followed by showing alternative views of the product with 66% and zoom with 61%. Additionally, according to an A/B test run by visual website optimizer, larger product images increase sales by 9%. Using large, quality images is often a key factor in increasing conversion. They allow the customer to view the product in more detail.

Just to give you an idea, color ads have a 62% higher visibility rate compared to black and white ads. Colors also have the ability to attract audiences to a particular type of location:

- **Red**: Attracts impulsive shoppers, much used in fast foods and settlements
- **Yellow**: Aims to capture the attention of consumers in store windows, attracting impulsive consumers
- **Blue**: Widely used by corporations and large departments, can be seen in banks, seeking to bring a sense of security and confidence
- **Green**: Can be found in clinics and hospitals, also associated with money and wealth
- **Orange**: Aims to attract attention, also attracts impulsive buyers
- **Purple**: Associated with aesthetic clinics, beauty products, and fine environments, it attracts sophisticated consumers

We will go deeper into these elements in `Chapter 5`, *Using UI and Content For Better Communication*, but remember that all these elements might influence user satisfaction and pleasure when using your website, app, product, or service and can have an impact on conversion.

Using good call-to-action

Another crucial UX element for conversion is **call-to-action** (**CTA**). In addition to appropriate sizes and colors, choose the text carefully as action verbs get more results. You can find in an article by Wishpond a great list of 25 good words to use for your CTA. Design your call-to-action to be personal and communicate value and convey urgency. When it comes to the standard e-commerce funnel, three of the four steps (landing, product, checkout) should have only one primary action.

Make it clear, unambiguous, and use white spaces to make it noticeable. Users should feel confused at no point, during any action, about what steps to take next or the best path to take. Make certain that users know/understand exactly what will happen when they perform an action. Be clear, precise, and simple; for example, use verbs such as *Subscribe to our Newsletter*, but don't be too obvious by saying *click here* (the CTA should in itself be understood as something clickable). Use urgent language when writing the copy for your CTA buttons, especially if you're making a limited time offer, as suggested by the CoSchedule blog:

54 Proven Words And Phrases To Use In your Calls to Action

Verbs To Kick it Off:	Hope And The Answer For What's In It For Me?
Get	Me
Download	My
Start	You
Stop	Your
Build	Results
Grow	Returns results
Join	Guarantee
Learn	Free
Discover	New
Add to cart	Safe
Try	Proven
Find	Rick-free
Save	Because

Exclusivity To Make Your Audience Feel Special:	Urgency To Entice Them To Act Now:
Limited supply	Ends tomorrow
While Supplies last	Limited time only
Only a few left	One-time offer
Featured	Expires soon
Exclusive	Urgent
Advanced	Deadline
Secrets	Now
Access	Only available to ___
Special Offer	Only X days left
Request an Invitation	Offers ends on ___
Members Only	Closing Soon
Now Closed	Today
Pre-register / Pre-order	Today Only
Limited Spots	Last chance
	Hurry
Words to avoid:	Immediately
Submit	Before
Order	Ends
Our / Ours	

To give you an idea, StubHub discovered that the CTA *See details* link, which was designed to take visitors to the ticket purchase page, was too ambiguous and was causing confusion to the user.

After watching visitors run into the same issue over and over again by using the platform `UserTesting.com`, StubHub changed *See Details* to *Go* and conversions increased 2.6%. For StubHub, a 2.6% increase in conversions is worth millions of dollars in revenue per year.

Also, it's very important to give your CTA button a prominent placement, which can be critical to drawing the eyes of visitors. Placement in prominent locations (distinguished area, top or center layout, in the angles for form's buttons) can lead to higher conversions because users will likely notice the call to action button and truly take action.

Buttons that are included in CTA elements should be different from the rest of the buttons on your website. The explanation is that CTA buttons, rather than simply serving as a functional UI element, should be designed to encourage a specific action.

Buttons should stand out. Buttons that aren't clearly buttons may experience a markedly lower click-through rate. Make sure that all buttons that perform a similar action have a similar design, being consistent. Think about the shape of the CTA buttons (rectangular buttons are better than circular ones) and consider a color pattern of feelings related to a specific action:

- **Blue, Green**: Positive (CTA: save, send, download)
- **Red**: Negative (CTA: delete, block, reset)
- **Black**: Neutral (CTA: see more, alternatives, discover)
- **Grey**: Disable

Regarding color, also mind the background color across our CTA's. An effective primary CTA should be a button in a contrasting color to your main website color scheme to help it stand out. It is also interesting to run A/B tests to learn what works better for your users. The CTA button has to be intuitively clickable.

The **Add to Cart** button, for example, can determine whether or not the user will add the item to your shopping cart. Aspects to consider are the color, format, size, text, visibility, ease of clicking, and loading speed. You can use, for example, a contrasting color button with the rest of the page, drawing the customer's attention.

Summary

In this chapter, you had the chance to understand how UX can be important to fix issues that are dropping the conversion for a website or app, impacting the business results.

You saw how to identify conversion issues by doing a UX analysis, such as quantitative/data analysis, and deeply understanding the users by doing researching, interviewing, and usability tests, besides testing solutions to fix the issues you have identified.

You also saw practical examples of how to fix UX issues by considering building responsive and accessible websites, improving loading time, saving time for your users, and following design trends.

In Chapter 5, *Using UI Elements and Content For Better Communication*, you will see how to use UI elements and content for better communication, being careful with writing and content, chasing the right typography, and using consistent iconography.

5
Using UI and Content for Better Communication

Even an experienced UXer might think that typography, colors, and icons should be UI designers, or content producers, concern. But the truth is that these elements can impact user experience.

In Chapter 4, *Increasing Conversion with UX*, we saw a how important elements such as CTA, copy, colors, and UI can be crucial for conversion. In this chapter, we will explore the following topics:

- Identifying UI and content issues
- The importance of UI for good UX
- Color, iconography, and typography as part of communication
- Content strategy for UX
- Real examples, or case studies
- Practical advice

Identifying UI and content issues

If you ask developers about the importance of the visual aspects of a project in defining user experience, you might commonly hear that they are important for the satisfaction and pleasure of the users. The truth is that a bad use of UI elements and content can result in different UX issues.

First of all, it is important that we know the difference between UI and UX (you will be asked about this a lot!): While user experience design corresponds to the continuous improvement of the usability of its system, it is concerned with producing a simple and intuitive interaction between users and machines, which translates into user satisfaction when when task are performing in an uncomplicated way. The goal of user interface design is to incorporate the company's identity into the application's DNA. UI designers are responsible for how the customer sees their product, which goes beyond the color scheme, fonts, and buttons. Instead the customers sees their product as a graphic development that incorporates a certain perception about the company itself (is its brand is sober, solid, reliable or is it more accessible, close to the customer?), through animations, responsiveness, tips, and visual cues that guide interaction and even market analysis.

When we talk about UX, or user experience, we're talking about something subjective. That is, no matter how much a designer or web designer strives, they cannot have 100% control over what people will feel when they try out a product they have designed. A part of people's opinions will always be emotional, temporary, and even impulsive in some cases. This means that there is a certain degree of unpredictability in the acceptance of this product.

The acronym UI stands for user interface. In this case, we are talking about something much more objective and controllable. The UI designer takes care of the part where the user interacts with a website (in the case of web design), layout, or product. Are the on and off buttons on a cell phone visible? Does the layout and colors of a graphic work show all the information the audience should see? Is the software intuitive? Does the order of the commands remain in the user's memory between one use and another? All of these questions are part of UI design.

The UX and UI are used together to enhance the design's effects on those who have contact with it. So a didactic way of looking at your differences would be to think that you can improve the **user interface (UI)** in order to create a better **user experience (UX)**.

The model proposed by interaction designer Dan Saffer, one of the pioneers in this area, puts UI design at an intersection of interaction design and visual design. These two areas, in turn, are part of the large group of experience design, which also encompasses information architecture and industrial design, among other fields.

We can say that, in general terms, UX design is concerned with macro issues—that is, the whole and not just the interface—while UI design focuses on the micro. UI design transforms the results of UX design into something palpable, visual, that is, it is the bridge that will turn into reality everything that was designed for the user experience. Hence, the ideal would be for the UX design to come before the UI design.

If we were dealing with a web application, for example, the UI would be the *design* part of the site and the way it would be presented to users, including aspects such as the color palettes to be used, fonts, and everything else. The UI is responsible for trying to seduce the user with its appearance. Aspects related to how the user will interact with the application are also embedded within the UI field.

Note that the UI is an important aspect, since it is usually characterizes the first contact that the user will have with the website or web application. Humans are very much guided by visual aspects and sensations, so a well-designed and thoughtful user interface can be the first step in keeping a user within a website. If the website were of a cake, this is the first step in persuading someone to eat it.

We can say that UI design is the means by which a person interacts and controls a device, software, or application. This control can be done through buttons, menus, and any element that provides an interaction between the device and the user. Also, as part of the user interface, you can consider typography, iconography, color scheme, and so on, besides content such images, graphs, copy, and text. These elements will have a huge influence on the communication with the user, and will result in a good or bad experience. Using these elements incorrectly might can cause misunderstanding and consequently drive the users to make mistakes; the users in completing their tasks correctly.

The importance of good UI for a great UX

There are two different, but similar, examples of how these simple elements can have a huge impact on the right communication and drive a user to commit mistakes. The way two winner cards were designed meant that the event presenters found themselves at the center of really embarrassing moments at two important award events: Miss Universe 2015 and the 2017 Oscars.

After the epic miss of the 2015 Miss Universe competition—the occasion when host Steve Harvey announced the winner as Miss Colombia when, in fact, it was Miss Philippines—perhaps few people imagined that another mistake of the same kind and at event of that scale, could repeat itself. Then we get to the 2017 Oscars and the awarding of the title of Best Picture to **La La Land**, when the winner was actually **Moonlight**, marked the first time that an error of this magnitude was committed in the history of the awards.

Speaking about the error of the winner's announcement at Miss Universe, as explained in the Digital-tutors blog (which you can see at: `http://blog.digitaltutors.com/miss-universe-2015-lessons-bad-graphic-design/`), we can see that the basic errors were due to the person who produced the card with the name of the winner and the misalignment of the information on the card—the second and third place names were on the left, while the winner's name was on the right.

There is a break in consistency, which ends up creating confusion. Another breach of consistency is that the names of second and third place are soon after their respective titles, while the name of Miss Universe is below the title. The second basic error is communication failure. Why write Miss Universe 2015 when one could simply say Winner? Since Harvey was presenting Miss Universe, it was very easy for him to confuse Miss Universe 2015 with a simple identification of the event. Another basic error was that the format of the program was already confusing, since it presents the second and third place before the winner. Also consider that they do not use the terms *second and third place*, but *first and second runner up*. Is the number one not always associated with the winner? Look who's on the side of the number one on the card—Miss Colombia. In addition, the producers wanted Harvey to read the names of the participants from top to bottom, when the winners are usually placed at the top of the list. That being said, it remains to be seen if Miss Universe 2016 will simply have a new presenter or will think more about the graphic design.

The Oscar 2017 card was developed by PricewaterhouseCoopers, the company responsible for keeping the names of the winners secret. At the top of the page is the Oscar logo, the largest element on the page. Then comes the winner's name, centered and in quotes, as reproduced by designer Brandon James:

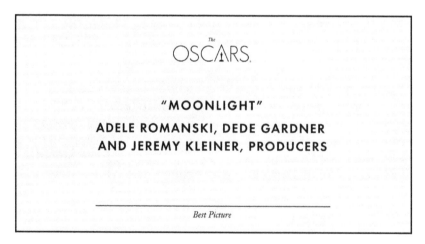

Redesign by Brandon Jameson – pbjameson.com

Note that the winner has the same weight and size as the list of names that follows just below. Already the category—as Best Picture—is listed last, with shy and small print. A seemingly simple layout, but one that was done with serious visual hierarchy problems.There are some questions and lessons to learn here:

- What is the most important information on the card? Undoubtedly, the category title and the name of the winning movie. Ironically, the category is the smallest information on the card.
- Is it really necessary to include the names of producers? If so, they should be smaller than the name of the movie.
- The logo in this case is the least important information. It should come under everything and with a reduced size (just like they did with the category title).

For Fast Co.(https://www.fastcodesign.com/3068535/this-simple-design-change-would-have-saved-the-oscars), the award winners' cards are layer upon bad typographic design layer. To begin with, the award logo is the biggest element of the layout. Beneath the logo is the winner's name, centered and in quotes which makes sense, but it would do much more if it were in larger, bold letters, for example, especially considering that all the names listed below are presented in exactly the same way. As a consequence, the winner does not get the attention they deserve. To make matters worse, the category names—*Best Actress, Best Picture*, and so on, appears below, small and in lowercase letters. *Of course it does not matter when it all works out. But the role of design is not to be a solution for when things are okay, but when things go wrong*, the site notes. In short, if the card inside the envelope were clearer—if it had the proper typography and a hierarchy of logical information—then the person in charge of announcing the winner would have realized the error.

Thinking about it, designer Brandon Jameson remade the card. At the top, he put the category name, Best Picture, in large print, assuring the presenter that he had the correct card in his hand. Next comes the name of the winner—in capital letters, bold and in quotation marks. The names that follow, the directors and producers, are written in uppercase and lowercase letters. And finally, the Oscar logo was shortened and put down there. For Fast Co., this example illustrates how subtle changes in design can help prevent a specific human failure. *People reading these cards are sometimes older, have probably been drinking, and are in the spotlight in front of their colleagues delivering some of the industry's most important information in the year—these cards need to be bulletproof*, says Jameson:

Redesign by Brandon Jameson – pbjameson.com

Another suggestion would also consider the envelope opening as part of the experience. In this case, the category would come first and be visual as soon as the envelope is opened:

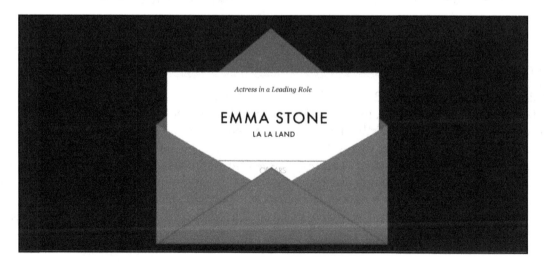

UI elements for good UX communication

Both examples, Miss Universe 2015 and the 2017 Oscars, presented problems of typography, hierarchy, and copy. As we have seen, simple solutions could have avoided the embarrassing mistakes. In the following pages, we will better understand how to focus on these elements as part of the user experience.

Minding the hierarchy of the UI elements

The visual hierarchy is one of the key principles of design. Whether creating print or digital pieces, you will have to deal with the content, and it needs to be well organized in the layout. More than being creative, you must take into account the subtleties required in composition, whether in the choice of colors, sizes, contrasts, orientation, positions, types, and especially what to include and exclude from your layout. The visual hierarchy is the organization and prioritization of the content in order to communicate the message well to the public.

As designers, we need to make well-intentioned decisions regarding content prioritization. With the massive amount of information available and the time the user spends gaining a first impression of the site, if the message is not thoughtfully placed, your message will not have the impact that you would like. You should put yourself in the user's shoes, creating paths to guide you along the route you want. It is necessary for you to pay attention to the elements that are most important graphically and distribute them in order to guide the user along the most important paths.

In the following figure, the hierarchy shows its power by structuring the same text in different ways:

- **Level 1 - Headline**: Or title! It is precisely that part of the text that must be seen immediately, which must attract (or shock) the reader
- **Level 2 - Subtext**: Here is a brief summary of what it is all about, to convince the reader to move on
- **Level 3 - Text**: Here is the bulk of the work, where the previous levels are explained in running text (which, unfortunately, is often the only level of the hierarchy)

To get the most out of the information and give the user the best experience, you should know the six principles of the visual hierarchy:

- **Patterns for viewing pages**: Most cultures read from top to bottom and from left to right (Arabic, Farsi, Hebrew, and over 20 other languages are read from right to left. Twitter, for example, accommodates users who read/write right to left). In addition to this information influencing the creation of a page, the task is much more complex than that. Recent studies show that people first look over the page completely before they start reading. Display patterns tend to have two forms—F and Z.

  The F pattern generally applies to pages with a lot of text, such as articles or blog posts. The reader scans the left side of the page, searching for interesting keywords in left-aligned headings or initial topic sentences, and then stops and reads (in the right direction) when they find something that piques their interest:

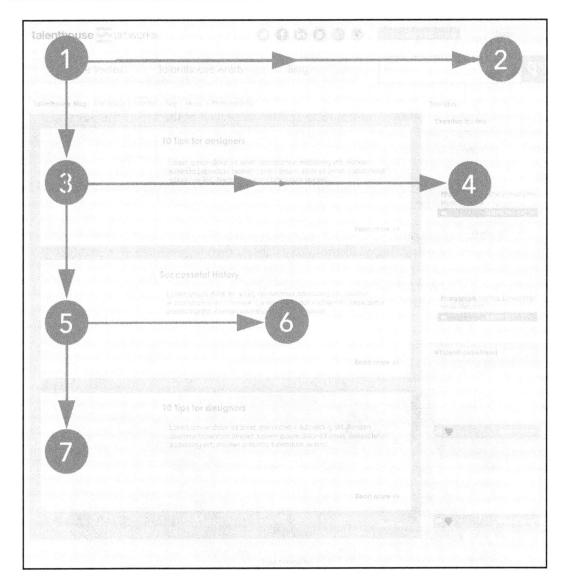

"F" reading pattern

To use this principle in design, align the important information to the left and use short, bold titles, text markers, and other ways to draw attention to breaking paragraphs throughout the text.

In summary, the F pattern suggests that:

- The user first reads in a horizontal movement, usually the upper content part
- Next, the users descends a little and reads in a second horizontal movement
- They then scan the contents of the left in a vertical movement
- The most important information should be placed at the top of the page (certainly within the first two paragraphs, according to NNG findings) or design where it is usually read
- We must use the left side of the layout to put highlighted phrases (using bullets, for example) where a large, horizontal eye movement is not necessary to take in the information

The Z pattern generally, applies to pages that are not centered on the text. And the way many pages are being designed these days, this group is getting larger, including pages such as ads or websites where information is not necessarily presented in paragraph blocks. The reader's eyes first check along the top of the page, where important information is more likely to be found, then head down, in the opposite corner on the diagonal, and do the same across the bottom of the page:

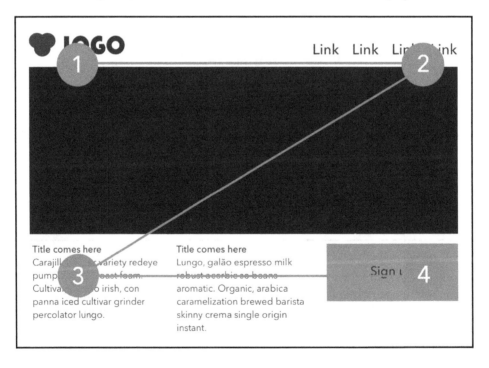

However, studies says that when presented with text-heavy content, we often follow the Gutenberg diagram:

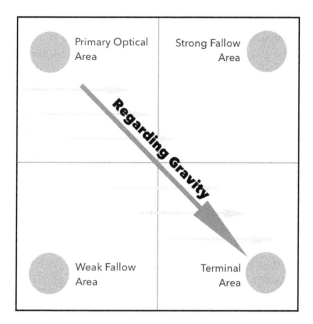

The Gutenberg diagram is a method used to understand how cultures that read from left to right visually navigate of content (the pattern of our eye movement), and how to optimize the layout as a result. This demonstrates a user behavior known as **Reading Gravity**, our habit of reading from left to right, top to bottom, in horizontal motions. Our eyes move from a primary area to a terminal area.

This diagram divides the layout into four quadrants:

- **Primary Optical Area**, located at the top left: That's where our eyes focus right away.
- **Strong Fallow Area**, located at the top right: It's used as a great place for pull-out supporting messages, secondary level offers, or cross-links to supporting content.
- **Weak Fallow Area**, located in the lower-left corner: It is the so-called diagram blind zone, the area that the user will pay less attention to.
- **Terminal area** (**Area terminal**), located in the lower-right corner: When the user arrives here, there is usually a pause in reading. It's a perfect place to include a button action.

The Gutenberg diagram suggests that areas of strong and weak rest will receive minimal attention from the user because they are furthest from the natural reading axis, unless they can visually detach them in some way.

For this very brief analysis of this theory, we can say that the most important elements must be placed along the axis of reading gravity. For example, place the logo or titles in the upper-left corner, a relevant image or text in the middle, and a CTA in the terminal area.

While it is interesting to consider these reading patterns, eye-tracking devices have shown that each human traverses the layout in a different way, and the path that the eyes follow is as unique to the person as their fingerprint. So, never disregard the usability tests, A/B, and so on that we have talked about in the previous chapters.

- **Size**: This is the simplest and most direct rule possible: People read the big things first. On the following Google Creative Lab site, it is very likely that the words **HAPPY PARTY** were your first focus of attention. This is intentional and focused on the main message that the company wants to convey. That is on the Google Creative Lab site: www.globalhappyparty.com.

Size, especially for texts, is a powerful tool in that it circumvents traditional rules of reading from left to right and from top to bottom. This means that a large word or phrase may be in the lower-right corner and will be the first thing a person reads. In addition, size can emphasize the message or content, making it more meaningful.

- **Space and texture**: Another way to get attention is to give the content a large space of respite. If there is a substantial negative space left around a button, or the lines of a block of text are well spaced, these elements will be more readable to the reader.

Spacing can be a stylish alternative or an addition to using large sizes in creating a website. Reducing visual noise will create clearer points of evidence for its creation. White space also makes the content more readable. A 2004 study found that using white space between paragraphs and right and left margins increases readers' comprehension by 20% as they find it easier to focus on content.

The texture refers to the total or default arrangement of space, text, and other details of creating a website.

- **Typography**: The choice of types is key to establishing a good visual hierarchy. Among the most important attributes we can select are the weight—the width of the strokes that make up a letter—and the style, with or without serif. Other attributes such as italics can be important as well. We will see more about this in the following pages.

- **Color**: Applying color to a composition has an immediate effect on the hierarchy. For example, if the main information is composed of a vibrant orange, while the secondary information is composed of a cold gray, the two levels of the hierarchy are visually separated to an even greater degree. Color can also be used to connect related informational components within the composition.

  Here is another simple and well-functioning rule: Bright colors stand out in soft or grayscale colors. You can explore this to get the user's attention wherever you want. Also, certain colors can help set the site's mood (blues are quiet, reds more aggressive, and so on).

  The Fitbit website uses colors, within the Z layout pattern, intelligently. The use of bright magenta immediately places the user's attention to the top of the visual hierarchy by also linking to the **get active** button, signaling that the two concepts are related.

- **Direction**: Page layouts are typically designed according to vertical and horizontal grids, both by convention and by the most readable formats. In this system, a new form of hierarchy emerges: breaking the existing grids. Texts placed in curves or diagonals will automatically stand out against the blocked texts of the remaining layout. This has been an effective strategy in ads and also on websites.

Choosing the appropriate typography

Typography is the soul of graphic work, be it in a physical or virtual environment. It has a lot of importance in the weight of the information and in the way that the users will perceive the content that it is meant to transmit. According to Oliver Reichenstein, web design is 95% typography. An ill-chosen type can ruin all the previous work of visual strategy design.

The first point is to know that typography for the web is different from that chosen for paper. The medium, the time, and the way of interaction are different, so the types have to be carefully chosen so that the user has the best experience with the site, be it through the phone, tablet, or desktop. That being said, it is worth remembering that typography is not only about the type, but about analyzing all textual content that will be presented: contrast, length, size, hierarchy, readability, reading, spacing, and composition end of the textual structure.

So, let's look at the sections of a typical website (structured according to the creation of content of the sites) and try to understand the best ways to use typography at every step of the design of the site.

Headline

The headline of your site is extremely important, since, according to surveys, most people only read titles when they are on the internet. The right thing is to bet on the highlighted headlines to gain the attention of the user, encouraging the later reading of the body of text.

According to a study done in 2013 by Smashing Magazine, sans-serif types are the most popular, with 51% occupying positions of use in the headlines of sites. However, recently, serif types have become more widely used due to the belief that they stand out in headlines, creating a more readable structure.

The most popular serif types for headlines are Georgia and Chaparral Pro, while the sans-serifs are Arial and Freight Sans Pro. A good tip is to use standard fonts, regardless of style, and to keep the number of fonts you use to a minimum and certainly no more than three on any website.

The trend, which has been used for some years and which remains popular in 2018, is that of sites with very large and bold type, with a strong visual impact, simple and effective, justifying the attention focused on the headline of the site.

Body of text

The body of text is one of the most important parts of your site content, since it is where the user will absorb the information you need to pass on. Although in headlines the difference between the use of serif and nonserif types is small, according to research, in the body of the text the question is different. Approximately 61.5% of sites use serif types in the text body versus 36.5% of nonserif use.

The same study indicates that most websites nowadays do not use standard types (such as Times New Roman, Arial, Helvetica, and Courrier New) either in the headline or in the body of text. This is due to the fact that brands have to differentiate in the choice of types, opting for services such as Fontdeck.com and TypeKit.com that run away from the standardized possibilities of using types for the web.

You can also use the Adobe Edge Web Fonts service (`https://edgewebfonts.adobe.com/fonts`) or `FontSquirrel.com` for more non-standard options.

Background

A good background choice for a website is one based on a color that allows contrasting text to be highlighted. This makes it easy and quick for the user to read the headline and text body more clearly. It is important to note that many sites are now betting on less hard but still legible contrasts, providing a comfortable reading that allows the simple identification of each line of text.

When it comes to body text, it is still very common for the white background pattern and black text to be used as it has enough contrast and refers to the classic color format of newspapers, making this contrast more popular.

Responsive typography

It is inevitable: Everything in web design has to be thought of from the perspective of responsive design. There are no more fixed widths, and the word of the hour is to adapt. Today, 42% of websites are already conceived of in terms of responsive typography. They are prepared to change shapes and scales when the size of browsers changes. These changes include the repositioning and adjustment of images, menus being replaced by icons, multiple columns becoming one, and fonts being repositioned and resized.

There are several methodologies for applying responsive typography on a website, especially if you write your CSS in SASS; The most recent way to do it, there is a platform called Flowtype.js that uses JavaScript to adjust the font size and height lines according to the width of the specific containers. Although it works very well and is an excellent tool for prototyping, optimization, and adjustments, Flowtype does not offer the refined control over the typography that would be necessary for the requirements of a large and complex project.

Fonts

Typography is much more than just the typeface or the text of a composition. It is about balance, positioning, hierarchy, and structure. Still, your choice of font is an important part of this process.

Some important features to consider when choosing your source are as follows:

- **Legibility**: Are the characters very different from each other? Highly modular or geometric fonts may be less legible than those with more organic and individualized shapes. Many types do not have a good distinction between the il, 1l e Il, glyphs, such as the Gill Sans font.
- **Reading**: Is reading the font comfortable in the text body? Does the font work in long texts? A good typeface for a UI has to be extremely readable in small sizes. As the text gets too small, we need a type with a large height-x. Height-x is the size of the letters in the lowercase.
- **Flexibility**: Does the font work in different sizes and weights? Would it work well for both titles and body text? A versatile source is able to solve many types of problems and express a rich hierarchy.
- **Charisma**: Are your details unique? Does your appearance look attractive when magnified?
- **Adaptability**: Is it screen-optimized?

Do not forget that each of the sources has its characteristics and history. For example:

- **Georgia**: This was built to order on-screen in 1996. It has a high height-x. Because it is already available in virtually every modern operating system and has meticulous hinting—adjustments for maximum readability on computer monitors—Georgia maintains its popularity on the web. It works great in smaller sizes, but its personality in the display mode (in large sizes) is not very expressive. Because it is a serifed font, it convey the sense of a classic, elegant, and traditional font.
- **DIN**: This became a standard source for signposting in Germany in the 1940s, often used on railroads and highways. With its rigid angles and square geometry, the DIN is suitable for headlines whenever a striking and architectural appearance is required. Its large height-x and its open shapes make it an appropriate choice for body text as well, although it can be tiring for long readings. It is a nonserif font, which passes the idea of a modern, minimalist, and friendly font.

It may sound like bullshit, but knowing the story behind a font can be crucial to the message you want to get across in your layout. A spoiler from Tim Brown's article: He says he used the Minion font in his layout because it's based on Renaissance ideas. He also chose to use the golden ratio for historical connections. As the project was about the history and typographic tradition, it made sense to use elements related to cultural roots.

To understand the impact that typeface can have on what readers thought, American film director Errol Morris ran an experiment in the New York Times with the title *Are you an Optimist or a Pessimist*. He wanted to understand whether typeface could affect how people perceived the information that was presented to them, so he put in front of readers a passage from David Deutsch's book, followed by a yes or no question inquiring from the respondents whether the respondents supported the claim presented in the book and just how confident they were about their answers.

A total of six different typefaces, namely Trebuchet, Comic Sans, Georgia, Baskerville, Computer Modern, and Helvetica, were tested among 45,000 readers on nytimes.com. The results showed that statements in Comic Sans had the least amount of credibility—Helvetica was a close second. The majority of respondents agreed with and trusted the statements in Baskerville typefont.

A study run by Michael Bernard of *Usability News* compared eight popular online typefaces—namely Courier New, Arial, Times New Roman, Comic Sans, Tahoma, Century Schoolbook, Verdana, and Georgia. All the fonts were examined at 10, 12, and 14-points sizes with a total of 60 people participating in the study. The results revealed that Times New Roman and Arial were read the fastest and that Arial and Courier were found to be the most readable. Though it is hard to figure out whether serif or sans-serif is better, the general opinion is that sans-serif texts are much more readable, even when present in smaller sizes.

The correct choice of typeface is crucial to the readability of your site, as well as the number of characters per line (it is suggested between 44 and 75, with 66 considered ideal), the size of the lines, and how the text is organized in pages (blocks, justified, left-aligned). Line length is the distance between the side margins of a block of text. Excessively long lines (over 100 characters) are a very common problem. Shorter lines will make a big difference in the legibility and professionalism of your layout. Because the length of a block of text may vary according to the font size used, the most effective way to control this measurement is by controlling the amount of characters. Shorter lines are more comfortable to read. Longer lines—as our eye needs to travel further from the end of a line to the beginning of the next—are more difficult to keep up with and keep engaged with reading. Try to use an average line length of 45-75 characters, including spaces and punctuation. In practice, space limitations or special use orders may require longer or shorter lengths. In any case, keep an eye out to see when the block is extremely long or short, enough to detract from good reading.

Line spacing, also called line spacing or line height, shapes the appearance of paragraphs and page structure, giving vertical rhythm as the user follows the text. A text composed by very tight interlacing stimulates the vertical movement of the eyes, and the user can easily get lost; this style can be used to convey an idea of urgency or exaggeration. Likewise, composite types with a very long line between them create streaks that also distract from reading.

As a general rule, your body content should be 12-point font. A study from Wichita State University determined that older adults prefer 14-point fonts for legibility and reading time. Keep in mind that a size that looks ideal on a mobile may appear to be small on a computer screen, and vice versa. People tend to hold a cell phone close to their face, as they sit farther away from the desktop screens. A good starting point for a desktop is 16 pixels. On mobile devices, the types can be smaller because the user can adjust the distance between the screen and their face to get the size most suited to their needs. Already for mobile, the size can start at 12 pixels:

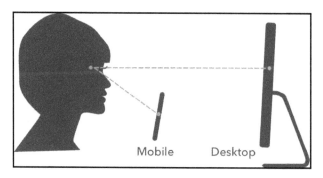

Mobile   Desktop

The study *Make It Big! The Effect of Font Size and Line Spacing on Online Readability*, by Luz Rello, Martin Pilot, and Mari-Carmen Marcos (`pielot.org/pubs/Rello2016-Fontsize.pdf`), which used eye-tracking to measure comprehension among people who read Wikipedia articles of varying text sizes and line spacings, found that 18-point text has the best readability and comprehension, and between 1.0 and 1.4 line spacing was ideal. The most important thing is to ensure that the text is in a comfortable size for reading. Believe in your perception.

One helpful tool that you can use to discover determining typographic tips based on font size and content width is the Golden Ratio Typography Calculator (`pearsonified.com/typography/`).

The font size will also help to determine hierarchies, in addition to differentiating the body text from titles. Formatting such as bold or italic can be used to define subtitles and photo captions. The important thing is that there is standard formatting and consistency.

An important tip is not to use more than two typefaces, one for body text and one for the buttons. Sticking to a basic typeface scheme of two to three different typefaces is the best way to encourage visitors to read your content. You can use Google Fonts (`https://fonts.google.com/`) to try all kinds of fonts on your website copy. Choose one typeface for your body text and another for titles and headings to establish a clear hierarchy that helps convince all the *scanners* who jump around your content to dive in and explore it further.

Keep these principles in mind:

- Mixing fonts is never a requirement—it's an option. You can build hierarchies using variations of size, weight, and contrast.
- A combination of two sources is acceptable. In some cases, three will work. But a composition with four types or more will almost never have a satisfactory result.
- You can mix any two fonts as long as they are visibly different. If you have ever heard someone say that you can only mix a serifed font with a nonserif font—that's not true.

- Font mixing has a better result when each font has consistent paper in the document. For example, in the following image, one source is for the titles and another for the text body:

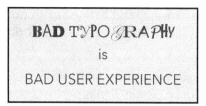

Picking the right color scheme

Colors carry a variety of psychological messages that can be used to influence the verbal sense of typography. Selecting a color for specific words in a composition can influence the user in their actions. But this is true not only for typography—colors can have a huge influence on communication, and can result in a good or bad user experience.

The power of color in marketing and advertising is a known fact, and it has been studied exhaustively in recent decades. With the emergence of the internet, it was only a matter of time before these studies included websites, and that web marketing realized the power that colors have in influencing behavior in converting leads. Believe that the colors you use in a CTA can influence the number of clicks you will get, for example.

Some time ago, Hubspot ran a test to see if changing the color on a button would impact conversion rates. They didn't change the text or outline—the only change or variation was the red or green color on a button. Despite the initial perception that the green color is more neutral and friendly, and would get better results, the fact is that the red buttons had a conversion rate that was higher by 21%. That is, even without changing texts, diagrams, and images, the page conversion can go up with a simple change of color on a button.

Of course, this does not mean that the use of the color red is always the solution. We should only take into account that a CTA should stand out clearly from the rest of the page to draw attention and make the user's eyes move to that specific area. And above all, we should not be afraid to test.

Three factors that are good to keep in mind when thinking about color combinations are-the complementation (how colors interact with each other), contrast (used to create a sense of division between elements), and vibrancy, aka the brightness or darkness (used to dictate mood).

You can define the color scheme in partnership with the UI designer. To choose the best color scheme, you should understand a bit more about colors and different groups of color schemes:

- **Monochromatic harmony group**: This is the harmony resulting from the same color of the chromatic circle. The shades may change, but they all stay in the same color.
- **Analog harmony group**: This is the harmony resulting from a primary color combined with two adjacent colors in the chromatic circle. A color is worked as dominant, while the adjacent ones are used to enrich the harmony.
- **Complementary harmony group**: This is the resultant harmony when we combine opposite colors in the chromatic circle. They are colors that are symmetrically positioned relative to the center of the chromatic circle. Hue varies by 180 degrees from one color to another. This harmony works even better if cold colors and warm colors are combined.
- **Triadic harmony group**: This is the resultant harmony when we use three colors equidistant in the chromatic circle. It is very popular with artists because it offers a high visual contrast, while maintaining the balance and richness of colors.
- **Divided completion group**: It is the harmony resulting from the selection of two pairs of complementary colors. Called by some tetra or rectangle by some, these combinations are the richest of all harmonies, because they uses four colors in complementary in pairs.

But it's a very difficult harmony to work on. If the four colors are used in equal proportion, the set will appear unbalanced, so a color should always be chosen as the dominant one over the others.

To help you to choose the best color scheme for your project, you can use examples from the `colorhunt.co` website:

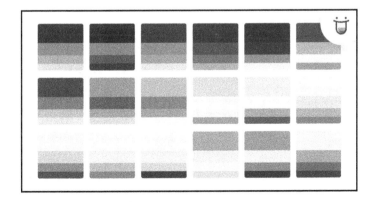

Developed by the Devbridge Group agency, Styleguide (`livingstyleguide.devbridge.com`), it lets you create beautiful, functional style guides for digital products, or as they often say, live style guides:

Like the Styleguide shown in the previous screenshot, Frontify (`https://frontify.com/`) allows you to create style guides for brands and digital products, but it comes with a few more tools to create prototypes, design specifications, and other features for developers.

To inspire you, you can use FINDGUIDELIN.ES (`findguidelin.es`), a directory with links to great brand guidelines for digital products. It serves as a great reference for you to create your style guides, or even for proper use of well-known brands. The cool thing is that the site can work using a collaborative process—that is, you can also collaborate by sending the link with the brand manuals.

Using consistent iconography

The amount of information displayed on an interface and the amount of screen space are often inversely proportional. When we take this experience into the *mobile world*, this discrepancy is even greater. With this, there is a need to optimize and organize the interface design of your site or system more easily and simply. One way to solve this problem may be to use icons.

Icons are elements that, in addition to playing an important role in communication between users and digital interfaces, are also responsible for guiding the way the user navigates, helping them to memorize the paths for information searching, helping the most intuitive interface becoming more intuitive, helping in the fluidity of the interaction, and creating good experiences for the user.

An icon can represent objects, processes, and actions/operations as long as they are correctly designed. It will help human-computer interaction because the user will identify and choose quickly, easily, and directly the action they want to perform on the system. It has the function of indicating what will be done when it is triggered. Therefore, the icon, besides playing the role of a button, also plays the role of indicating the next actions within a metaphorized environment.

Therefore, the icon is an important element for communication in digital interfaces, since it has the function of guiding the user in the search for information, helping them to memorize paths by making the digital medium more friendly and intuitive; facilitating communication and interaction between the user and the system, mainly for acting as elements of information synthesis; and privileging interfaces with small proportions and content, such as smartphones, tablets, cameras, and other digital devices that contains little space for interaction.

Using visual aids to facilitate the transmission of an idea is very common when our intention is to optimize communication by reducing what could be long phrases into a single image, or, more precisely, an icon. In traffic signs, information boards, or labels, we use the presence of icons to convey an idea. However, this communication is not always effective. Abstracting an idea, or a concept, from an image as simple as an icon is not an easy task. More complex still is trying to define which icons will be easily interpreted by people. Who ever wondered what all those icons really mean on clothing labels? Looking at the following image:

The icons are images that are used to simplify an idea, and the understanding of them depends very much on the experiences and repertoire of each one. To be more challenging, this idea is not always well absorbed by people, generating more difficulty than understanding. The web is no different. We found a huge variety of icons used in websites and apps that have been used over time, creating a very specific icon culture for that context. Still, we have many cases where the idea of the icon is lost by the user.

However, icons can be great for universal communication, as we have seen in `Chapter 1,` *Understanding UX and its Importance,* when looking at the solution used by the Japan Restroom Industry Association after a survey showed that tourists are often unable to understand the many controls on Japanese toilets, making going to the toilet very complicated for them. Concerned about being more tourist-friendly for the 2020 Tokyo Olympic Games, Japan's Restroom Industry Association (`http://www.sanitary-net.com/global/`) has agreed to create a set of standardized icons:

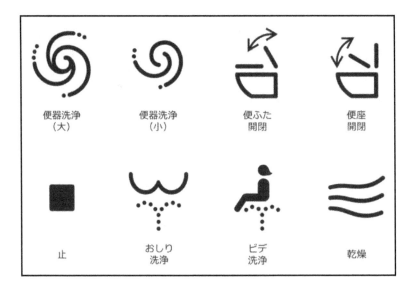

To use them effectively, we must pay particular attention to the connection between their form and the action that will be performed by pressing their corresponding button. The graphic sign must have a direct or metaphorical identification with what will be executed. To illustrate this, we can cite the pencil as the icon that will edit any document. A pencil is an object that humans use to write on paper, so it is an excellent representation for editing documents, just as a recycle bin represents deleting the document—that is, *throwing the document in the trash.*

When we talk about a system or website, it will not only have an action, a link, or an item to select. There will be several actions within an interactive interface where the icon will not come alone. It will be accompanied by a grouping of icons in the same pattern, called an iconography, which will be specially designed to be identified by the user as part of that system.

It is important that the iconography of your website is consistent and standardized so users know their meaning. Your users shouldn't be spending time trying to interpret the icons. Icons should give users a point of reference. A very good project related to iconography is the Google Visual Assets Guidelines, published on Behance.net. This project consists of an application manual, standardization, and development of icons based clearly on flat design. You can see more of Google material design at: `https://material.io/icons/`.

A website that can help in this task is the Noun Project (`https://thenounproject.com/`), where you can find thousands of great icons created by designers from around the world.

If you are looking for a set of icons with the power to use CSS, try: `fontawesome.io`.

In general, whenever we want a clearer and more objective communication of an idea, we use text to describe it. When reading a title or a phrase, we are much less likely to fall into ambiguities and doubts, once the intention has been described in detail. However, if this change of an icon to text ends up causing discomfort to the user experience, we can solve the problem of understanding, but we add another visual in its place.

There are two important pieces of information to consider here:

- Icons are good for optimizing space and achieving a more pleasant visual effect
- Texts make clear the idea that we want to convey

In a study conducted by the User Testing Blog, 88% of users correctly predicted what would happen when they clicked on an icon with a label. This number drops to 60% on icons without labels:

> *"Icons are, by definition, a visual representation of an object, action, or idea. If that object, action, or idea is not immediately clear to users, the icon is reduced to mere eye candy — confusing, frustrating, eye candy — and to visual noise that hinders people from completing a task."*

> *– Nielsen Normam Group*

According to studies conducted by the Nielsen Norman Group, to improve the usability of an icon and avoid ambiguity, a good practice would be to add, whenever possible, captions or labels to each icon. This way, we avoid wasting time that the user would have used to decipher an icon and greatly improved their experience of interacting with this interface. In other words, icons should never be purely decorative. If they are not immediately recognizable, or if they increase the cognitive load, then you need to consider their utility.

Remember that there are already some well-known icons on the web, such as the play/pause and close button, and so on, which can be applied to the layout without these subtitles, since the meaning is already widely known in the web community. That is, we can more securely use some icons that have already been used a lot on the web, and which consequently have become a standard to represent certain ideas.

There is no official documentation that determines exactly what these icons are because there are no truly universal icons, although you can find icons that are consistent across platforms and design systems that improve accessibility. A good way out is to always do usability tests with the icons that you use, asking other people what they understood of that icon, or even the user him/herself.

You can run an A/B test not only to choose the best icons, but also to ensure that the use of an icon can be the best alternative. For example, you can use an icon in variation A, and plain text for variation B. This will show you whether the icon is even necessary in the first place:

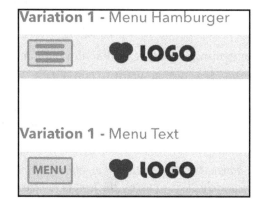

James Foster did a similar A/B test and found that it was actually hurting usability: The text-only version resulted in a 20% increase in conversions. In this case, the icon was not necessary.

Here are some quick tips for choosing iconography:

- Evaluate whether the icons meet the needs of the sender, the receiver, and the medium in which it will be used.
- Start by identifying the icon proposal and its use.
- It is recommended that you use real-world metaphors. This facilitates user recognition, identification, and association of the icon, which can use previous experience and learning to interpret the icon.

- Sort the icons by styles. Consistent stylistic treatment has great importance. Styles should be set so that all icons are grouped by a consistent approach or by their appearance.
- Use the 7 +/- 2 rule to group icons—that is, never use more than nine icons in a single grouping. Above this number, it is very difficult to memorize the metaphor and its spatial position, requiring the user to make extra effort every time a certain screen is used.
- It is recommended that the icon has a simplified appearance. It is much easier to memorize them when their metaphors are represented by graphic syntheses.
- Evaluate the iconography choice by showing them to potential users.
- It is recommended that you use color with discretion. For the creation of an icon, it is enough to use five colors, or even less, including black, white, and/or gray. A lot of color variation distracts the attention of the user.
- Well-designed, systematically designed, and effectively organized icons should be easy and quick to recognize in a complicated visual context.
- Use simple icons—they are much more aesthetic and understanding, and your metaphor will be understood much quicker by being more obvious.

Content strategy and microcopy

Content is not a web writer's only responsibility: Having good copy and text makes a huge difference in the user experience, and the wrong use of them can lead to UX issues. Well-written texts and images with high quality convey credibility, and engage and encourage your user to complete the task. Thinking about all this will be your content strategy.

The content strategy is the process that ensures content is published, edited, republished, rethought, and archived when necessary. It's also the process of planning content creation and ensuring that it appears in the right place, at the right time, and for the right users.

There are some basic components to content strategy focused on content and content strategy focused on people:

Components focused on content:

- **Substance**: What kind of content do we need (topics, types, sources, and so on) and what messages does that content need to communicate to the audience?
- **Structure**: How is content prioritized, organized, formatted, and displayed? (This description of the structure can include communication planning, information architecture, data modeling, link strategy, and so on).

Components focused on people:

- **Workflow**: What processes, tools, and human resources are required for content initiatives to be launched and maintained successfully?
- **Governance**: How are content and strategy decisions made? How are changes initiated and communicated?

The main goal of the content strategist is to think about these four aspects. Usually, they are involved in the initial stages of the project, whether in the planning or research phase.

But for content strategists to be able to make accurate recommendations about how content should circulate across multiple channels, pages, and devices, there are certain activities that they need to do. Let's look at some of them:

Content audit:

- The content audit is usually a repository of all content currently available in the site/app/system/ecosystem that is being redrawn
- In the case of a website, for example, this document takes the form of an organized table of links

The following are some common questions the content audit tries to answer:

- What content already exists on the site?
- How is this content categorized?
- What is important to maintain?
- What will be added again?
- Where is this content linking to?
- How dense is this content?
- In what format is it presented?

Content analysis

Once the content is properly audited, it's time to analyze the results to be able to make recommendations for the new content strategy that should be adopted. It's time to think a bit more about the goals that each piece of content (or content group) is trying to achieve—both the business goals and the goals of the user. And it is precisely here that the intersection with the world of UX begins.

Common questions that this method tries to answer:

- What are the different types of content that exist?
- How does this content compare with competitors?
- What are the objectives of each type of content?
- Which content works better? Which ones are not working?
- Where does this content live and how is it organized?
- Where does the information come from? In what **content management system (CMS)** does it live?

Strategic recommendations

The strategic recommendations are the summary of the opera. It usually takes the form of a deck or presentation, where the strategist analyzes the current state of content, identifies problems, makes recommendations for improvements, prioritizes those recommendations, and plans how these recommendations can be implemented in terms of people and processes.

The following are some common sections of this document:

- Current content state
- People
- Failures/gaps in content
- Competitor analysis
- Future status of content
- Strategic recommendations
- Content versus channels
- Content versus formats
- Governance
- Voice tone
- Workflow

- SEO
- Editorial calendar

This document is usually the most important definition of the content strategy, and it circulates among various stakeholders until there is consensus on the way forward for that project.

Editorial and tone of voice guide

This is the document that informs the creator's work. How should titles be written? What words and which tone of voice should they use/not to use? It is an especially important document in projects where content will be created by several different people. It is a way of establishing a consistent language for the entire product/brand, regardless of who the person on the other side of the screen is, by creating the content that the user consumes.

Organization

In addition to written text, with a tone and appropriate voice, it is also important to note how the text is organized on the page and throughout the site navigation. The text format and how it is organized helps the user understand the navigation better. Make sure that you write clear, useful, meaningful, and concise user-interface text (labels, explanations, tooltips, messages, and so on) that helps users complete the task at hand. You can always change or revise the copy to minimize friction.

SEO

You will want to consider **search engine optimization** (**SEO**) for conversion optimization. Although this is not exactly work for UXers, it is definitely something that we should take a close look at and likely ask a specialist to help us with.

The first search engines understood the context when analyzing keywords and backlinks. Sites were ranked by the number of keywords and synonyms found across their pages, which helped in the relevance of the searched for terms, and web backlinks ranked the popularity of a site.

Search engines now use machine learning to understand the context of a search and the quality of a website, and then deliver the best search result.

Enhancing the performance of any site within search engines is directly related to user satisfaction. The higher the satisfaction, the better the performance. In this equation, the relationship between the two variables (SEO and UX) is increasingly added to the following points:

- Volume of research
- Quality and relevance of content
- General structure
- Customer sentiment

Visitors won't engage with it because the content looks intimidating and it's too hard to read. You can avoid this issue by applying solid content fundamentals:

- Use short paragraphs
- Use short words (write like you speak)
- Scrap filler words and get to the point
- Break up your content with subheadings, lists, and bullet points

Copy and microcopy for UX

A few years ago, we talked a lot about the fact that users do not read. But let's face it, this was at a time when most digital interfaces (mostly sites) used large blocks of text to communicate messages to users, perhaps an inheritance of magazines, booklets, or instruction manuals, when it was assumed that the user was willing to read texts in depth.

Years later came mobiles, a paradigm shift that has affected not only how systems are designed, but also how users behave when interacting with them:

- **From a system point of view**: Mobiles have extremely small interfaces with limited text space and a much shorter, brief, small-dose interaction
- **From the user's point of view**: Mobiles have much more fragmented use of technology throughout the day, and encourage a habit of multitasking, and a much diminished level of concentration on what is being done

According to studies, users will have time to read 28% of the words if they devote all of their time to reading, but realistically, will read about 20% of the text on the average page.

Back in 2008, researcher Jakob Nielson and Harald Weinreich found that most people would scroll around halfway down the page for longer content and only spent enough time on the page to read less than 20% of the text. From these findings, they were able to calculate a formula that describes the amount of text that users would probably read from articles that ranged in the 200 to 1,250 word count. As shown in the graph, as the word count increases, the percentage of people reading not only decreases, but becomes more erratic around the halfway mark:

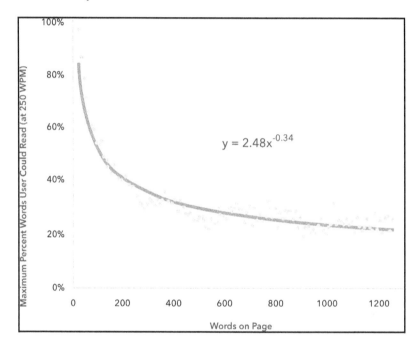

With this in mind, it is natural that people are much less willing to *read* interfaces.

This is why we use the term *microtext* (microcopy in English). In practice, this refers to the art of being able to transmit a message in small fragments, in a limited space of text, with conciseness, clarity, and personality. This can be in the form of a button name, an error or success message, an instruction line displayed above a form, a help tooltip—any interface text.

It is interesting to observe the use of microtext in two dimensions: a functional and an emotional one:

> The **functional** dimension is the one I described in the previous paragraph: a simple action where all states are clearly transmitted to the user. No error. No noise or ambiguity.

> The **emotional** dimension is a bit more abstract, obviously. The microtext helps not only the user to understand what is happening in the system, but also to form in their head the perception they have of that product/brand.

The functional value of microtexts

In addition to explaining an action (*registering*), a microtext can be used to guide the user in performing a task (*your password must be at least six characters long*) or give feedback on an action they performed that was created successfully.

It is also possible to use microtexts to anticipate needs, wants, or concerns that the user will have when performing a particular task.

In his most recent book, Dan Saffer addresses the subject of m*icrocopy* and gives some useful tips when writing such types of text:

- Avoid very vague stock names such as *Submit*. What happens after the user *Sends* the form data?
- Is instruction text absolutely necessary? You do not need to add a *Please login* above a login form.
- When the text is too long and needs to be truncated in the interface, make sure the user can read the full text easily.
- Test your texts on real users. Show them a microtext interaction and ask them to say out loud what they think will happen when they click or interact with the UI.
- Use human language, not system language. *Posted 3 hours ago* is much easier to understand than *posted on 03/03/2014 at 2:33 PM*—a detail that ends up being forgotten by many designers out there.

Tips for good microcopy

To improve the UX from a copy perspective, follow these quick tips:

- **Communicate benefits, not features**:

  If you explain to people why you are asking them to do something, it is much more likely that they will do it. It's a little text trick you can do to immediately sound smarter. In writing, there are always two elements: functionalities and benefits. The first is about what a product does. The second is about what it allows you to do.

- **Speak the language of your users**:

  People respond well to words, phrases, and tones of voice depending on their own personality, not why you chose the right word. That's where people are useful. They help you communicate with users in a natural and logical way for them, and this results in a better user experience. You do not say to a child *this statement is illogical and therefore invalid*. You say *this is not how it works, let me explain*.

- **Keep the text short**:

  Here, we return to the concept of *microtexts*: keep your text short. Clients often ask for more words on a page, but the text can always be shorter, and in most cases, shorter text yields better results. Whenever possible, reduce.

  Text is a cornerstone of the user experience, sometimes neglected by UX professionals after *wireframe with lorem ipsum* was delivered.

Accompanying the development of the texts that will be displayed in the interface is important not only to ensure good usability, but also to make sure that text and images are working together to convey a message in line with the tone of the brand.

Summary

In this chapter, we learned about the importance of different content and UI for great user experience. We also saw how these elements can create big issues in terms of communication between your website, app, product, or service and your user. I hope you learned how all these aspects and elements, such as hierarchy, typography, iconography, color, copy, and so on, are interconnected and influence each other.

Although content strategy and text creation can be a job for a copywriter, and the choice of color scheme, typography, iconography, and so on can be a job for a UI designer, as a UXer, you should influence those decisions and make sure that all of them will allow for a great user experience.

Understanding these aspects of UX and UI in depth, it will help you to identify the UX issues that are impacted by these elements, and you will be able to make wise suggestions as to how to fix them.

6
Considering Accessibility As Part of the UX

Unfortunately, many design projects neglect the importance of accessibility in order to create more inclusive products and services. Keep in mind this aspect when you are building your product or service as it is becoming more relevant and it should be part of every project from the very beginning. In this chapter, you will learn how to analyze accessibility issues and how to fix accessibility issues that you might find, besides seeing a few cases not only online but also in the offline environment.

In this chapter, we will look at the following topics:

- What accessibility is and its importance
- Different demands in accessibility
- Accessibility as an inclusive UX
- Real examples or case studies
- Analyzing your website or app

What accessibility is and its importance

The story of accessibility is very similar to physical spaces in the real world. A building, to be accessible to wheelchair users, for example, needs access ramps, more spacious elevators, and bathrooms with grab bars. A building only becomes 100% accessible when anyone can get access to any of the spaces available there.

The same thing happens with websites. To say that a website is accessible means that anyone on any device and with any type of disability can navigate the site with ease and without restrictions.

Many of the aspects that make accessible websites are implemented with ease when designed from the beginning of the project. It is much easier to incorporate accessibility into your website or application when you are starting from scratch, than trying to fit accessibility into a website that already exists. Think about the work you do to incorporate larger ramps or elevators into a building after it's already built.

The complexity of making an accessible website/app can vary greatly depending on factors such as content, number of pages or templates, content dynamism, development tools, and the platform used.

When planned from the beginning, accessibility features are implemented more easily. That's because the whole design is already thought to make content accessible to more people.

On the other hand, trying to fix inaccessible sites/apps may require more effort, especially if the code was not developed with standard HTML tags.

Another challenge is that of interfaces that have a lot of multimedia content. That's because the whole content needs to be adapted to contain captions or text transcripts. Depending on the volume of such content on the site, you need to create a dedicated team to tailor that content—or develop a content creation flow that you already take into account.

In any of the preceding scenarios cited, once the site is implemented, there are a number of procedures that must be done to test and verify the real accessibility of the system:

- **Validate your HTML**: If HTML is used incorrectly, assistive technologies will encounter problems interpreting page content, which will obviously cause problems for users. Use an HTML validator to check the quality and standardization of the code.
- **Test with a keyboard**: Leave the mouse aside and try browsing your site with the Tab key. You should be able to interact with all the features of the site (menus, links, forms, buttons, and controls), and use them by pressing *Enter*, Space, and Arrows Directional. If you cannot reach a specific section of the site or a specific page module, this may mean that the site still has accessibility issues.

- **Use an accessibility checker**: There are several online tools that check whether a site is accessible or not—some of them are free and available immediately.
- **Test with users**: In addition to the technical tests, it is always important to validate with real users. It does not have to be a very formal test, but it is important to bring users with different levels of skills and characteristics.

In this chapter, you will not only see how to fix UX issues related to accessibility, but also you will understand the importance of knowing this target group better and that focusing on them allows you to present more inclusive projects.

The WCAG documentation

In 1999, the **Web Content Accessibility Guidelines** (w3.org/TR/WCAG10) was published by the **Web Accessibility Initiative** (**WAI**: w3.org/WAI), a project by the **World Wide Web Consortium** (**W3C**). Since then, this document has been widely accepted as the definitive guideline on how to create accessible digital projects. In 2008, WAI made a set of updated directions for internet accessibility, officially known as WCAG 2.0 (w3.org/TR/WCAG20).

Although we have this document that has filtered through the entire digital community, the article *How the internet still fails disabled people*, published by The Guardian, highlights that

> *"According to the Office for National Statistics, in May 2015, 27% of disabled adults had never used the internet, compared to 11% of non-disabled adults."*

A survey by PewResearch Center found that 38% of disabled Americans use the internet, but only about 19% of them say their disability makes using the internet difficult. Also, the survey states that of the 62% of disabled people that do not use the internet, 28% said their disability impaired or made impossible the use of the internet.

According to W3C, accessibility is defined by providing conditions for the use, security and autonomy, total or assisted, of spaces, furniture and urban equipment, buildings, transport services and devices, systems, and means of communication and information, for a person with reduced mobility.

The UN Convention on the Rights of Persons with disabilities recognizes access to information and communications technologies as a basic human right. In order to provide equal access and equal opportunity to people with diverse abilities, it is crucial that any design project, digital or not, be accessible. Keep in mind that as a UX designer, you must put people at the center of your project. By not considering accessibility to your design projects you are neglecting an important group of people.

"Neglect Accessibility is like delivering a site with only the English version and ignoring all users who are not fluent in the language. By delivering a non-accessible site you are excluding users who need to navigate using assistive technologies."

- Fabricio Teixeira, Creative Director (UX) at R/GA.

The **Web Content Accessibility Guidelines** (**WCAG**) 2.0 is organized around four principles often referred to as the acronym POUR:

Perceivable

Can users understand the content? This helps us to keep in mind that just because something is noticeable with a sense, such as vision, this does not mean that all users can perceive it. To make this work, you need to include a segment in all research so you can establish how those with disabilities use the internet. Don't reinvent the wheel—find examples of websites that provide for accessibility and learn from them. Make sure to:

- Offer text alternatives to non-text content
- Offer subtitles and other alternatives to multimedia content
- Create content that can be presented in different ways, including assistive technologies, without losing meaning
- Make it easy for users to watch and listen to content

Operable

Can users use UI components and browse content? For example, something that requires a cursor passing interaction cannot be operated by someone who cannot use a mouse or touch screen. Reconsider how you use automatically playing audio and video content and make sure it does not disrupt accessibility technologies and can be accessed easily. Make sure to:

- Ensure that all features are accessible from the keyboard
- Allow enough time for users to read and use content
- Do not show content that can cause convulsions
- Help users browse and find content

Understandable

Can users understand the content? Can users understand the interface and is it consistent enough to avoid confusion?
Make sure to:

- Make the text readable and intelligible
- Make the content appear and operate predictably
- Help users avoid and correct errors

Robust

Can content be consumed by a wide variety of user agents (browsers)? Does it work with assistive technology? Assistive technologies are resources and services that aim to facilitate the development of daily activities by people with disabilities such as screen reader, electronic loupe, screen magnification software, keyboard with enlarged letters, or navigation assistant. They seek to increase functional capacities and thus promote the independence and autonomy of those who use them. Make sure to:

- Maximize compatibility with existing and future tools

Although WCAG provides a comprehensive view of what content is accessible, they can also be a bit overwhelming. To make it easier, the WCAG guidelines were simplified, by the **Web Accessibility in Mind (WebAIM)** group, into an easy-to-follow checklist specifically targeted at web content.

The WebAIM checklist (`webaim.org/standards/wcag/checklist`) can provide a brief high-level summary of what you need to implement while also linking to the underlying WCAG specification if you need an expanded definition.

With this tool in hand, you can chart your accessibility work and make sure that as long as your project meets the criteria described, your users will have a positive experience while accessing your content.

Different demands in accessibility

According to MIT, 15% to 20% of the world population has some type of disability; 53 million of the adult population in the US has a disability according to figures from 2015. In order to create an all-inclusive web experience for all users, it's helpful to understand the ways different types of people with disabilities access web content and what you need to do to make your website more accessible to them:

- **Hearing impairment (deafness or disability)**: Hearing impaired users can use the web if subtitles are offered for multimedia content (any video content that also has audio) and transcripts for audio-only content. Without subtitles or transcripts, only visual content can be accessed.

- **Motor deficiencies (physical deficiencies)**: Users with motor disabilities tend to use only the mouse, keyboard, voice, or other inputs to control and navigate the web.

  Websites developed with flexible input options are more accessible to these individuals. The requirement to use only mouse or keyboard only creates barriers for these individuals.

- **Visual disabilities (blindness or low vision)**: Users with visual impairments rely on functions for screen widening, keyboard-only navigation, and/or the use of screen reader technology. Access to information through these forms depends on: font sizes of considerable size, good color contrast, a well-structured website that has identification for all graphics, icons, buttons, and multimedia, using web standards when writing code for tables, forms, and structure.

- **Cognitive disabilities**: Users with cognitive disabilities depend on a consistent navigation structure. Designs with overly complex, flickering, or flashy presentations can be confusing to these users.

It is important to keep these types of disabilities in mind when you test the design subject. Also consider creating personas to also cover these target groups. A persona with special needs has the same characteristics, demographics, level of experience with technology, and level of personal detail as other people. It is common for this type of persona to describe what its limitations are and what accessibility considerations should be taken into account when designing products for them:

- What is the limitation that they have (example: blindness, difficulty in using the mouse, difficulty operating in noisy environments)

- Special tools or technologies you need to use (example: magnifying glass for reading small texts, screen readers, and so on)
- Level of experience with these assistive technologies
- Frequency of use of these tools and technologies

Accessible as part of the universal design

In general terms, when we say that a website is accessible, we mean that the content of the site is available, and its functionality can be operated, literally, by anyone. If we wrongly assume that all users can see and use a mouse, a keyboard, or even a touchscreen, interacting with page content the same way we do, we will be led to an experience that works well for some people, but creates problems ranging from simple hassles to unpassable obstacles to others.

Accessibility, then, refers to the experience of users who may be outside the narrow typical user bandwidth, who can access or interact with things differently than expected. Specifically, it refers to users experiencing some kind of disability—and keep in mind that the experience may be non-physical or temporary.

For example, although the trend is to focus the accessibility debate on users with physical disabilities, we can all identify with the experience of using an interface that is not accessible to us for other reasons. Have you ever had a problem using a desktop site on a mobile phone, or have you ever seen the message *This content is not available in your area*, or could not find a familiar menu on a tablet? All of these are accessibility issues.

Accessibility is part of a broader concept called *universal design*, which claims to make design accessible to everyone, not only including disabled people, but anyone with any kind of difficulty. The universal design covers seven principles and can also be applied to products other than online or digital service ones:

- **Equalization in the possibilities of use**: Can be used by any user in equivalent conditions:
    - Provides the same means of use for all users, which will be identical whenever possible and equivalent when not
    - Avoid stigmatizing or segregating any user
    - Provisions for security, privacy, and safety should be equally available to all users
    - Make the design equally appealing to all users

- **Flexibility of use**: Caters to a wide range of individuals, preferences, and individual abilities:
  - Provide choice in terms of use methods
  - Accommodate both right and left-handed options to be accessed and used
  - Facilitate accuracy and precision of users
  - Provide adaptability to the user's pace
- **Simple and intuitive use**: Easy to understand, regardless of user experience, knowledge, language skills, or level of concentration:
  - Eliminate unneeded complexity
  - Be consistent with expectations and intuition of users
  - Accommodate a wide range of language skills and literacy
  - Arrange the consistency of information with its importance
  - Provide effective prompting and feedback during and after task completion
- **Noticeable information**: Effectively provides the necessary information, whatever the existing environmental/physical conditions or sensory capabilities of the user:
  - Use different ways (such as verbal, tactile, pictorial) for redundant presentation of essential information
  - Provide adequate contrast between essential information and its surroundings
  - Maximize legibility of essential information
  - Differentiate elements in ways that can be described (that is, make it easy to give instructions or directions)
  - Provide compatibility with a variety of techniques or devices used by people with sensory limitations
- **Tolerance to error**: Minimizes risks and negative consequences arising from accidental or involuntary actions:
  - Arrange elements to minimize hazards and errors: most used elements, most accessible; hazardous elements eliminated, isolated, or shielded
  - Provide warnings of hazards and errors
  - Provide fail safe features
  - Discourage unconscious action in tasks that require vigilance

- **Minimal physical effort**: It can be used efficiently and comfortably, with a minimum of fatigue:
    - Allow users to maintain a neutral body position
    - Use reasonable operating forces
    - Minimize repetitive actions
    - Minimize sustained physical effort
- **Dimension and space for use and interaction**: Adequate space and dimension for interaction, handling, and use, regardless of height, mobility, or user posture:
    - Provide a clear line of sight to important elements for any seated or standing user
    - Make reaching all components comfortable for any seated or standing user
    - Accommodate variations in hand and grip size
    - Provide adequate space for the use of assistive devices or personal assistance

Simple and intuitive use:

- Easy to understand, regardless of user experience, knowledge, language skills, or level of concentration.
- **Noticeable information**: Effectively provides the user with necessary information, whatever the existing environmental/physical conditions or sensory capabilities of the user.
- **Tolerance to error**: Minimizes risks and negative consequences arising from accidental or involuntary actions.
- **Minimal physical effort**: Can be used effectively and comfortably with minimal fatigue.
- **Size and space of approach and use**: Appropriate space and size for approach, handling, and use, regardless of height, mobility, or posture of the user.

Accessibility as an inclusive UX

The book *A Web for Everyone—Designing Accessible User Experiences*, by Sarah Horton and Whitney Quesenbery, can help UXers on the mission to make accessibility happen. The book gives practical advice and examples of how to create sites that everyone can use.

Creating a website for everyone is combining good design and usability with accessibility to create inclusive design, according to Rosenfeld Media's Guide to accessibility principles at UX.

The principles of accessibility in UX are based on three main sources:

- W3C content and accessibility guide, which provides the basics for web accessibility and best practices
- The principles of universal design, seven principles that work for the full spectrum of human abilities
- Design thinking, an approach that emphasizes grounding the process on human needs

By using accessibility principles in your UX projects, you will have a chance to create websites and apps that work for everyone—including people with disabilities. On the book's website, you will find interesting information and extracts from the book (such as personas of people with disabilities), besides tools to help you to think more objectively about accessibility, without sacrificing design or innovation. As Jesse Hausler, principal accessibility specialist at Salesforce said, accessibility shouldn't be a barrier to innovation or force you to make an ugly, cluttered, or boring project, as many might think.

Also, as highlighted by DUX MAG, we shouldn't consider accessibility only as part of social projects, but also as an innovation! Siri is one example of innovation brought by the author in this field. He highlights that Siri was developed for a group of people with no specific deficiencies or special needs, but it became a major solution for disabled people.

Although for most companies accessibility is still not a priority, the author reminds us that, as professionals seeking to improve user experience, we should start thinking of accessibility as a way to be innovative and make sure that companies understand that this is also good for their brand and visibility.

Accessibility analysis

In order to analyze the accessibility of your website or application, start by verifying all these points as a check list:

- Content is noticeable in multiple ways
- Audio content is subtitled for those who cannot perceive audio through hearing alone
- Alternatives in text are offered for non-textual content

- Content is operable in multiple ways
- All features are available through the keyboard
- Users can browse and find information easily
- Content is understandable
- Text is readable and understandable
- Content appears and is operable in predictable ways
- Content is robust across multiple platforms
- The site interacts with mobile devices and assistive technologies

The validation of the accessibility of a page should be done through automatic tools and direct review. Automatic methods are generally fast, but are not able to identify all the nuances of accessibility. Human assessment should help ensure clarity of language, good use of textual equivalents, and ease of navigation (usability), for example.

The important items in the validation method that follow are discussed in more depth in the validation section of the WCAG 1.0 External Website techniques document, and they are as follows:

- Use an automated accessibility tool (list of web accessibility assessors in the next topic). It should be noted that these tools do not address all accessibility issues, such as the clarity of a text, the applicability of a textual equivalent, and so on. Thus, such tools are only one of the 11 points of this methodology. There is no point in being *zero error* in these tools if the rest of the methodology is not applied.
- Validate the syntax (for example, HTML, XML, and so on, in: W3C Site HTML Validator External). HTML (X) HTML errors can lead to poor downloading of the page, avoidance of web standards required for assistive technologies, errors in semantics and page rendering.
- Validate style sheets (for example, CSS, validate in: W3C Validator External Site). CSS code errors can lead to leakage of required web standards and errors in page rendering.
- Use a Color Contrast Analyzer External Website to ensure good page visibility, including for low vision and color blind people.
- Use a text-only browser (Lynx or Webvox) or an emulator. These types of browsers and simulators will not let you load JavaScripts and images and most of your users will use keyboard navigation. It becomes a basic test to know if the HTML (X) code of the page is independent and functional.

- Use multiple graphical browsers with sound and active images:
    - **Deactivating the images in the browser**: This allows the descriptions placed in the ALT attribute to become apparent, in order to be able to verify if they are adequate.
    - **Without sound**: One can check if the absence of sound on the page changes the quality of the information and navigability (in the case of a podcast, it is appropriate that there is the textual equivalent of it).
    - **Without mouse**: One can check if the keyboard navigation is adequate.
    - **Without loading frames, interpretable programs, style sheets, or applets**: This means that one can navigate the content independently of the presentation (CSS) and layers of behavior (scripts and others).
- Use multiple browsers, old and new.
- Use a screen reader, screen magnification software, a small screen (cell phone), and so on.
- Use spelling and grammar checkers. A person who uses a voice synthesizer to read a page may not be able to decipher the best approximation of the synthesizer to a word that contains a misspelling. Eliminating grammatical problems increases the degree of understanding of the page.
- Review the document for clarity and simplicity. Ideally, ask an experienced literary reviewer (Web Writing) to review written content and evaluate clarity of writing. If you do not have this feature, try to have someone else read the page to see if it is understandable.
- Ask people with disabilities to review the documents. These users, with or without experience, are an invaluable source of information on the status of documents, with respect to their degree of accessibility and ease of use.

Automated accessibility tools

There are a few tools that you can use to help you to analyze if a website follows the WCAG 2.0 standards of accessibility on the web. It is worth remembering that all these tools are only auxiliaries, and that there needs to be a human assessment to give a final verdict on the subject:

- **LowVision** (`http://lowvision.support/`): Focused on vision problems, the tool allows you to test your site for users with common vision problems (cataracts, glaucomas, color blindness, and so on).

- **ColorBlind Page Filter** (`http://colorfilter.wickline.org/`): Focused on color blindness, allows you to view a website for users who have this type of visual limitation.
- **Valet** (`http://valet.webthing.com/`): Allows you to validate a website's code to verify its accessibility.
- **TAW** (`http://www.tawdis.net/ingles.html?lang=en`): Detects potential accessibility issues by showing your locations directly on the analyzed page.
- **Accessibility Developer Tools** (`https://chrome.google.com/webstore/detail/accessibility-developer-t/fpkknkljclfencbdbgkenhalefipecmb?hl=en`): Chrome plugin offered by Google with various accessibility verification functions on websites.
- **WCAG Contrast Checker** (`https://addons.mozilla.org/EN-US/firefox/addon/wcag-contrast-checker/`): Tool that specializes in testing the contrast of websites.
- **Wave** (`http://wave.webaim.org/`): Free web accessibility evaluation tool provided by WebAIM. It is used to assist programmers in the process of assessing accessibility. This tool, instead of generating complex reports on the page, simply shows the original content of the page, but with indicators of the zones of the page that reveal problems or accessibility features.
- **Image Analyzer** (`http://www.etre.com/tools/colourblindsimulator/`): Examines all images found on a web page to check for any accessibility issues. The width, height, alt, and longdesc attributes are examined for appropriate values. Learning from errors pointed out using this service could improve accessibility issues.
- **Readability** (`http://www.online-utility.org/english/readability_test_and_improve.jsp`): Is the key to accessibility. It is hard to test, however. This online tool evaluates text based on different reading scales and also suggests which complex sentences to take another look at. Great for those writers who commonly write in a way that is just a little too complex.
- **AccessColor** (`http://www.accesskeys.org/tools/color-contrast.html`): The AccessKeys site tool tests the contrast and brightness of the colors between the page and the background of all elements of the site, to ensure that the contrast is high enough for people with visual difficulties. This tool finds the relevant color combinations in the HTML and CSS documents, preventing the programmer from having to do so by testing various combinations.
- **Cynthia Says External Website** (`http://www.cynthiasays.com/`): It has a report that is not so simple for the new users to understand, but it is also well known and used internationally.

If you need a more specific tool, take a look at the official list of accessibility testers created by W3.org: `https://www.w3.org/WAI/ER/tools/`.

The importance of colors

Within accessibility, color may be one of the easiest aspects to address, and yet one of the most neglected. The main reason is because the choice of colors is often restricted to an aesthetic decision on the part of the visual designer. Even the marketing department might have a big say in this, as well, and they tend to optimize for conversions rather than accessibility. It would be good for websites to try and get UX and marketing to work together. A more accessible website is equal to more engagement and ultimately more conversions.

The only way to break down this stigma is to understand more about how color choices impact the experience of anyone who visits your site or uses your application, and how some simple best practices can change that scenario. To do this, we need to understand some of the most common limitations.

Color blindness

It impossible to talk about color and accessibility without starting with color blindness. Everyone has seen a comparison between how a colorblind person and a person with normal eyesight sees a macaw or a box of colored pencils. These photos are great for explaining what this visual impairment is all about, but how does it impact the most basic parts of a digital interface, such as a form?

Our retina has rods, which capture light, and cones, which recognize the colors. Three types of cones - specializing in recognizing blue, green, and red - are responsible for forming the entire spectrum of visible colors. You can check the graph here: `http://wearecolorblind.com/article/a-quick-introduction-to-color-blindness/`.

Color blindness, a deficiency present in 8% of men, occurs when there is mutation in one or more of these types of cones, limiting the visible color spectrum. The most common type (90% of cases) is deuteranopia, which limits the perception of the color green.

In the following diagram, it is easy to see that the distinction between green and red may be difficult for a colorblind person. Just the universal colors for success or error, right or wrong, victory or defeat, going or stopping. These are the colors present in 99% of forms out there.

If you access the page
`www.providr.com/how-people-with-color-blindness-see-the-world/2/`, you will see
easily that the distinction between green and red is very difficult for a colorblind person.
Just the *universal* colors for success or error, right or wrong, victory or defeat, goes or stops.
Just the colors present in 99% of the forms out there.

You may also understand the difference more via the following comparison. You can also
see the difference better with the comparison on the page: `http://www.color-blindness.`
`com/coblis-color-blindness-simulator`

Another example is the following chart, which tries to show which team has won and who
has lost in the last 10 games:

Other disabilities

Color blindness is not the only reason to take the choice of colors in an interface seriously:
there are other visual deficiencies, such as cataract and low vision, common in the elderly,
which is in an increasing share of users; and even with normal view, the context affects how
one perceives and sees the colors: brightness and contrast of the monitor, the lighting of the
environment, and the time of day.

This becomes critical when a design is set on a Cinema Display and users have another type
of monitor to access, regardless of their age and whether or not they have any type of visual
impairment.

Of course, that gray text on a slightly lighter gray background looks stylish, but an ordinary
computer monitor will not be able to reproduce the nuances of brightness and contrast of a
professional monitor. Also, the display of a brand new smart watch can be difficult to see
on a sunny day. Resolution, font size, icons, and even the context of use can affect the color
perception and the accessibility of the content.

One of the first good practices for choosing colors is: do not just rely on colors to pass on
information, also use icons and text to ensure the message is conveyed. Ensuring a
minimum of contrast to allow the distinction between colors and elements is another good
practice. Another good practice is to make sure that colors are identifiable using their
saturation and brightness.

This third one may seem complicated, but that basically means darker dark colors, lighter whites, and an increased color saturation to make an element easily identifiable compared to the colors around it.

To summarize the three mains good practices related to color:

- Do not rely on a color to pass on any important information. Use icons, text, and even texture to leave clear information. That's right there at W3C.
- Ensure a good contrast between colors and elements. Take into account the size of the elements, sources, and context of use. The W3C requests a minimum contrast of 1: 4.5 (or 1: 3 for larger text).
- More brightness, more saturation, more hue, more everything! When you begin to set the color palette to be used, be sure to consider the brightness, saturation, and even hue of the colors. This way, all users can have the same visual experience that was designed.

What about apps?

Much is said about web accessibility, but apps can and should be accessible to any user. In general, UX designers should try to feed accessibility into design systems as much as possible. A first step is to check the accessibility guidelines for the operating system for which you are designing: iOS or Android.

Although responsive sites are accessible from a variety of device types (the most common of which are smartphones, phablets, tablets, laptops, desktops, and TVs), the fact that a site is responsive does not automatically make it accessible to all types of users. Understand that responsive design makes apps accessible to multiple devices and screens and not to users.

These are different issues. While responsive design focuses on how the layout and features will adapt to various devices, accessibility focuses on how different types of users will interact with a particular interface.

There are areas of accessibility that have nothing to do with how the layout fits into different devices—such as contrast, readability, form work, and other themes that we've talked about here in this chapter.

At the end of the day, you may have accessible sites that are not responsive, and responsive sites that are not accessible. One thing is not directly related to the other. And there are cases where responsive design can make apps less accessible, especially on mobile devices.

Of course, creating websites that can be accessed from any type of device is a good start, but that's just one aspect of accessibility.

One of the common problems when designing responsive sites is that designers and programmers end up taking shortcuts in how the site is built—and these shortcuts can affect the accessibility of the product. For example:

- Scrollbars need to appear when content does not fit on the screen. Blocking scrollbars using overflow: hidden means violating the accessibility rules of WCAG.
- Pages need to work properly with or without CSS enabled.
- Pages need to be readable without specific colors being set. Whenever the background color is manually set, the text color must also be set to avoid contrast problems.
- The positioning and the reading order need to remain the same on desktop and mobile.
- Using CSS to hide content at a particular resolution hinders access when users are using screen readers.
- The user should be able to zoom the screen naturally by up to 200% in mobile. No need to force the zoom lock.
- The level of contrast between background and content needs to be even higher on mobile devices. While on desktop the contrast ratio needs to be 4.5 to 1, and on mobile it needs to be 7 to 1.

You can check if the mobile app you are working on is OK for accessibility by using the Quick Accessibility Check tool which you can find on OneVoice on their website: `http://www.onevoiceict.org/first-seven-steps-accessible-mobile-apps/quick-accessibility-test`

It is also highly recommended to check out the W3C Mobile Standards: `http://www.w3.org/WAI/mobile/`

On the W3C website, you can also find a step-by-step on how to apply Accessibility to Mobile: `https://www.w3.org/TR/mobile-accessibility-mapping/`

Accessibility and IoT

The current **IoT** (**Internet of Things**) scenario presents a number of different systems that do not talk to each other, and that ignore the most basic principle of Accessibility: making experiences accessible and inclusive to any type of user, regardless of what their point of entry into this ecosystem is.

With the Internet of Things, the term accessibility takes on a whole new meaning. In addition to ensuring that experiences are accessible to any user profile, there is also the basic concern of creating consistency in the way that operations are performed.

Think of browsers, and the standardizations dictated by the W3C that today we find obvious. None of this is a reality with respect to how connected objects interact with each other.

Now think of devices that measure user health (for example, smart balances, diabetes meters, heartbeats, and so on): it is to be expected that minimum accessibility requirements are included in these platforms, such as the ability to control button size or to translate the experience into different languages.

Can I give you some practical examples?

- Viewing the small numbers on your Withings scales or your FitBit smart bracelet when having vision problems
- For the same reason, having difficulty seeing the current temperature when rotating the Nest thermostat
- Failing to reach Nest's smoke detector because of being in wheelchair

As mentioned by McAfee (`https://securingtomorrow.mcafee.com/business/accessibility-requirements-in-the-internet-of-things/`) in the article *Accessibility Requirements in the Internet of Things*:

> *"To ensure accessibility, IoT devices would need to automatically identify their usage context, talk to the server, and then serve the best experience and best use conditions for users (example the amount of light on the screen, language captions different from English, or interface tips for novice vs. advanced users). But getting connected objects to control experience through a server (not locally) would greatly increase the price of IoT devices, given the number of requirements that come with this new kind of interaction."*

Good practices

As you have seen, when we are designing any product services, it is important to consider accessibility in your solutions. Now we will look at a few things that you have to keep in mind.

Screen readers

Screen readers are software that is used to get a computer response through sound, mostly used by the visually impaired. The program goes through texts and images, reading aloud everything that it finds on the screen, as well as the operations that the user performs with the alphanumeric keys and the commands entered.

How does navigation work?

Navigation through screen readers works essentially in three ways:

- Reading the entire page (navigation with the arrows):

- Reading the links (*tab* navigation):

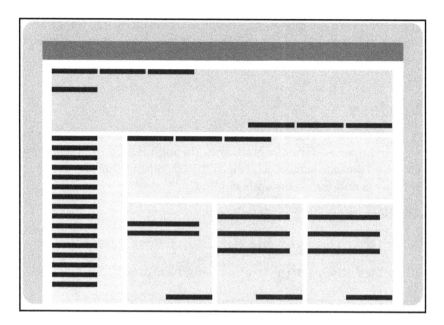

- Reading the headers (navigation with the *H* key):

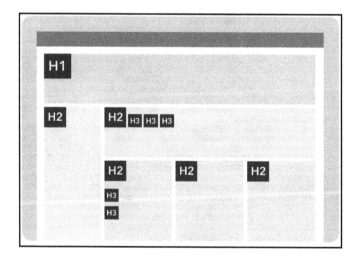

From these three main commands, the user is able to be guided by the structure of the page while following the human speech emitted by the software when reading its content.

It is therefore important that both the design and the code are ready to receive the user browsing using screen readers. A simple broken or poorly implemented header can cause the user to get lost on the page and have difficulty understanding how the information is organized hierarchically.

There are a few softwares to do it:

- **Jaws** (http://www.freedomscientific.com/fs_products/software_jaws.asp): Paid screen reader for Windows
- **Virtual Vision** (http://www.virtualvision.com.br/): Paid screen reader for Windows
- **NVDA** (http://www.nvda-project.org/): Free screen reader for Windows
- **Window-Eyes** (http://www.gwmicro.com/): Paid software for Windows
- **Orca** (http://www.gwmicro.com/): Free screen reader for Linux
- **VoiceOver** (http://www.apple.com/br/accessibility/voiceover/): IOS screen reader that comes with Apple devices

Do not rely on colors as the only way to explain something
Affected users: those who are partially or completely color-blind

One of the main points that accessibility tries to ensure is the ability of users with vision problems to be able to navigate normally through the web:

- 1 in 188 people are blind
- 1 in 30 people have low vision
- 1 in 12 men are color-blind (partially or completely)

Well, that last group is more common than it looks. And that's exactly what you need to think about when choosing colors for certain interface elements.

A common mistake on the part of designers is to rely only on the use of colors to communicate something to the user. A classic example is error messages in forms. This is just one example of many—of a design flaw that is more common than you might think. But the good news is that the solution is also simple: just use some other element along with the color to indicate the error: be it a phrase, an exclamation icon that is easy to understand, or tooltips or balloons pointing to the error.

Focused tips

Check out a few great tips focused on types of users who can be affected by specific accessibility issues:

Pay attention to the contrast
Affected users: Those with low vision

According to the **WCAG (Web Content Accessibility Guidelines)**, the contrast ratio between text and background should be at least 4.5 to 1. If your font size is 24px or 19px bold, the minimum ratio drops to 3 to 1.

This means that when your text is 24px or larger, the lightest gray you can use on a white background is #959595.

For texts smaller than this, gray needs to be even darker. With a white background, the lightest gray you can use is #767676:

> **This is a big text**

Remembering that this is on a white background; the more the background darkens, the more the text needs to darken as well:

> This is a normal text

They are very tight guidelines, but they help ensure that even users with low vision can see what is written on the screen. And in the end, remember that these improvements not only enable more low-vision users to navigate your site, but also provide a more enjoyable reading experience for users who have completely normal eyesight.

Visually indicate which item is selected by the keyboard
Affected Users: Browsing using a keyboard

Some users with motor limitations navigate the web using the keyboard. When a field is in focus, it is common to see an outline around it indicating that it is the currently active item. You may have already seen this in forms and navigation menus:

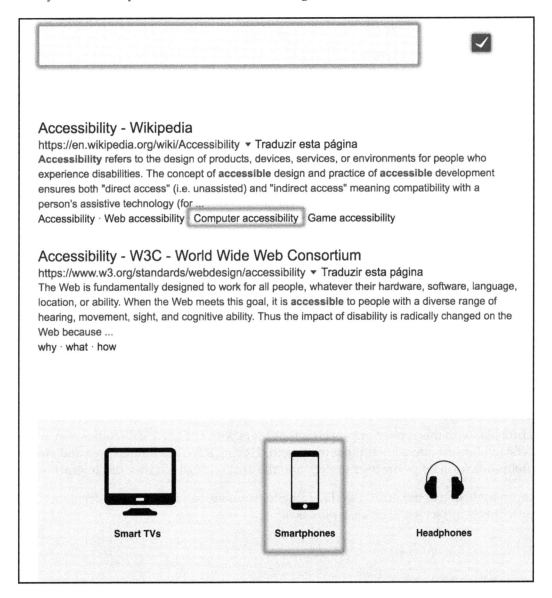

Outline is a native CSS function, but many designers and programmers end up manually removing this function for aesthetic options. The problem is that without this indication, it is practically impossible for the user navigating the keyboard to understand which field, link, or part of the screen is in focus. It is something simple to fix, but it can cause many problems for a certain group of users.

Be clear on forms

Affected users: with cognitive difficulties

Recently, designers and developers have decided to innovate in the way forms are designed and presented to the user.

Instead of the traditional text field with well-delimited borders:

Label

The trend seems to be the fields that blend with the background:

search notes

searching in you notebooks

The problem with this type of approach is that users with cognitive difficulties may not understand how to interact with that form field. Having a well-delimited area and size in the fields of a form helps the user understand the area with which they can interact.

Medium itself, one of the most used blogging tools today, has very serious problems in this regard. This is the screen to create a new post:

lisandramaioli
An Italian-Brazilian journalist passionate about #UX and #UXresearch — http://uxpressocafe.com
Draft

Title

(+)   Tell your story...

Another important point in the form is the clarity of the labels. It is important that the labels are visible at all times, even when the user clicks inside the text field to start filling it.

Do not trust the hover states
Affected users: with motor limitations

Some users navigate through the interfaces using only the keyboard—or even using some voice recognition software, where commands are given out loud and then converted into interface clicks.

The hover states problem, in this case, is that it *hides* the options available to the user. If the user cannot see that a button exists on a page, it will not be able to give the voice command to the system to click on that option.

The same thing happens when there is no mouse: how will the user know that when you hover over an item, more options will be revealed?

More accessibility tips

Also check out this list of quick suggestions to make sure your website is accessible:

- Be careful with text superimposed on images, however cool it may seem. It can be done correctly, but it is very difficult.
- Decorative images must have an alt attribute (alt = ""). However, non-decorative images should have alternate text. This text is read by screen readers (and also by search engines); it must provide relevant information about the content of the image. To see if an image is decorative or not, ask yourself if the content would still make sense if the image was removed.

- Icon fonts are bad for accessibility. It is better to opt for SVG as it is an accessible image format.
- The underlining of links is useful for users who have difficulty in contrast discrimination.
- Forcing the opening of links in a new window is not something expected. If you implement this functionality, the link must have an obvious and explanatory iconography (CSS `pseudo-element :: after`).
- Links should be descriptive. Avoid *click here* and other non-informative anchors.
- Do not present overly long paragraphs. Some users tend to get lost quickly in large blocks of text. Long content is not necessarily better.
- The layout structure of the document (hierarchy of headers—H1, H2, ... Hx) is important. This hierarchy is used by certain programs to navigate within a document.
- Extravagant layouts can become tricky, because they can make it difficult to understand how content flows. It is very important to hit the content hierarchy.
- Disable CSS and evaluate the layout structure. See if your content continues to make sense.
- Be careful with infinite scrolling. It can be problematic for users using a keyboard. Allow to replace scrolling by paging.
- Parallax scrolling and heavy animations can cause nausea or malaise. Use with caution, or disable these effects.
- Beware of infinite, even subtle animations. They can be considered a distraction for people with **Attention Deficit Hyperactivity Disorder (ADHD)**.
- Test whether content flow is adequate and keyboard navigation works. These features help advanced users who want to get things done quickly and efficiently.
- Test whether the interaction with your site is easy enough. A good way to test the interaction with your site, application, or software is to use the mouse/trackpad with the other hand.
- Include a *skip-to-content* link at the top of the page. This helps users with screen readers not have to go through their entire header.
- Dialog windows, light boxes, and so on. They should be able to be closed by clicking outside them or by pressing ESC. This prevents people from having to get the little cross – yes, I know there are those who do this on purpose.
- Avoid justified text, especially in large numbers. Justified text makes reading difficult, and for some people, it makes reading a confusing process.

- Make sure the line spacing is at least 145-150% larger than the font size. The lack of spacing between the lines of text (line height) usually causes serious reading problems.
- White space is free! Do not be afraid to use it.
- Do not disable the zoom. Some people need the functionality to consume their content comfortably – some unusual situations require users to expand content.
- Do not be afraid to use a large font. It is unusual for users to zoom out, which means that the fonts are usually very small on the web.
- Repeat usability tests. About 7 in 10 users leave a site when they find it difficult to use (CAP16 data).
- JavaScript is not an enemy of accessibility. In fact, some patterns can only be really accessible with JavaScript.
- Avoid *CSS-only* solutions. They can be elegant; but they often ignore the accessibility aspects of a resource, making it suboptimal.
- Make sure that mouse-over (`: hover`) effects do not limit access to content. Keep in mind that not all users have a mouse/trackpad.
- Never forget to indicate which elements have focus. This is not to say that you cannot change the default browser outline in buttons, forms, and text selection.
- Test your keyboard navigation. A good way to test is to turn off the mouse or turn off your trackpad.
- Think about the position of your call to action on the screen. Not everyone has a long thumb. In some cases, not everyone has both hands available.
- Radio buttons must be grouped—preferably within a fieldset, with a caption serving as a label for the group.
- Content with animations and heavy effects should be introduced with a warning to protect people suffering from epilepsy. There is already a prefers-reduced-motion media query.
- Some people use screen magnifiers for surfing the web. Designing for them is not too difficult. I recommend reading the text: How to make your site accessible to people who use screen magnifiers (`https://dev.to/_bigblind/how-to-make-your-website-accessible-to-people-who-use-a-screen-magnifier`).

Real examples and case studies

Although we have focused a bit on websites and apps, it is important to notice that accessibility goes beyond online services and products. In the following section, you will find a few cases to illustrate how well companies have been designing their products and services based on accessibility knowledge.

Fukuoka City Subway

In a 10-year project, the Fukuoka city subway in Japan made public transportation accessible to millions of people. The idea was to create an environment of good mobility and fewer barriers, in addition to making information easily understood by everyone, as you can see in the following image:

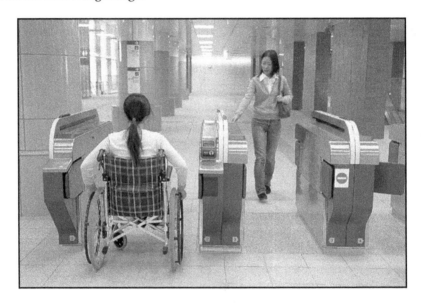

Institute for Human Centered Design and DOGA (Design and Architecture Norway)
Project director: Toshimitsu Sadamura, GA-TAP. Inc
www.inclusivedesign.no

Some of the improvements include:

- **Universal line movement**: The station layout allows passengers to move freely through the architecture using the shortest route possible. Tickets and exits always lead to an elevator or subway escalator in cars equipped to carry wheelers.

- **Universal facilities**: Ticket machines were mounted below normal to accommodate wheelchairs as well as standing passengers. The magnetic tip of the white cane used by visually impaired users automatically calls the elevator and opens the doors through sensors, as you can see in the following image:

Institute for Human Centered Design and DOGA (Design and Architecture Norway)
Project director: Toshimitsu Sadamura, GA-TAP, Inc
www.inclusivedesign.no

- **Space comfort**: Large atriums and transparent materials are used to bring natural light into the basement and provide a sense of space.
- **Visual information**: Each station has its own color, wall material, and unique symbol, making it easy for children and people who do not speak Japanese to identify.

The Nanakuma line has attracted worldwide attention and has won several awards as an example of affordability:

Institute for Human Centered Design and DOGA (Design and Architecture Norway)
Project director: Toshimitsu Sadamura, GA-TAP. Inc
www.inclusivedesign.no

The de Young Museum

The de Young Museum in San Francisco has developed a unique program that will allow guided tours by a robot to those who cannot physically visit it.

While other museums have developed innovative programs to expand accessibility, such as special tours for the deaf and the visually impaired, de Young's robotic tour guides represent an important step towards the way organizations think about inclusion.

Oxo

Oxo was created by Sam Farber in 1990 to help people who, like his wife, suffered from arthritis and had trouble holding household items. The company is a success to this day and has also won over people who do not have physical problems, with its proposal to help make day-to-day life much easier.

Tuva

Like Oxo, Tuva ended up winning over everyone with its comfortable and ergonomic design. Tuva cutlery was stemmed from the belief that different people use cutlery in different ways. Thus, not all cutlery is suitable for people with different sizes of hands and different strengths in their hands, especially if we consider children, the elderly, and people with some physical difficulty. Today, Tuva is one of the best-selling brands in Sweden and Norway and is the winner of several awards for the beautiful design of its products.

Barclays

Thanks to a bank customer who reported to his manager that he was having trouble viewing his card, Barclays decided to create high visibility credit cards in partnership with the Royal National Institute of Blind People, the English Dyslexia Association, and the Barclays Reach network. Since 2013, more than 2,000 people have created their personalized cards.

Tesco

At a meeting with the UK's **National Institute of the Blind (RNIB)** in 2000, supermarket giant Tesco was told their site was not accessible to a sizeable portion of the population. With the perception that their practice excluded customers, they committed to improving the accessibility and usability of their site.

In 2001, a new, easy-to-access version was released, making online shopping available to more people. In 2002-3, digital businesses made a profit in excess of £ 12.2 million – more than 30 times compared to the previous year. The project continued in development, and finally in 2005, Tesco integrated the two sites, giving full access to the features and functions of the standard site. Today, the company continues to be one of the most innovative international retailers.

You can see more here: `www.tesco.com/help/accessibility`

Legal and General

As soon as the Tesco Accessibility project was launched, the `W3.org` website also mentioned the Legal and General website as an example of good practices on accessibility.

You can see more here: `www.legalandgeneral.com/accessibility`

Awake Labs' Reveal

The 2017 Accessibility Innovation Showcase, in Ontario, profiled innovative accessibility technologies and assistive devices through interactive exhibits. Awake Labs' Reveal was one of the examples shown during the event. It is a wearable device that measures and tracks indicators of stress and anxiety and corresponding behaviors in real time.

You can find more information here: `http://www.awakelabs.com`

AccessNow

Another project presented during the 2017 Accessibility Innovation Showcase was AccessNow, a mobile app that uses crowdsourcing to rate the accessibility of locations around the world.

You can find more information here: `http://accessnow.me`

TellMe TV

One more project which shown at the event in Ontario was focused on TV products. TellMe TV is the world's first 100% described video-on-demand service offering convenient audio description on demand for people with visual impairment.

You can find more information here: `https://www.tellmetv.com/`

eSight

Startup eSight (`esighteyewear.com`) developed a wearable technology that works with high-resolution image capture. The glasses are aimed at people who have low vision and, for example, cannot differentiate colors and depths, with an HD camera and two sensors on the outside, besides two OLED screens and prisms on the inside:

The images captured by the camera are linked to the information obtained by the sensors. Thus, all this data is displayed on the screens a few millimetres away from the eyes and have a design that allows the user to keep both hands free, it enables mobility, is versatile, and provides instant sight:

Summary

In this chapter, we discussed accessibility in detail, its importance, as well as how to consider people with any kind of disability as part of your target groups. You saw how to evaluate and analyze apps and websites to find if they follow the W3C standards for accessibility and how to fix UX issues related to it.

You also saw a few cases, not only from the digital and online universe, but also examples from the physical world, and we saw that accessibility is an important topic for not only designers, but for everyone who creates products and services for real people in the real world.

Now you are ready to implement accessibility into all your projects!

In Chapter 7, *Improving the Physical Experiences*, we will see how to improve user experience and fix UX issues in public environments.

7

Improving Physical Experiences

During the user journey, we can identify different touchpoints—ones which are part of public environments, as well. As professionals of user experience, we notice usability issues wherever we go. Jesse James Garrett proposed, *this attitude of always thinking about user experience is an acquired condition for which there is no cure.* Yet, for banal things, we generally assume that some are simply good enough, or we fail to see beyond superficial improvements in utility.

We all go through frustrations with bad design decisions in places such as public restrooms—from dispensers of toilet paper that are out of reach to faucet sensors that never seem to recognize our presence. These simple interactions symbolize a more endemic problem of ignoring the user experience as a whole. This chapter will show you how to fix UX issues in physical environments as well:

- UX can be applied everywhere
- How to improve ATMs
- Simplifying an elevator panel (but not much)
- Improving car panel design
- Creating a magic experience in parks
- Improving boarding passes
- Bus stops as part of the user journey
- Redesigning urinals to encourage men to wash their hands
- When online meets offline experiences

UX can be applied everywhere

It is common to relate UX with digital and online interfaces, such as websites and mobile apps. In Chapter 1, *Understanding UX and Its Importance*, we discussed how UX can be applied to any kind of interface with users, such as the *norman doors*. We also showed how the Japanese Restroom Industry Association improved user experience in public toilets by redesigning important icons. In Chapter 6, *Considering Accessibility As Part of the UX*, we also saw how the Fukuoka City Subway in Japan made public transportation accessible by improving the service design.

It is possible to improve the user experience or fix UX issues in any service or environment where we have user interaction. The first step, as in any UX project, is to observe the users and how they interact with the service, machine, or environment. There are many factors in the context of use that end up affecting the way people experience a particular product: the time of day, the day of the week, the geographical location, the environment, the people around, the physical configuration of the space where the interaction takes place–the list is long. We will understand their context, pain points, and needs. We will use the techniques and the methodologies already discussed in Chapter 2, *Identifying UX Issues – UX Methodologies*.

In this chapter, you will find tips, ideas, and a few cases of bad user experiences in public environments, and with physical objects.

How to improve ATMs

Since ATM machines appeared on the streets about 50 years ago, their basic function has hardly changed. However, to attract a younger audience and save money, banks have updated not only their ATMs, but also the meaning of the word bank.

Finally, the banks have started offering features, such as videos, touch screen, custom applications, and menus, that we have seen in smartphones for some time. There are products for the new generation who do not want to go to a physical bank and prefer to use technology services with the aid of technology. However, there is still space for improvements.

A survey by ACI Worldwide and YouGov with more than 8,000 consumers around the world found that people are looking for easier, more intuitive, and secure ways to access their accounts. In all, 43% of consumers in Italy, 38% in Spain, and 28% in the US want ATMs to offer better and safer forms of authentication. They also stressed that they would like to see more detailed information about their accounts, such as alerts for future payments or withdrawal fees. Another innovation mentioned was the possibility of issuing a new credit or debit card from the equipment. Among the problems of ATMs, however, the most cited by consumers were the fees charged for its use.

Germany leads the use of ATMs—48% of respondents said that they used the equipment, even with the availability of new digital forms of payment. This is followed by Spain with 47%, the United Kingdom with 42%, France and Italy with 40%, the USA with 34%, and Hungary with 29%.

This is how it works in Argentina: in some ATMs, the machine delivers the money before returning the card. The problem is that many users leave the machine as soon as they get the money in hand (after all, that's exactly what they went there for) and forget to take the card back after the transaction has taken place.

If people are preoccupied with other things (such as the children who were left alone in the car or a movie that is about to start), they forget to remove the card after the service has been completed. To correct the problem, a simple change in the flow order of ATMs as follows would suffice.

The following is how it happens in Israel (and in other countries around the world): first, the machine returns the card, and only after the card has been withdrawn does it deliver the money. After all, no one will leave the ATM without the cash in hand.

This is a small change in flow that can help the bank save hundreds of thousands of dollars with lost card problems.

It is interesting to think as well about the applicability of UX methodologies and techniques in a public environment. One of the digital and online interfaces with which we commonly have to interact, for example, is service-service terminals, such as bank **Automated Teller Machines (ATMs)**.

What if banking self-service machines were redesigned from scratch? What if they became a little more human?

These were the questions IDEO asked when developing a new model of ATMs for the Spanish bank **Banco Bilbao Vizcaya Argentaria** (**BBVA**). The project, which began in 2007, took more than 2 years to get ready and was an excellent opportunity to bring innovation to a company that was truly willing to pay for it.

This can be considered a simple and true innovation. Focused on people experience with a positive Branding experience as a consequence.

Many of the changes implemented in this project show how much the market accommodates existing solutions and forgets to look at the human need that gave rise to the technology in the first place. Therefore, what we see is a bunch of companies scrambling to be the first to *innovate,* when in fact they are just reheating ready-made solutions that had emerged in another era, in another technological context, in another zeitgeist. The interface explores the metaphor between virtual and physical.

Self-service terminals are increasingly used to serve customers or end users easily and quickly, without the need of an attendant, bringing agility to the process as a whole.

They have been common since at least the end of the last century, when ATMs became popular as a standard means of querying basic information on bank transactions, withdrawing money, making deposits, among other simple and independent analysis operations of a financial operator.

In all these cases, the service is through a human-machine interface in which, the customer, often without any knowledge of information technology, needs to interact with a screen and certain devices (biometric sensors, cameras, card slots, and so on) in order to carry out the desired operations.

Considering that many users are unfamiliar with so much technology and yet we still must meet their needs, the development of any self-service system should take into account basic usability issues that make terminal experience as easy and intuitive as possible.

This post will talk a bit about usability and decisions that guide the creation of self-service systems, with a case of a terminal for rental of vehicles used as an example.

Usability

In general, it can be said that usability is concerned with creating systems that are easy to learn and use. Among the usability evaluation methods that can guide the construction of a self-service solution are the 10 heuristic interface evaluation principles proposed by Jakob Nielsen and Rolph Molich.

The 10 principles, as quoted by Robson Luis Gomes dos Santos (2006) and revisited by Edson Salerno Junior (2008), are as follows:

- **System status visibility**: This keeps the user always informed about system actions and gives procedural guidelines in each situation
- **Equivalence between system and the real world**: The system must speak the language of the user, using words, phrases, and similar concepts, besides following the conventions of the real world, presenting the information in a natural and logical order
- **User control**: This provides subsidies so that the user can do or undo actions
- **Consistency and standards**: This offers the user a navigation pattern, from the previously agreed concepts
- **Error prevention**: For a careful design, the occurrence of errors must be minimized and checked before the incident and, if necessary, presented to the user with a confirmation option
- **Recognizing instead of remembering**: Objects, actions, and options that help the user to find what they want
- **Flexibility and efficiency of use**: The design of an interface should serve both experienced and novice users, allowing, also, mechanisms to adapt the system to the user's needs
- **Aesthetics and minimalist design**: Information presented (verbal and graphic) should be relevant and directly related to the subject at hand
- **Assist users in recognizing, diagnosing, and recovering wrong actions**: Error messages should be presented clearly and objectively and, in addition to indicating the problem, need to suggest a solution
- **Help and documentation**: Help and documentation tools are needed to help you find system information

Considering these principles and the expertise gained from developing a car rental solution, take a look at these four key tips that will improve usability in self-service terminals:

- **Direct to the point**: Limited options—systems must direct customer actions rather than requesting data entries that may potentially lead to errors. If the customer has only a limited amount of options to choose from, it is best to display the options as predefined buttons rather than have the customer enter the chosen option.

A classic example of this type of problem, as reported in UX Magazine, is an ATM that only delivers $ 20 bills, but asks the customer to enter the amount desired. This eventually leads to errors when the customer requests non-matchable combinations with $ 20 bills.

In the car rental system, one of the features offered was the choice of a vehicle model. The interface that was defined offers, in the format of carousel figures, only the options available for rent at the time of use of the terminal. The client is left to navigate the options through left and right buttons to the desired model.

The use of buttons with a checkbox, in a small amount, also symbolizes well the range of options and gives the user visual control of their choices.

- **Navigation**: The self-service interface must be accompanied by information in a logical layout and options that allow the user to do and undo actions, following the most intuitive navigation to fulfill their need.

It is suggested to place screen-to-screen, **Back** and **Follow**, **OK**, and **Cancel** buttons, giving the user control of the flow in a binary way.

Before finalizing the operation, it is interesting to explain to the user their choices and their resulting values. For example, in the car rental solution, an estimation screen is displayed, detailing the contracted items and the price of each one. The user only proceeds according to the result of their interaction with the system.

- **User messages**: Messages should always guide the user, indicating a problem and suggesting a solution. In self-service systems, special attention should be given to messages, since communication is made directly from the customer interface. One major issue with UX at the moment, for example, is the use of messages, which actually get in the way and are difficult to remove or close. It should be super clear how to remove them.

Exception codes or business rule messages that prevent an operation from completing must never be displayed on the interface. These can cause confusion to the user or even some wrong impression of your relationship with the company providing the service.

For example, a customer with negative credit should never be informed of this by a machine, which does not have any attachment for a personal relationship. In this case, the guideline followed in car rental is to direct users to a desk in case there were any impediments to operation in the terminal.

- **Filling forms**: Forms require users to fill in a quantity of data required for simple storage or navigation of the system.

  Depending on the size, forms have the disadvantage of confusing and tiring users, leading to errors (since, in terminals, typing is done directly by a user who is, in general, in a hurry), and increasing the time of use of the terminal.

  In self-service, forms should be avoided and, if necessary, minimized. In the car rental scenario, due to the need to update the customers' address, it was decided to display the current address only for confirmation. A form for filling in a possible new address can be replaced by requesting only the telephone number or email so that the residential update is completed through another channel.

Simplifying an elevator panel (but not much)

Besides digital and/or online interfaces, UX can also help us to identify and fix bad experiences with more analogue interfaces, such as elevator panels.

Basically, a good design should make the user have the least doubts and think as little as possible about what procedure they should use to achieve the result they want, except where doubts are intentionally created and make sense in the context of design. For the most part, if in doubt, the design is probably not clear enough.

Look at this elevator buttons:

Now, imagine the situation: someone might have stopped and thought that in this arrangement, the aesthetics of the button frame would look better. This person might be thinking: "But and now? Does the arrow correspond to the button that is aligned vertically or horizontally? How do you know?" You can even push the two buttons to ensure that the elevator you want will arrive; it's not as if you would get stuck in the building for that. However, the moment you looked, saw unclear action options, and had to stop to think of a solution of its own is a clear example of bad usability.

Designer Brian Scates (http://sxates.com/), for example, was tired of using the confusing interface of the elevator in the building he lives in—something he does five to six times a day.

The following are some of the problems of the current elevator design:

- The numbering is inconsistent, as there is no button for each floor. The panel skips numbers 2, 3, and 8
- Of the four elevators in the building, only two go underground and to the top floor.
- Since it has many floors, visitors take a long time to find the desired floor and even understand where the special floors are (subsoil, cover, floors of service, and so on).

This is how the floors of the building are divided:

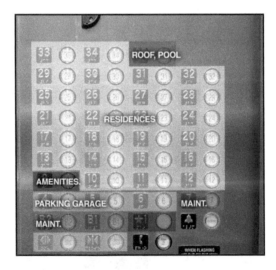

Most users go to residential floors (from 10th to 35th), others go to parking (4th to 6th), and some to public spaces such as the 9th-floor gym or the 35th-floor pool.

In addition to the preceding problems, Brian noted a recurring problem with elevators in his building (and many others). People often missed the elevator because they could not reach it before the doors closed. Also, the people inside the elevator could not find the DOOR OPEN button in time to hold the door for whoever was coming, since this button was mingled with so many others available on the same panel.

The following screenshot is Brian's suggestion for an ideal elevator panel:

Of course, Brian knows that elevator panels are made in scale and that customizing them for each building would cost a fortune.

However, he argues:

> *The time saved in trying to find a button, multiplied by the hundreds of thousands of elevator routes that people perform each year, saves valuable time for residents and visitors to the building. Not to mention the energy and time lost when someone pushes a button by mistake.*

You will also like to check out this video of Billy Hollis analyzing a bad elevator panel design: `https://youtu.be/xqf1SfMRaBk`

Improving car panel design

A brilliant concept project was created by Matthaeus Krenn (`http://matthaeuskrenn.com/new-car-ui/`) that brings a new look to the interfaces of the panels of the cars:

Even in newer models that have digital interfaces, the controls are an amalgamation of buttons and controls side by side that require the driver to look at the interface to find the desired button. In that context, a second of distraction can pose danger to the user and the other drivers around them:

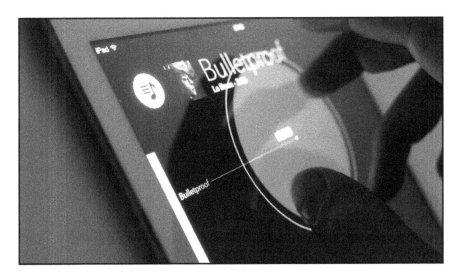

Several automotive companies have begun replacing traditional physical controls with touchscreen interfaces. Unfortunately, their ambition to dictate new trends in hardware does not fit very well with the software they create in this new context. Instead of exploring new limitations and opportunities, automakers simply replicate old button patterns on these new touch interfaces.

So basic controls like air conditioning and music players—which are commonly used by people while driving—now lose the tactile feel of feedback when activated, requiring even more attention from the drivers who operate them.

Creating magic experience in parks

MagicBand is a gateway to My Disney Experience, the digital system that integrates different Disney services. It is a plastic bracelet that has a built-in radio frequency chip, the so-called RFID. With this chip on the wrist, Disney can identify you inside its parks, shops, and hotels and offer you various personalized experiences.

Containing your personal information, Disney's MagicBand connects you to different services within the Orlando resort to ease your flow through the complex. It is worth saying that wearing the bracelet is a magical experience, like almost everything that is done there. On the front of the MagicBand, there is a symbol of a Mickey in high relief. Touching this symbol on the sensors scattered throughout the parks, which also has a Mickey design, makes this MagicBand work.

For example, to enter the park, just touch the Mickey of the bracelet with the Mickey that is on the *ratchet* of the park. When light turns green, you can enter. The same happens for the cardboard boxes for shopping, bedroom doors, and so on.

It is a product completely geared to enrich the *user* experience of the parks, one that can be used at various moments of the user experience and its journey:

- **Room key**: If you are staying at any of the complex's hotels, upon check-in, each person in your family/group will receive a MagicBand. With it, everyone can open the bedroom door. This is a safe way to ensure that only the people in your family have access to the room, as it is much harder to lose a bracelet that is attached to your arm than a card in your pocket or backpack.
- **Park entrance**: A few years ago, Disney abolished the use of paper tickets in its parks, since they wet, tear, knead, and only create problems. That's why, today, visitors can only enter the parks with the magnetic card (read more about it at the bottom of this page) or MagicBand. It is linked to the ticket you buy online or at the box office, and is where the days of use are counted.
- **FastPass+**: Disney's famous *queue -queue* works the same way as tickets and is stored on MagicBand. At the entrance to all the attractions that are in the system, you will find a post with a Mickey drawn. If you have a FastPass+ available for that toy at that time, the Mickey post will light up when you contact your MagicBand and the Cast Member will let you in through the shorter queue.
- **Memory Maker**: The new Disney photo package also works with MagicBand. When you buy it online, it links to your **My Disney Experience** account and automatically the package *enters* your bracelet. Using it with Disney Photopass photographers scattered around parks, restaurants, and photo-taking attractions (such as certain roller coasters), you'll be able to access everything through the site or the app. Note that **Memory Maker** only works with MagicBand when the two are linked to the same **My Disney Experience** account.
- **Shopping and dining**: If you are staying at one of the hotels in the complex, you can also link a credit card to your MagicBand for use during the day in the shops and restaurants. You can pay the bill with the bracelet, and at the end of the trip, Disney will charge everything on your card, so you do not have to walk around with your wallet all day long. You can choose whether others in your group can also use your wristbands as a method of payment and even set a limit on the amount they will be allowed to spend. It's a cool joke (and even educational!) to put a small boundary on the children's bracelet and leave them free to choose what they want to buy. For security reasons, MagicBand can only be used to pay bills and make purchases after being authorized by a password that you set at check-in and type in the machine every time you make a payment with MagicBand.

MagicBand was launched in 2014 and new services have been regularly added to the bracelet. The specialized media advances a multitude of uses that would be possible because of the RFID chip that exists within MagicBand, such as the characters calling you by name when they sign an autograph for you and take pictures, or the park staff congratulating you on the day of your birthday (without you needing to wear those pins).

Improving boarding passes

In Chapter 5, *Using UI Elements and Content for Better Communication*, we presented two examples of how the bad design of winner card can result in huge problems. During Miss Universe 2015 and the Oscars 2017, the presenters announced the wrong winners, which could have been probably avoided by a better design.

Tyler Thompson is one of those customers who are not content to make a complaint without giving a solution to the problem.

One day he was at the airport, bored while waiting for the flight time, when he decided to look for something to read. He ended up getting out his Delta Airlines boarding pass.

I looked at the card for a moment. Then I rubbed my eyes and looked a little more.

Discontented with all that lack of ticket hierarchy, Tyler took his moleskine and began scribbling some solutions to the problem. *First I need to know the flight number, then the gate, then my seat.*

A few hours later, Tyler posted on his blog his own re-reading boarding pass, with a little color to enhance the look of the brand and help identify easily to which company the flight belonged. The result?

A brand new interface for the boarding pass:

Interface is the medium capable of promoting communication between two groups or individuals in any medium.

Examples like these only remind us that it is past time to remove the *user* before experience design and stop thinking only in digital environments or the web. The experience is one, after all. From the purchase of the ticket, to the check-in, to the boarding pass, the barrier is increasingly invisible.

In a real-life example, we have the virgin boarding pass that was designed to optimize the standard size of US letter paper to the maximum, but at the same time has instructions for the user to fold the card so that it is the size of the passport—the item that normally accompanies the traveler at all stages of the trip.

You can find more examples on Tyler Thompson's website: `http://passfail.squarespace.com/`

Bus stop as part of the user journey

The experience in public transport includes much more than just the route; it is also related to the compliance with the schedules, the interval of the trips, the integration of the lines, and the comfort for the passenger. In this context, stops and stations play a very important role.

The transport system includes the sidewalks, crossings, access, and the interior of the stations, which also consider stops and embarkation and disembarkation points. These environments should provide information about the system, such as bus lines and schedules, in addition to allowing secure access and providing full user autonomy.

In parallel with accessibility standards, other initiatives can make these spaces more attractive or even give them a higher purpose.

In 2009, a similar project was carried out in the Netherlands, in the city of Eindhoven; the green space of the bus stop offers a pleasant environment for people waiting for boarding. In Kentucky, in the United States, a structure made from glass bottles also uses LED lamps powered by solar energy, which illuminates the parade at night; during the day, sunlight is filtered through the bottles, as in a stained glass. You can see this last project here: `http://brocoloco.com/urban-solutions/`.

Dubai, in the United Arab Emirates, is equipped with an air-conditioned bus stop to help passengers withstand the city's traditional heat; the structure also protects people from possible dust storms:

You can find more bus stop examples here: `http://bit.ly/CreativeBusStops`

Redesigning urinals to encourage men to wash their hands

In 1917, French painter, sculptor, and poet Marcel Duchamp inscribed the work *source* in that year's exhibition of the association of Independent Artists of New York. It was a crockery urinal signed by the pseudonym R. Mutt. At that time, he did not imagine that urinals would be a piece with different possibilities and needs of redesign.

UX methodologies can be applied, as you can see, to any user interface. The designer Kaspars Jursons (`http://jursons.com`) challenged himself to redesign public restrooms. The problem? About 1/3 of Americans do not wash their hands after leaving a public restroom, a problem more common among men than among women. Then, Jursons decided to propose a solution for this.

The solution proposed by the designer is a urinal with a sink attached to the top of it. This reduces the *distance* between the urinal and the sink, which in public toilets is usually a few steps away. Okay, those few steps do not justify the fact that they do not wash their hands, but by putting the solution in the face of the person, he realized that the rates of hygienic delinquency decreased a lot. The faucet still features sensors to activate automatically, as soon as the urinal realizes that the user has finished the service.

After all, the solution suggested by Jursons helped to save a great volume of water the design allows the same water from the tap to be used to wash the hands is also used to flush:

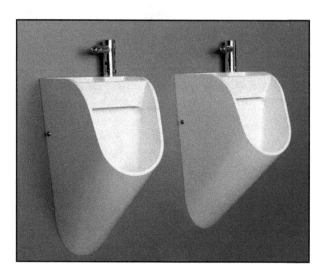

When offline meets online experiences

A study, *the Future of Luxury Retail Bricks-and-Mortar*, conducted by graduate students of the Fashion Institute of Technology class of 2015, had as a conclusion that despite e-commerce growth, physical storefronts still comprise 75% of the retail landscape. According to this research, bricks-and-mortar retail must rethink and reinvent its four key elements: assortment, service, navigation and product. Another study, *the Future of Luxury: Global Research Insights, Emerging Trends and New Business Models for 2030*, conducted by another group from the same school says that to maintain a competitive edge, brands must embrace technology integration into in-store models to meet the demands of consumers.

The cosmetic retailer Sephora, for example, makes sure that their customers have a similar pleasure experience while navigating both online and in the physical store, often coordinating their approach on one channel to drive results in another. They use shopper data to integrate the retail and mobile experience, for example, Sephora to Go is a mobile app, which was designed to emulate the knowledge of a personal shopping assistant or a Sephora sales associate.

Amazon is an example of a store that uses this online and offline integrated strategy. In 2015 the most famous online e-commerce platform opened its first bricks and mortar bookstore bringing UX concepts from their online store:

Rob Salkowitz in an article for Forbes highlighted that:

> *"It is cleanly designed and navigable but no one will be overwhelmed with the selection, and no one will mistake the shopping experience for an Apple Store or anything like it."*

The integration between physical and online goes beyond: Amazon says, *it stocks the location using data it collects from its website. The store stocks about 5,000 titles at any one time, compared with millions on its namesake website,* as mentioned Greg Bensinger in an article for WSJ *Amazon plans hundreds of bricks-and-mortar bookstores, mall CEO says.* Amazon's bricks and mortar store lets you use its app to check the prices and also showcases customers' online book reviews for some titles and curates sections featuring selections from employees, including chief executive Jeff Bezos.

It is interesting to see how Amazon is changing the game and influencing other online stores to also get into the physical world such as the fashion site Bonobos, eyewear retailer Warby Parker and online makeup subscription service Birchbox.

A few high-end fashion brands have also been improving the retail customer experience by adding technology to their store. iBeacon technology, for example, allows stores to interact with their clients by delivering geolocalized offers at the right moment once the customer enters the store's vicinity. There are lots of improvements to be made to *contextual UX* and the ibeacons in store themselves, but also the iBeacon app's design.

Staying with in-store technology, tech company OakLabs produced a touchscreen interactive mirror for fashion stores. Equipped with an RFID reader, it lets the customer know which items they have and offer the ability to request a different size or color without leaving the dressing room.

Fashion brand Ralph Lauren is already testing the new tech-driven fitting rooms at their store on Fifth Avenue. Virtuality reality is also being used to connect real and virtual. Moschino teamed up with VR platform Livit to stream its 2017 spring/summer show in 360 degrees VR. The customized Moschino headset was given to the first 50 shoppers to arrive at Moschino's New York and Los Angeles boutiques.

Moschino wasn't the first high-end fashion brand to use virtual reality though. Dior created its own virtual reality headset in 2015, with high-definition image resolution and integrated holophonic audio. It gives the customer a 3D immersion into the backstage world at a fashion show. Dior Eyes headset was designed entirely by Dior's own workshops in partnership with DigitasLBi Labs France using a 3D printer.

It doesn't matter if your project is for online/digital experiences, in a physical environment or for a integration of both. Focusing on the full user experience during the whole user journey, at all brand touchpoints, will be crucial to the business success.

In other words, besides making sure that all brand elements are present on the website or app, the experience online should be an extension of the offline experience considering:

- How are the sections of the stores organized on both experiences?
- Are the sections named in a similar way?
- Is the purchasing experience similar to both?
- Can the customer find the same products if they are using the app?
- Can they find their nearest store?

Summary

Although it is more common to think about websites and mobile apps when we talk about UX, it is important to understand that we can use the UX methodologies to identify design issues in any interface digital or physical, online, or in public environment to redesign it and improve user experience. You will find *norman doors* everywhere, so to find design solutions for those issues, keep the use at the center of your project and observe the users and how they interact with the service, machine, or environment.

In this chapter, you saw a few examples and you might find other examples in your day-to-day life.

In Chapter 8, *Improving IA for Better Navigation*, you will learn how to use Information Architecture methodologies to improve content organization.

8
Improving IA for Better Navigation

Information architecture is an extremely important part of the UX design process. The term was defined by Wurman in 1976 and is based on the organization of information within a visual space. Broadly speaking, the study of this discipline also predicts that information must be accessible and easy to find. In this chapter, you will see how to improve information architecture in order to improve navigability and findability by using UX methodologies such as card sorting, tree testing, taxonomy, and so on.

In this chapter, we will cover:

- Understanding IA as part of the UX
- Analyzing information architecture issues
- Using card sorting and tree testing to fix bad IA

IA as part of UX

According to the Information Architecture Institute, **information architecture** (**IA**) refers to the structural design of shared information environments" focused on how to organize and label content, but also on the search and navigation systems to support usability and findability.

> *"The organization, search, and navigation systems that help people to complete tasks, find what they need, and understand what they've found."*

> – *Peter Morville*
> *UX Specialist*

The information architecture that we know of today began around the 70s, long before the emergence of web and mobile applications, or the popularization of UX design. Like usability and accessibility, IA goes beyond the digital world. From the gondolas of a supermarket to a newsstand, it is crucial that the organization of items is recognizable and makes sense to most people. Good information organization reduces friction in user interaction, providing a smoother experience. So organization of information becomes even more fundamental when dealing with complex systems.

The user experience design process seeks to ensure that no aspect of user experience with the product happens without its conscious, explicit intent.
One way to tackle this complexity is to break the work of crafting the user experience into its constituent elements, facilitating the understanding of the task as a whole.

The user experience ends up being the result of a set of decisions taken in the creation of a product, system, or service: how it will appear, how it will behave, what can be done, and so on. Breaking down these decisions in layers helps you understand how these decisions are made.

Jesse James Garret in his book *Elements of User Experience* (2003) proposes five plans that make it easier to understand the decisions made in each of them. Every decision of a higher plane depends on the lower one. These plans are: strategic, scope, structure, skeleton, and surface. The first more abstract, until you reach the last, which is more concrete:

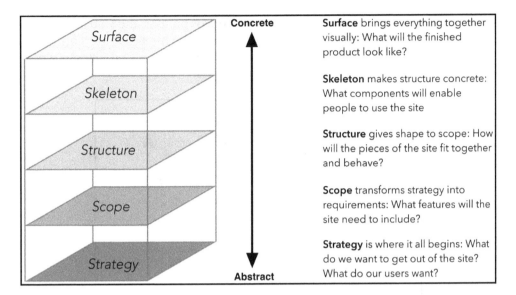

Surface brings everything together visually: What will the finished product look like?

Skeleton makes structure concrete: What components will enable people to use the site

Structure gives shape to scope: How will the pieces of the site fit together and behave?

Scope transforms strategy into requirements: What features will the site need to include?

Strategy is where it all begins: What do we want to get out of the site? What do our users want?

The user experience process, in Garrett's view, consists of layers whose overlaps range from a more abstract to a more concrete level:

- **Strategy**: Refers to what we expect for the product (website, system, application), but not just what we want, but what users want.
- **Scope**: Survey of requirements and specifications of functionalities and qualities that the product should have, and how the project will be conducted.
- **Structure**: How should content be organized? What is less and what is more important to be viewed and found by users? How can this fit into the technical, marketing, and usability capabilities and limitations of the product?
- **Skeleton**: It is the moment in which the organization of the elements that will constitute the interface, its components, is planned—including thinking about which types of components are best suited to display the information and enable functionalities for users.
- **Surface**: It is the final interface, what the consumer, client, user, will have before them, and with which they will interact.

The problem was still that of naming, because part of the community in User Experience dealt with problems such as application design with traditional solutions (transaction, security, scalability, and so on). The other part saw the web as a means of distributing and capturing information, applying solutions from the medium of publications, media, and information science (marketers).

To solve this duality, Garrett divided each plan into two contexts: the web as functionality (software interface) and the web as an information medium (hypertext system). For each context, an element stands out. So this process unfolds in some specific activities and knowledge:

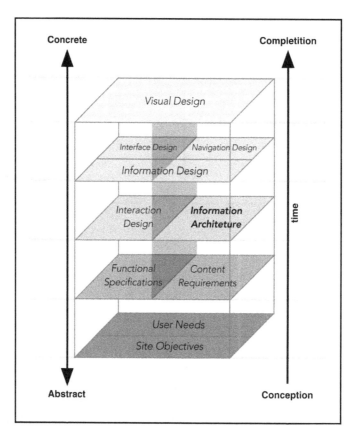

The web as a software interface (task oriented):

- **Visual Design**: Graphic treatment of interface elements (the *face* of the site)
- **Interface Design**: As in the traditional IHC, it is the design of interface elements to facilitate user interaction with functionalities
- **Information Design**: In the sense Tufteano *, is the design of the presentation of information to facilitate understanding
- **Interaction Design**: Development of application flows to facilitate the tasks of users, defining how this interacts with the functionalities of the site

- **Functional Specifications**: Set of features with detailed descriptions that the site must include to meet users' needs
- **User Needs**: Objectives of the site with external origin, identified through research with users, ethnic/techno/psychographic research, and so on
- **Site Objectives:** Business goals, creative goals, or other internal source goals for the site

The web as a hypertext system (information oriented):

- **Visual Design**: Visual text processing, graphical interface elements, and navigation components
- **Navigation Design**: Design of the elements of the interface to facilitate the movement of the user in the middle of the information architecture
- **Information Design**: In the sense Tufteano *, is the design of the presentation of information to facilitate understanding
- **Information Architecture**: Structural design of information space to facilitate intuitive access to content
- **Content Requirements**: Definition of content elements needed by the site to meet user needs
- **User Needs**: Objectives of the site with external origin, identified through research with users, ethno / techno / psychographic research, and so on
- **Site Objectives**: Business goals, creative goals, or other internal source goals for the site

It is possible to realize that UX is inevitably associated with the planning of Information architecture. With this, there are many abstract aspects that precede the visual interface. Not coincidentally, the greatest time consumption in the entire process (4/5 = 80%) corresponds to the validation of strategy, content, IA, and informational and navigational design, rather than the visual parts (UI).

In this very important phase that is IA, the user experience designer has at their fingertips a series of techniques and resources to build the information architecture of a website, application, or system, which will serve as deliverables throughout the product design.

According to Reichnauer and Komischke and Rosenfeld and Morville, the IA system can be classified into:

- **Organizational systems**: Based on this line of reasoning, people tend to organize information to take control of the world itself. And with that the way information is organized is better understood by others. It also involves the classification of words and concepts in a heterogeneous and ambiguous way.
- **Labeling systems**: The form of representation of information in computational and physical environments so that the cognitive and space needs where the information will be shown is the smallest possible. It is also how the information is grouped so that they are organized and construct navigation systems facilitating the recognition of the information.
- **Navigation systems**: As the name itself says, it is the ability to give a sense of direction in the environment in which the user is inserted. The navigation system is extremely important for the user to identify where they are and where they can go.
- **Search system**: Aims to provide tools and means for the user to find information clearly and objectively. Despite this, the navigation system does not solve all problems alone, because the environment must provide content and resources relevant to the user.
- **Taxonomy**: In turn, it is defined as the categorization of hierarchical relationships as well as equivalents that are useful not only for search systems, but also for effective navigation hierarchies.

Information access is an important aspect to the user experience. Keep in mind that people organize information differently, users have different mental models. Don't forget that cultures impact perception; even different parts of a single state (cities versus countryside) will classify differently (eastern versus western cultures as well). For example, we can say soda, pop, or coke to order the drink in different places.

According to Wurman, information can only be organized in five possible ways (LATCH):

- **Location**: Geography or proximity, particularly when combined with time, is one of the most useful ways of organizing information. The location can be concrete, such as a position on a map, a part inside a system diagram, or a step in a flow chart, or more abstract directions of space, such as a grouping of images together to convey their relationship with the others (for example, French wine, Argentine beef, and so on).

- **Alphabet**: This is one of the less used in visual communication, but it provides a way to organize large amounts of data. Although *A* fits nicely into its LATCH acronym, this dimension represents any scheme in which information is organized by an arbitrary symbol, such as a numerical index or table of contents (for example, phone book, list of websites, and so on).
- **Time**: Organizing things temporarily allows the suggestion of causality. This approach is most valuable when combined with other schemes such as location. Time is often represented by graphical schedules and calendars (for example, meeting of two hours, stays of two days, and so on).

- **Category**: When you classify an item as part of a group, this can help you to identify patterns in your data. You can consider as examples of groups, distinctions such as gender, color, or other item attributes. Once the items are categorized, they can be counted and apply statistical techniques to identify those patterns (for example, format, topics, and so on).
- **Hierarchy (or magnitude)**: The way items are related according to one or more factors will help you to find the internal structure and relationships between the data elements. For example, a hierarchy type would involve a simple item's attribute sorting, such as importance order, number, or its size. More complex hierarchies can be organizational charts, family trees, and other types of relational data (for example, price, size, and so on).

You can see for the following image how we could, for example, organize dogs under the LATCH principle. You can range the dogs by location, like by country or continent of origin, for example:

Or you could organize these dogs alphabetically, by their breed name:

Maybe by time, for example, the year in which the breed was officially recognized by the American Kennel Club:

You can even arrange them in a hierarchy by size or weight in pounds, for example:

Maybe by categories, like by color or hair size, for example:

" The dogs don't change, but the information about them does"

– Richard Saul Wurman

We can also understand information architecture as a process that helps us to build these relationships and organize the items of a system in a more logical way for the user to find more easily. We can divide the architectural process into three main stages: ontology, taxonomy, and choreography. This model, originally published as a short film by TUG co-founder Dan Klyn in 2009, stands as a framework for ensuring that information architecture is useful, relevant, and authentic:

1. **Ontology**: Ontology consists of establishing the meaning of each word that will be present in your system. For example, when we say the phrase, *her dress is blue.* Which blue is the transmitter referring to? In fact the receiver of this message can imagine a gigantic number of varied colors that fall within this specification:

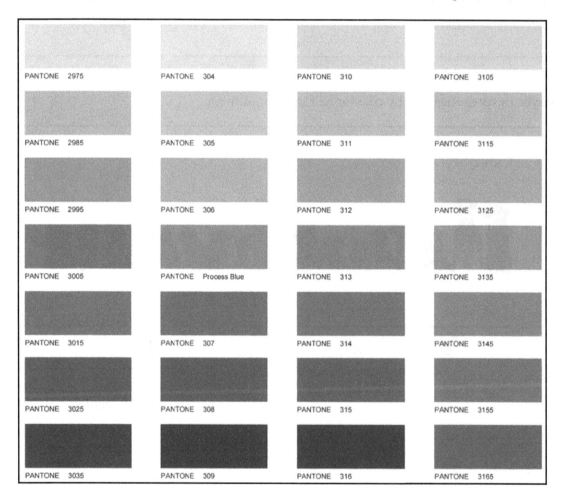

Although this type of information works perfectly for people's daily lives, it does not serve some types of activities that require specific information. Something like *her dress is turquoise blue* is something extremely specific. People who know the turquoise color immediately associate the information with color.

In the same way that pantone gives names, or codes for colors, it is necessary to classify the meaning of words of your system. When making the information architecture of a system it is good to have a system glossary that guides the designers. On the other hand, the choice of words should reflect common meanings since it does not make sense that the user needs a glossary to navigate their system.

2. **Taxonomy**: Taxonomy is the stage of grouping the contents and actions according to the meaning. In this step it is important to structure the information in the form of an organization chart, and its unfolding is a site map, a wireframe, or use flows. Taxonomy is a term of biology for the description, identification, and classification of organisms, individually or in group. For example, when we speak of mammalian animals, we are referring to a range of terrestrial and aquatic animals. In the case of information architecture it is important that every word, or action, of the system appears in an organized way so that the user can find what they are looking for. Therefore, taxonomy is structuring the information to reach an objective, grouping pieces of information by their meaning, and creating relationships between the items of the architecture.

3. **Choreography**: Choreography is the last stage of architecture. After grouping the meanings, or words, it is necessary to create one more level of relation. Each group of information that has emerged from the taxonomy must relate to each other. Choreography is the stage where we organize groups. This stage of the process consists basically of associating meanings and structure. In this way it is possible to construct flows in which the user can reach the navigation objectives through the meanings of the information and calls to action that the system presents, without being distracted by the content of the system itself.

IA and different fields

The activity of IA finds origins in librarianship and has roots in several fields and methodologies, including cognitive psychology and architecture. Here are some definitions about these methodologies:

Biblioteconomy

Librarianship is the methodology responsible for knowledge organization systems. This is a methodology that encompasses the study of how to categorize, catalog, and locate resources. It is used in traditional libraries, also in museums, science labs, and even in hospitals. When thinking of the digital world, probably one of the best examples would be search engines such as Google, which is basically a giant digital library where all information is digitally cataloged. This information must then be extracted in a logical, relevant, and organized way for the users.

Cognitive psychology

Cognitive psychology is the study of how the human mind works. Of the mental processes that occur during the consultation and processing of information. Information architecture is based on some different elements of cognitive psychology to influence how we structure information. The following are some of the key elements of cognitive psychology that information architects most value:

- **Cognitive load**: Is the amount of information a person can process at any time
- **Mental models**: Are the assumptions that people consider before interacting with a website or application
- **Decision making**: Is the cognitive process that allows us to make a choice or to select an option

Architecture

The founder of modern models of information architecture was graphic designer and architect Richard Saul Wurman.

Wurman believed that information should be structured in the same way as a building: building on a solid foundation. As in architecture, IA must be based on a precise, intentional structure and a solid foundation of ideas.

In summary, Information architecture is the discipline responsible for organizing, labeling, and designing the entire structural design. In the *polar bear* book, Louis Rosenfeld and Peter Morville describe the following basic definitions of information architecture:

- The combination of organization, labeling, and navigation schemes within an information system
- The structural design of an information space to facilitate task completion and intuitive access to content
- The science and art of structuring and ranking websites and intranets to help people find and manage information
- It is an emerging discipline and a community of practice, focused on bringing the principles of design and architecture into the digital context

Still in the *polar bear* book, Rosenfeld and Morville published a diagram containing what would be the three circles of information architecture:

- **Context**: Encompasses business goals and constraints, company culture and policy, resources and technology
- **Users**: Are the target audience for the information, including their needs, their behavior, and their experiences
- **Contents**: Can include texts, numerical data, images, videos, and documents

The seven principles of information architecture in Peter Morville's and Louis Rosenfeld's information architecture for the World Wide Web are:

- Organize (establish options for building the digital environment)
- Browse (learn from the user, either through information provided by them or by understanding their behavior in digital environments)
- Naming (identifying areas, whether through words or icons—or both)
- Search (how to index information for effective search)
- Research (path for content construction)
- Draw (elaboration of tests for validation of the nformation architecture, even before the construction of the prototype or interface)
- Map (visually structure the information architecture, for example, flowchart)

How to identify IA issues

When designing a website architecture, the information architecture principles should help users to understand where they are and where the information they are looking for is in relation to their position. Information architecture will help to create hierarchies, categorizations, taxonomies, navigation, and metadata. Whenever a menu, content, or a website's structure is organized, information architecture is being practised.

The following are some of the issues that we should consider each time we design a website:

- How are the users flowing on our website or app?
- How does the system help the user to categorize its information?
- How is this information presented back to the user?
- Does this information help the user make relevant decisions?
- Do the labels make sense to the users?

To help us to better understand, analyze, and identify IA issues, there are a few IA deliverables that we can start from:

Content tree

It is a diagram that allows structuring and hierarchizing the content of the product, be it an application, system, or website. Morville and Rosenfeld advise that the sequence of steps should be as objective as possible for the user to go from point A to point B. As you can see in the following:

▼ 🗋 0.0 Home
    🗋 0.1 Home (logged in)
▼ 🗋 1.0 Creative Invites
    ▼ 🗋 1.1 Art/Design CIs
        ▼ 🗋 1.1.1 Specific Art/Design CI
            ▼ 🗋 1.1.2 Upload Artwork
                🗋 1.1.3 Congratulations page
    ▶ 🗋 1.2 Fashion CIs
    ▶ 🗋 1.3 Film CIs
    ▶ 🗋 1.4 Music CIs
    ▶ 🗋 1.5 Photography CIs
▼ 🗋 2.0 TH Artists
    ▼ 🗋 2.1 Art/Design
        🗋 2.1.1 Artist Portfolio
    ▶ 🗋 2.2 Fashion
    ▶ 🗋 2.3 Film
    ▶ 🗋 2.4 Music
    ▶ 🗋 2.5 Photography
▼ 🗋 3.0 Blog
    ▼ 🗋 3.1 Success Stories
        ▼ 🗋 3.1.1 Featured Articles
            🗋 3.1.2 Article
    ▶ 🗋 3.2 Featured Artists
    ▶ 🗋 3.3 Meet Judges
    ▶ 🗋 3.4 Host Interview
    ▶ 🗋 3.5 Winner Announcement
    ▶ 🗋 3.6 Get Inspired
    ▶ 🗋 3.7 Tips & Advices

Site maps

Site maps are an organization chart that shows all the pages the site will contain. This document specifies the various screens and shows the hierarchical relationship between them. It is usually produced at the beginning of the project and refined during all steps according to the subsequent demands:

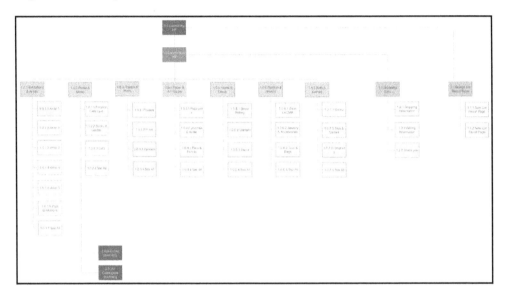

Site Map Structure

Flowchart

It is an above-average IQ site map where the flow of information is organized. This way it is easier to understand the transition of information on each screen. Flowcharts are fundamental for the realistic look of the project, because in addition to understanding the paths, it still allows us to find more objective flows for the visualization of certain sections or screens.

Navigational flows

Representations of the user navigation experience in the product, with the main points of contact of the individual with the interface and to where such points will take them along navigation.

Wireframes

These are the graphic interface layout structures. They allow us to imagine the informational organization of the content and the functionalities. Medium-fidelity prototypes are considered prototypes of the interface, ranging from low-fidelity (on paper) to high-fidelity prototypes (the interfaces are finalized in a graphic editor or directly in HTML). The most advisable way to plan the interface, because it is fast, economical, and collaborative is low-fidelity wireframes:

Visual of Wireframe

Content inventory

It is a rather authoritarian name, but deep down it's a nice one. When in the project, new or existing, information content is large and it becomes necessary to have global control of these texts that will be generated for the site.

It consists of a mapping of all the pages (predicted or existing) and the content of each one. In this way, we can see all the content holistically, which will be easy to organize the information (taxonomy, controlled vocabulary, and so on), to identify duplicate content (very common in sites with large amounts of information) and in the future to facilitate its finding:

Link ID	Link Name / Page Title	Link URL	Subject Type (not summary or keywords)	Document Type
1.0.0	About	http://mysite.cc	Nav	
1.1.0	Our offices	http://mysite.cc	Nav	
1.2.0	Client at a glance	http://mysite.cc	Marketing	paragraphs
1.2.1	Corporate backgrounder	http://mysite.cc	Marketing	list w/ description
1.2.2	Awards	http://mysite.cc	Marketing	list w/ description
1.2.3	Corporate history	http://mysite.cc	Marketing	
1.2.4	Corporate reports	http://mysite.cc	Marketing	
1.3.0	Community connection	http://mysite.cc	Nav	
1.3.1	Charutable contribuitions	http://mysite.cc	Marketing	paragraphs
1.3.2	Volunteering to make a difference	http://mysite.cc	Marketing	paragraphs
1.3.2.1	Volunteer request form	http://mysite.cc	Marketing	form
1.3.3	Giving guidelines	http://mysite.cc	Marketing	paragraphs
1.3.4	Proposal process	http://mysite.cc	Marketing	paragraphs
1.3.5	Computer product contributions	http://mysite.cc	Nav	paragraphs

Navigation schema and nomenclature

A navigation schema specifically focuses on the navigational structures and the relationships between these structures present within an interface. A very practical example of this as a deliverable would be: the global navigation (top nav), tool bar, and left rail (in various states) for a product facet search on product pages. These are important to tease out separately from other UI elements for many reasons, one of which is because they need to appear in a style/developer's guide.

You can also analyze the navigation schema in parts:

- **Global Navigation**
- **Primary Navigation**
- **Secondary Navigation**
- **Breadcrumb Navigation**
- **Footer Navigation**

As you can see here in the following image:

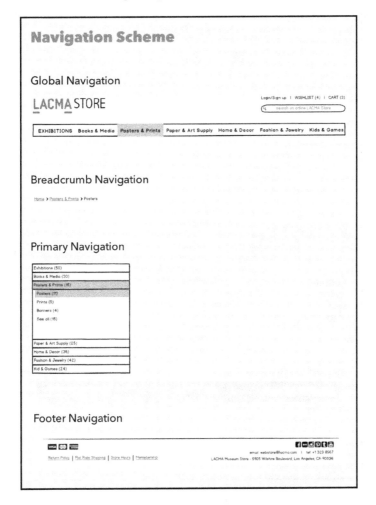

Different Navigation scheme

A good way to analyze the navigation schema is to do a competitive analysis, as you can see in the following image, the comparison of different museum online stores global navigation:

Global Navigation scheme

Besides the **Global Navigation**, you also will want to compare the **Primary Navigation**:

Primary Navigation scheme

Besides the navigation schema, you will want to closely analyze the nomenclature. A good way to do it is again through a competitive analysis of the menu items and adding them in a spreadsheet. You can also organize the menu items as descriptive and active, for example:

Task flow analysis

It is a descriptive analysis of how users perform tasks using their product. It can be a step-by-step, a table, or even a text document that contains the narrative of the main tasks performed. It is very useful when defining which tasks are most important and to assess if any of them are too complicated for the user:

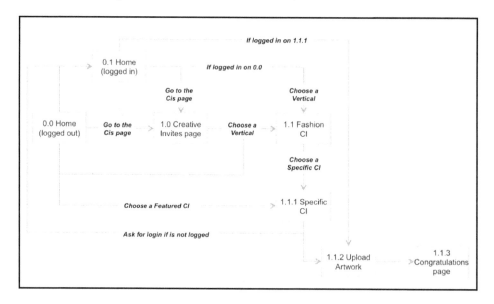

You can also do a competitive comparative task analysis, like this one comparing the checkout flow of different museums stores:

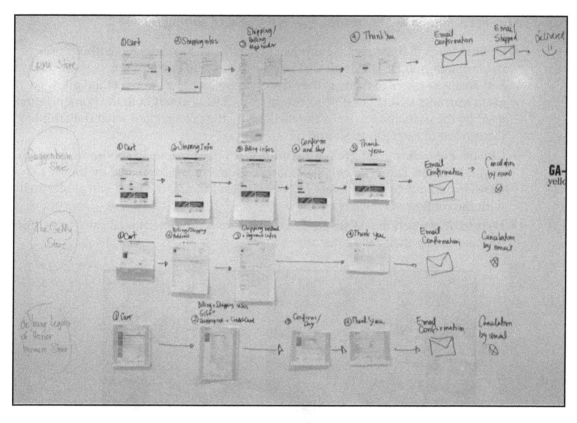

Visual representation of Comparative Competitor flow on the wall

Using card sorting and tree testing to fix bad IA

Two simple, but powerful tools will help you to fix bad IA based on the users mental models.

Card sorting

Card sorting is one of the techniques used to better define and test the taxonomy (labeling) based on the users mind map. There are a few types of card sorting:

- **Open**: Means that the participants can group the contents freely, without pre-determined groups. They will also be able to name the groups any way they want and create as many of them as they deem necessary. The open method allows more learning, as it is possible to obtain information about both the nomenclature used by the participants (since they will name the groups) and what they think the content of each group should be.

- **Closed**: Pre-determined groups are offered for participants to choose where each card is to enter. This type helps validate the nomenclature created by the project/company team, as it lets you see if users identify the label and associate it with the content to which it belongs.

- **Hybrid**: It is when the participants sort cards into pre-determined categories, but they can create their own categories as well:

And they can still be subdivided into:

- **Individual**: Each participant makes their grouping alone. Then the data of all the respondents are compiled to generate a kind of *site map* and, mainly, to show which cards correlate more often. The sorting card of the individual type is more scalable, especially if an online tool is used, which helps when compiling and analyzing the data.

- **In a group**: The participants, divided according to their profile, must arrive together in an ideal grouping. Like other group discussion techniques, this type of sorting card generates discussion, makes participants have to defend their point of view, talk about what they are doing, discuss ways to group cards, and question the meaning of content. It is obtained learning that goes beyond the suggested final structure:

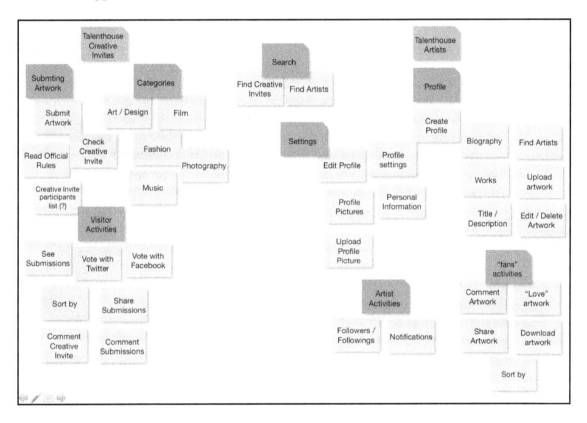

You can also do an image card sorting to understand how users would classify products, for example.

The card sorting process

The goal of working with information architecture is to propose a better way to organize the information and functionalities of the project that we are working on. It is crucial that user understanding is efficient when we organize the information and that it is consistent with the content and accomplishment of the task in the final product.

The card sorting process consists of three steps:

1. Before beginning the card sorting session, it is important to conduct an inventory of project features and content. Each of these features are made up of one card. These cards can be represented by means of physical material (for example, post-its) or by digital means. There are online tools that help in this process, such as ConceptCodify.
2. The set of cards is then presented to the users and then they must regroup the different cards according to their point of view and in a coherent way.
3. At the end of the session, the results are analyzed by the professional who conducted the card sorting (either manually or through online tools).

It is good to keep in mind the following:

- This methodology allows users to view and organize information in the way they see it. With this, the professionals have the inputs to define the best organization based on the users' standards.
- It is a simple and playful method and should be clear to the users.
- This technique is relatively inexpensive. You do not need special materials for its execution.
- Each session lasts between two and three hours and can take from two to three days depending on the amount of users and complexity of the project.
- This process is not definitive. Users will influence the perception of information organization and the professionals involved will make the best decisions for the project.

Content selection and card preparation

Organize an exploration meeting to align the client's understanding of the project's context, content, audiences, goals, and metrics. Make a content inventory in case the service is intended to evaluate the architecture of an already deployed project.

Establish a test plan that will define test variables, user profiles such as age range, level of web browsing experience, gender, and professional activities, among other characteristics—and the procedures to be followed. Also, decide whether the sessions will take place remotely or in person and still be closed or open—when the participant can propose new cards or labels for the categories. Perform a pilot test for checking and adjusting the proposed test plan.

The content of the cards can be composed of individual pages, groups of pages, or the whole navigation system of the site. Make use of easy-to-use papers of preference with heavier weight than sheets of sulfite, use short labels for the user to identify quickly, if it is necessary to put additional information on the back of the card, identify cards with numbers to facilitate analysis later.

Use an average of 30 to 100 cards, less than 30 cards makes it difficult to identify categories, more than 100 cards can make the activity time consuming and tiring for the user, it is worth providing additional cards and pens for the user to write suggestions of labeling case required. Keep in mind that the card sorting can be applied individually or in groups, studies show that applied in groups of three or more users the results become more representative. For the selection of users are valid all recommendations made to select users for usability testing.

You can use a room with tables and chairs for the participants, it does not have to have much secrecy, the technique is simple to apply and it only requires a little attention of the applicators to follow the reaction of each user who is practicing the activity, assisting in any doubts, and noting important information that sometimes comes up in group discussions. Make sure to take pictures in order to make it easier to input the results in a document.

The analysis of results basically seeks to answer the following questions:

- How *close* are two items? (that is, how often they were cited in the same category)
- How close is an item in a pre-defined category?

The results of the groupings of each participant are combined and treated statistically as needed. The goal here is to try to identify patterns of behavior in order to work out an efficient mental model for all profiles simultaneously This task is not easy and the consultation with other team members is valid for better interpretation. Data analysis of a session is part science and part magic. It can be done in two ways: by looking for general patterns or by using cluster analysis software. Cluster analyzes are statistical comparisons of the trees generated in the sessions in search of similarities of associations.

It is recommended to use software for analysis, for this we have some alternatives websort, optimalSort, or the good old excel worksheet. Using a spreadsheet we can make comparisons between each participant or group of participants by placing all the categories one below the other and the frequency with which the labels appear in each category group to obtain an average, and from there we define the best taxonomic positions for each group in the site navigation system.

In case of an open or hybrid activity, when you add the labels written by the participants into the spreadsheet, try to identify the similar ones and define the same label for all of them. For example, in an open activity, a few users can define a label as a *car* and others as *automobile*. In this case, you will want to group them and input the data in a spreadsheet. You can find a great template by Donna Spencer, author of the book *Card Sorting - Designing Usable Categories* here: `http://rosenfeldmedia.com/books/card-sorting/#resources`.

Participants frequently use similar labels, but they are not identical to name groups. It is important to define a standard label to be consistent. You should choose the most mentioned term by the users and you can create columns on your spreadsheet: *Most common terms, variants*", "standardized term". For example, a most common term can be *cars*, a variant can be *automobile*, and the standardized term would be *cars*.

If you are using an online tool to do the card sorting, such as OptimalWork, the platform will give you all the results organized, ready to be analyzed. Observe the groups that were created by the participants, how they organized the labels, the used terms and labels, highlight trends, what is similar, consistent, different, and so on. Don't let out of your analysis the participant comments and your notes during the activities.

With OptimalWorkshop (`https://www.optimalworkshop.com/`), for example, you can get a graph analyzing the online cardsorting activity:

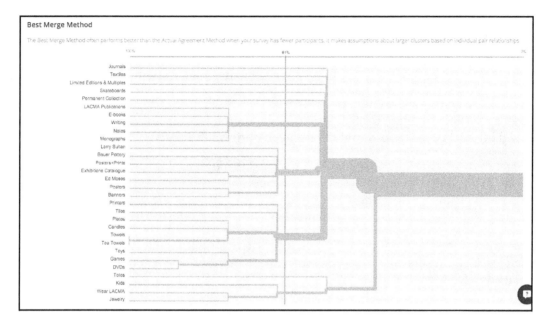

Card sorting test result visually on the optimal workshop

As an alternative, it is to use Trello to let users organize the cards online:

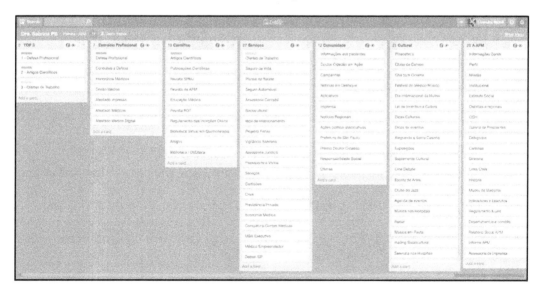

Card sorting using Trello

Tree testing

Card sorting is very important for sorting content, but when it comes to structuring this content, it may not be as efficient as users are organizing content with no reference in mind.

As in tree testing they are invited to perform actions (such as finding a specific product) through a clickable sitemap, content structure validation is much more accurate as it is analyzed in practice whether or not the user can perform the tasks.

If navigation problems are subsequently identified through usability tests, these problems are likely to be related to other factors on the page, such as poor word processing and poor usability and element distribution, but these problems are unlikely to be related to the structuring of pages, since the site structure has already been tested in tree testing.

Tree testing is a great validation technique for content structure, which allows you to validate users' performance by finding particular content or performing a certain action without any visual interference.

Tree testing allows you to:

- Visually test the navigation and findability of your site/app
- Let you identify navigation problems before building a prototype
- Let you review all attempts and problems that users had to navigate before beginning to build a prototype or test version
- Let you analyze the ease with which users complete tasks successfully

Tree testing generates quantitative data that measures the performance of the structure. The main measures of performance are:

- **The success rate**: The percentage of participants who completed the task correctly
- **Speed rate**: the average time to complete each task
- **Directness rate**: the percentage of users completing the task on the first attempt

In general, the first step in structuring content for a large website is card sorting. Card sorting will generate an initial structure, receiving the categories and labels of each content, usually resulting in a sitemap. For some projects, the structuring of navigation ends after card sorting. But so far, you have just got a sitemap.

Once the tree testing is a variant of the usability test, the only variable to test is the site structure. Thus, participants are invited to find different information as well as perform certain actions through a clickable sitemap. Asking participants to complete tasks reflects user behavior better than just using card sorting, where users are invited to sort and organize content.

There is no visual interference, just a clickable sitemap, where the user can navigate. Through the sitemap the user indicates on which page they would find the information corresponding to the question. In addition, each click on an item or subitem is computed so that the recruiter knows exactly the paths that users have traveled to get on the page they think is the correct one:

Tree testing can be done online through numerous available software, and you do not need to download any software. The best applications for online tree testing allow moderate to moderate, non-moderated face-to-face sessions, and it is recommended that each section has a maximum of 15-20 minutes, so the user is not distracted after some time using the same sitemap.

It is very important to formulate the tasks correctly, because the chances of misinterpretation are greater since the users only have a sitemap to represent some type of content. That is, it is necessary to write a scenario around a real task and reduce the risk of misunderstanding, and avoid using words that are represented in the sitemap so as not to confuse or stimulate any path to be taken.

A great tool is Treejack, by OptimalWorkshop (`https://www.optimalworkshop.com/treejack`). It generates countless reports, most of which are graphs, making interpretation of the results faster. It also generates a success graph, which shows the path taken to complete a given action, the percentage rates of users who performed the correct path the first time, how many users returned to the previous page, and more.

Summary

In this chapter, you had the chance to better understand what is IA and how to re-organize it in order to improve navigability and findability by using IA methodologies such as card sorting, tree testing, taxonomy, and so on. We saw how important it is to label and categorize the content in order to help users find what they need and accomplish their tasks with no problem, in an easy and intuitive way based on their mental models. As shown by Rosenfeld and Morville, we must consider, besides the users, the context and the content. IA tools and deliverables such as task flow, navigation schema, content inventory, navigation flow, flowchart, sitemaps, content tree, and so on.

In Chapter 9, *Prototyping and Validating UX Solutions*, you will learn how to validate UX decisions and potential solutions.

9
Prototyping and Validating UX Solutions

Once the UX issues are identified through UX research and extensive analysis, you will have defined a few potential solutions for those issues. Now it is time to test and validate them before the Dev and Design teams start working on the implementation. It is also a good moment to refine the solutions you have designed based on quality feedback.

In this chapter you will learn about:

- Testing, validating, and refining
- Choosing the right tools to create prototypes
- Running tests with prototypes
- Tools to run usability tests
- Five ways to do mobile usability testing
- Tips to run usability tests with a prototyping tool
- Using TreeTesting to validate the IA

Testing, validating, and refining

In this stage of the project, you might have already sketched, wireframed, or prototyped a few solutions for the UX issues you have identified through UX research and different analyses. It is important to validate and refine them before delivering them to the Dev and Design teams.

Remember that it can be up to 100 times more expensive to change a coded feature than a prototype, according to Web Usability, and the IEEE *Why Software Fails* report points out that about 50% of the reworking time could have been avoided if the tests had been run in the early stages of the project.

There is not a single best time to run usability tests; some propose first-step testing with paper prototypes, while others speak of high-fidelity prototypes complete with interaction, animation, and test capabilities on the device.

It is also possible, and sometimes desirable, to run several rounds of testing as you move through loyalty prototypes. Wireframe usability testing can ensure testers focus on the actual nuts and bolts of the information architecture and navigation streams, where you can then iterate through a high-fidelity prototype and test again.

As a suggestion, you can start testing a paper sketch before turning it into a low fidelity prototype, and then test it again, before turning it into a mid or hi-fi prototype, in a refinement process, until you feel confident delivering it to the dev/design teams.

Before we talk about the test itself, let's better define each type of prototype:

Conceptual prototype

A conceptual prototype is one that does not look at all like the final product version; the visual details and the interface layout are not a priority.

What should be taken into account is the interaction and navigation streams. This type of prototype can look like anything and be made using any kind of material or tool.

Conceptual prototypes are usually used at the beginning of a project in order to validate an idea or function. The most common is the paper prototype, or paper sketches.

Low-fidelity (lo-fi) prototype

This usually includes layout details and other tangible aspects. The intent of a low-fidelity prototype is to quickly and dynamically create a way to iterate and make quick changes to the most basic aspects of the product. It may be considered a higher version of a wireframe; the difference here is that it must be interactive and have basic functions that are possible to test.

Medium-fidelity (mid-fi) prototypes

Depending on how advanced the project is, low fidelity may not be appropriate, especially if the team has begun refining the visual concept of the project.

Usually, a prototype of medium fidelity is digital, with the advantage of being easily shared online.

Medium-fidelity prototypes are usually made from the middle to the end of the project, and in many cases are refined using graphical software such as Photoshop and Sketch app. It is also common to see professionals already working with HTML/CSS in this step. It is interesting to start using branding graphics such as symbols, logos, institutional colors, brand images, or image banks, and so on.

This type of prototype is great for the type of customer or employee who wants to see more details about how your product is going. Sometimes it is much easier to show something almost in the state of art than a few sketches.

It's important to note that there are certain types of customers who cannot quite understand wireframes or low-fidelity prototypes.

High-fidelity (hi-fi) prototypes

This is the stage in which the entire visual identity of the product has already been defined, and the time has come to create something as faithful as possible.

This mockup will be used not only for usability testing, but also as a guide for developers to get started with the product.

The high-fidelity prototype should be mostly similar to the final product and should be navigable and interactive, thus facilitating the work of developers and testers.

Choosing the right tool to create prototypes

The truth is that there is no best tool of all, but rather the right tool for you, the type of project, the stage of the project, and your needs.

Before choosing the best tool for you, it is important that you ask yourself a few questions. Who knows, you may discover a better option that will greatly help your work:

What is the learning curve?

How long would it take you to learn to tinker with this tool? How long would it take you to create a prototype? Avoid picking heavy tools with many functions you will not even use. If you're spending more time trying to figure out the program rather than putting together the prototype, there's something wrong.

What kind of interface are you prototyping?

Is it a website, a mobile app, a desktop application, an application for a wearable (Apple Watch, Android Wear)? Depending on the type of interface to which you are prototyping, one tool or another may best fit your needs. In addition, some prototyping programs are available for Mac only; others run in the browser.

What are the requirements for prototype fidelity?

This is a very important factor when choosing the tool that you will prototype, as there are several differences of fidelity. Do you just need wireframes that show the structure and layout, or do you need something that shows more detail and complex interactions?

Do you need to share the prototype?

Collaboration is a very important part of design, so it is crucial to consider the possibilities of collaboration offered by the tool. If needed, some tools allow you to share your prototype with your team or even work collaboratively on the material.

What are the necessary skills?

Are you an expert in the field or are you still getting started? Are programming notions necessary for this project or more the part of the visual design? Depending on your professional profile and your role in this project, whether you are prototyping and programming or are going to do the visual part, certain tools can serve you better.

Finally, what is your budget?

How much can you or your company invest in the tool?

With all these questions answered, let's take a look at some tools.

Prototyping tools

There are many different tools to create prototypes. Here you will find a few options most popular among UX professionals.

Paper

The cheapest and easiest way to create a prototype or wireframe.

I use a super-practical method to create mobile wireframes on paper: picking up my cell phone and placing it with the screen facing down on an A4 sheet. Using a pencil or pen, I make an outline about three or four times. That way, I can create a mobile screen to make sketches.

The advantage of the role is that it is more agile and much easier to stimulate creativity and collaboration. Creating something of low fidelity is interesting, gets rid of the details, and creates something more conceptual in an efficient way.

Fluid UI

Fluid UI is a prototyping online tool focused on early stage mockups and idea validation for use by UX researchers, product managers, and startups. If you have pre-existing designs you can upload them; otherwise, it's easy to work from their built-in libraries and design capabilities. Fluid UI also allows for live online user testing with built-in video calling and interactivity and real time collaboration between designers, UX researchers and product owners: `https://www.fluidui.com/`:

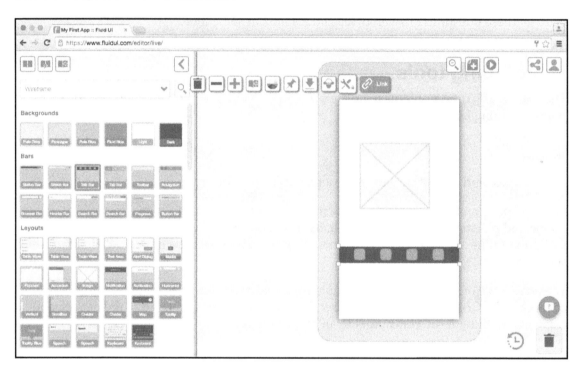

Visual representation of FluidUI

POP by Marvel

Bought by MarvelApp, POP is a really great tool to create prototypes by using paper sketches; it turns hand-drawn wireframes into interactive prototypes. Just take pictures of your sketches and upload them to POP, or upload PSD files to Adobe Creative Cloud. Then you can easily add transitions between views, gestures, and interactions. POP is synchronized with Dropbox, so you can easily share your work with others. Essentially, it's made for low-fidelity interactive prototyping, right alongside paper prototyping: `https://marvelapp.com/pop/`:

Marvel app

The Marvel app is a very simple prototyping tool, but one that can please both UX designers with advanced knowledge and beginners. It allows for the creation of prototypes of high and low fidelity, in addition to being integrated with Sketch. Similar to Invision, but with fewer functions, it makes it possible to make navigational and interactive flows. You can use Marvel app as a replacement for InVision, since it is cheaper: `https://marvelapp.com`:

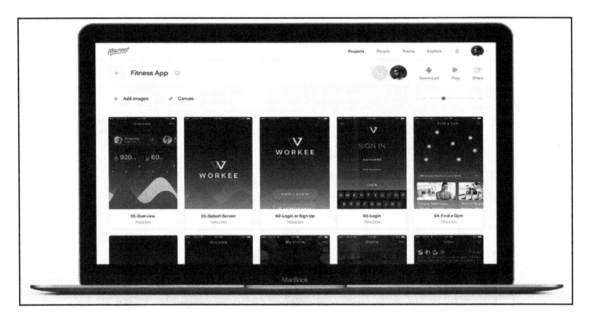

Visual representation of MarvelApp

Axure RP

Axure RP is a very complete tool, already well known in the area of design UX—perhaps the most popular and most requested software in the professional environment. You can create low-fidelity or high-fidelity prototypes with interaction and file-sharing options for collaborative work. It also has drag-and-drop functions and scrolling rules. Axure allows the designer to make clickable and interactive wireframes that customers like. However, if you are not very familiar with the system, interactions can take a little time to learn. Along with prototypes, UX designers use Axure for sitemaps and user flow throughout the UX process. This tool can be used to create the simplest, bare bones, low-fidelity wireframes as well as extreme high fidelity wireframes, depending on the needs of the designer: `https://www.axure.com/`:

Visual representation of Axure

InVision app

this is a prototyping tool that runs on the web and allows you to have collaborative and interactive prototypes in order to receive feedback from clients and colleagues. It is suitable for projects that need lower fidelity, but accepts uploads of PNG, JPG, GIF, AI, and PSD files. Using InVision for projects with many screens to design, and when you need to test/validate micro-interactions, can be a very complicated and uninteresting task: `https://www.invisionapp.com/`:

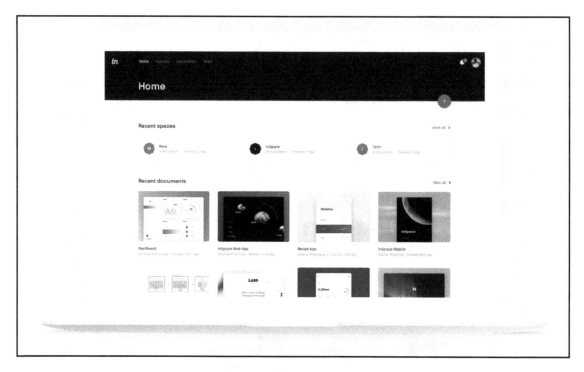

Visual representation of InvisionApp

InVision Studio

The new software intends to aggregate the most commonly used tool functions, covering the product design cycle from end to end, encompassing design functions (competing directly with Sketch), prototyping (the current InVision core business), and motion (contending against Framer). It also contains real-time collaboration tools for designers and handoff functions for designers and developers, competing with tools such as Zeplin and Figma: `https://www.invisionapp.com/studio`.

Adobe XD

This is the new software from Adobe that came to compete with Sketch app and InVision. In Adobe XD, you can create prototypes that can be made available online. It is lightweight and easy to use, but it is still in beta and has many bugs and problems. It allows for the creation of interfaces as well as prototyping. In the Design tab, you can create interfaces using text and vector tools, and in the Prototype tab you can see a preview and share the interface. It's great for creating high-fidelity prototypes: `https://www.adobe.com/pt/products/xd.html`

Zeplin

Zeplin is the most famous plugin for Sketch. It is used for collaborative work between designers and developers. It helps developers easily check UI specifications—developers do not have to keep asking designers for interface details (color, font size, spacing, and so on). The plugin exports all properties to a CSS file: `https://zeplin.io/`:

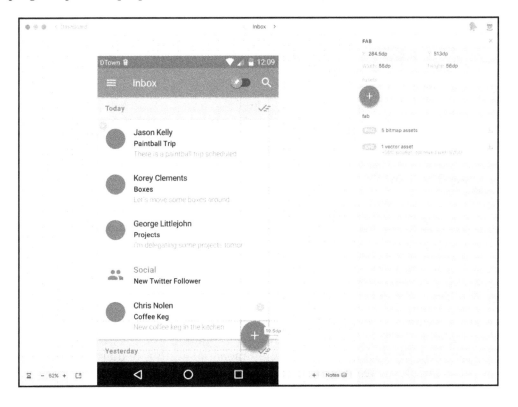

UXPin

UXPin is a tool that is also very complete and has several advanced functions, including the creation of responsive layouts. It is a highly collaborative tool that features rapid prototyping features, low or high-fidelity prototypes, code snippets, and many other very interesting functions: `https://www.uxpin.com/`:

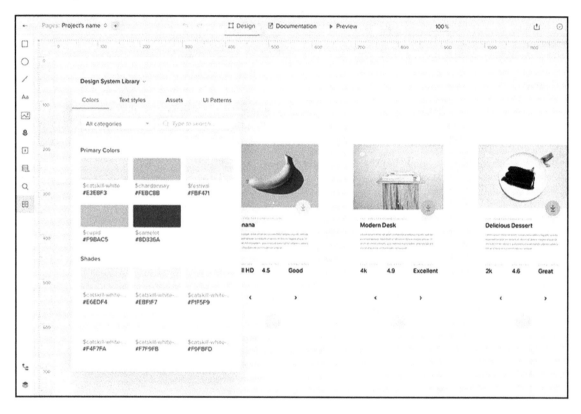

Visual representation of UXpin

Figma

Figma is an online and collaborative prototyping platform. It's like a mix of Sketch and Photoshop, only online. Figma stands out due to its collaborative resources in real time. Designers can work together remotely. Programmers can add/write their own code in a real-time project while the team is giving feedback: `https://www.figma.com`

Flinto

A great tool for high-fidelity prototypes, especially for user testing. It makes your prototype look and feel like a real app: `https://www.flinto.com/`:

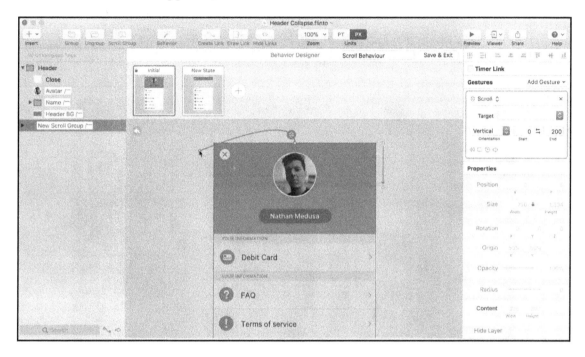

Visual representation of Flinto

Framer

Framer is one of the main tools used by Facebook; it has some nice integration with other tools, such as Sketch app and Figma. Framer allows you to create extremely detailed animations with few lines of code (it uses a simplified version of JavaScript called CoffeeScript): `https://framer.com/`

Origami Studio

This is the Facebook design tool, however it is only available for Mac OS, and is more focused on animations. You can import interfaces created in Sketch and insert animations. Plus, it has preview apps for iOS and Android: `https://origami.design/`

Principle

Another unique tool for Mac OS, which also allows you to import files created in Sketch and apply animations. It has a preview app for iOS—very interesting for creating and checking animations for mobile apps. Principle is a very easy-to-learn tool, as well as relatively lightweight software. You can import Sketch files and also have some animation functions. This tool fits well in projects that have lots of interaction or animations between one page and another, but that are without great features: `http://principleformac.com/:`

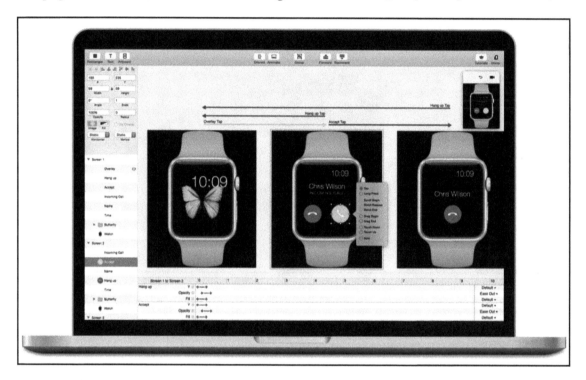

Visual representation of principle

Balsamiq

Balsamiq is a simple, easy-to-use installable tool that is mainly used to create wireframes: `https://balsamiq.com/:`

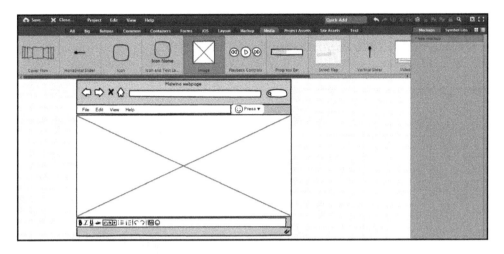

Visual representation of Balsamic

JustinMind

JustinMind is useful for developers to inspect a project. It is possible to see every detail of pixels and sizes in a very friendly way. It's an excellent desktop application, and although not as well known as Adobe XD or Sketch, it's fairly easy to use. It enables the fast creation of clickable wireframes and high-fidelity prototypes. It's very good for web and mobile apps: `https://www.justinmind.com/`:

Visual representation of JustInMind

Proto.io

Also web-based, Proto.io allows you to build your prototypes from your own library of elements: `https://proto.io/`:

Visual representation of Proto.io

Sketch app

Made exclusively for Mac OS X, it is one of the best known tools in the international market for creating interfaces, websites, and icons. It's very similar to Illustrator, but easier to use. You can see a preview of the interface on your mobile or tablet using the Sketch Mirror app. When integrating with InVision or Marvel, it is possible to create prototypes quickly. You can also print the screens and run paper tests: `https://www.sketchapp.com/`:

Running tests with prototypes

Usability testing is one of the most classic test types: you sit down with a user and learn how he really uses your website or product. You determine some tasks that he needs to perform and watch to see if he has difficulties at some point. This is the ideal type of test for making strategic decisions and to create product improvement hypotheses.

Recording the session can help you further when you are going to discuss what you have learnt with your client, or even to remember the problems that users had when proposing improvements to the interface.

- **Moderate usability testing**: This is the most traditional type of test, and can happen in person or remotely (via video). Large companies here in Silicon Valley (and also in Brazil) have immense laboratories equipped with cameras, screen-recording software, and one-way mirrors so project stakeholders can follow the test without the participant knowing and feeling pressured. The moderator guides the user through the test script, asking questions and assigning tasks that they need to accomplish using the product or interface being tested.
- **Non-moderated usability tests**: These tests can be performed online by the user through tools that automatically guide the user through the tasks. Users are encouraged to say aloud what they are thinking and why they are clicking on each item on the screen so that a person can then analyze the results.

When you are testing on prototypes, keep the relevant limitations in mind, and when looking at the data you collect, think about how any specific prototype factors may have played a role. For example, if you have included lorem ipsum text as a placeholder in your prototype, this may hinder some users' browsing abilities; a more or less messy color scheme may not have the intuitive elements that users depend on. Keeping these potential issues in mind will help you both set your usability tests and better understand the results.

Running usability tests

Enough theory; here's the practical side to running usability tests on high-fidelity prototypes. You will need:

- Sample users
- Interactive prototype with friendly test features
- A facilitator
- Observers

Sample users

Find participants who actually represent the users of your app or site. You must have your user persona chosen and ready to act. Choose users from these target groups with the help of user testing tools or your own resources. The key at this stage is the size of your test sample; you may think it is wise to do usability testing on as large a sample as possible in one go. The more users you use, the more flaws you'll get, right?

According to usability guru Jakob Nielsen, *the best results are by testing atleast 5 users and running as small as you can afford*. As we saw before, the basic premise behind Nielsen's assertion is that tests without users give you zero knowledge during the test, and only one user gives you an exponential increase. Each additional test user brings an increasing number of repeated ideas, and a decrease in the number of original ideas.

So whatever your budget for groups of users, it's best to distribute it across several smaller groups evenly spaced throughout the design process, rather than investing all of the stakes on a huge testathon.

As well as testing your top target users, it can be very helpful to bring together some novice users—people you do not expect to use your application or software—and find out if there is a market for your product beyond. These newbies can tell you more about usability than your main market could.

Finally, the way to communicate with your testers is the central axis for effective usability testing. They have to be able to figure out the tasks on their own; an objective and neutral mode should be used when giving tasks. A descriptive statement (*you want to buy an XL blouse*) will always get the test results more usefully than a normative statement (*go to the Menu tab and click 'Blouse' in the drop-down menu*). Only descriptive instructions will let you know if your users are intuitively navigating the interface or not.

Interactive prototype with friendly test features

Depending on the type of test and the product you are developing, your prototyping tool needs different testing characteristics. The minimum is a simulation of scenarios, obviously. The simulation button should allow you to work with the prototype directly in the browser, which allows you to conduct tests remotely or in person. In addition, realistic interaction, device testing capabilities, and data table simulation are also vital if you want users to really try out your end product. If you want to run formal usability tests, you will probably need a prototyping tool that is integrated with a user testing tool.

A facilitator

Someone with usability game experience. The facilitator needs to know enough about the users and their habits to establish when to go deeper into a problem during the tests and to be able to manage groups of people who may have conflicting views about their experiences.

Observers

It is appropriate for design and development teams to observe usability testing so that they can understand user reactions without mediation.

Tools to run usability tests

As for prototyping tools, there are a lot of options for tools to run usability tests. You will need to choose the best one for your project based on your budget, time frame, and whether you will do a moderated or unmoderated test, online or in person. As you saw before, most of the prototyping tools allow you to run tests. A few more options of great toolsare described next:

Lookback

Using a mobile phone or webcam, you can record the screen of the device used and, at the same time, record the face of the person. This material goes to an application dashboard, so you can then analyze how the session went. With a notebook or mobile phone, you can capture many insights over the course of developing your project. You can download the program at the page `https://lookback.io/download`; there are several options for devices. Another step is to integrate the prototypes into tools like Invision, Marvel, and Proto; they all have a way of integrating with lookback.

WhatUsersDo

The WhatUserDo (`https://www.whatusersdo.com/`) service is very simple and you will receive feedback in a short time. Determine tasks, select the audience, and voila—you will receive videos from users during the tests.

User testing

Integrated with Invision, the tool delivers the results of the test with a user within 5 minutes. You can buy credits to perform the tests, and set up tasks and activities that you plan to validate in the site or app. The process is similar to What Users Do: select the audience based on demographic and configure tasks. User testing gives you access to more than one million people, so it's easy to filter your target audience. The best of these tools is that participants will use their own devices and environments. Take a look: `https://www.usertesting.com/`

UsabilityHub

The UsabilityHub (`https://usabilityhub.com/`)tool allows you to create three test types:

- **Five seconds test**: the layout is shown to a user for five seconds and then he answers a series of questions about what he saw
- **Click test**: the layout is shown to a user next to a task, and the system records which region of the screen is clicked
- **Nav flow test**: you upload a series of images and test if people can complete certain flows of navigation

Skype/GoToMeeting

Prepare a session using Skype or any other platform that allows desktop sharing.

Start by asking your friends and family (within your target audience) if they want to be a part of the study. Ask, too, if they know anyone who could participate. After getting this list of participants, prepare the sessions according to their availability and send invitations (use Doodle to help you at that time). Do not forget to ask them to install the appropriate platform before the test day. On the day, share the prototype link and ask them to share the desktop. Go ahead, start a test session! Note that something (essential) to have in these sessions is a recording application. The QuickTime application is one that you can use to record your sessions for later review. If you cannot do this, make notes during the session.

Other tools

You can also try these other tools: Userlytics, TryMyUI (mobile friendly), Userbrain, Watchband, UserThink, Loop11, UsabilityHub, UserZoom, and others mentioned in `Chapter 4`, *Increasing Conversion with UX*. For screencapture, you can consider Camtasia, ScreenFlow, Jing, Morae, Silverback, and UX Recorder (for iOS devices). You will find more suggestions here: `http://remoteresear.ch/tools/`.

Five ways to do mobile usability testing

The script, the sample, and the analysis do not change that much when it's a test with mobile devices—you'll just test on a different screen after all. What changes is the way you watch and film what the person is doing on the small screen.

For tests of usability in the computer, there are very good tools that account for recording the screen and face of the participant and the audio of the participant, all synchronized. The most famous are Morae and its more modest cousin, Camtasia. But what about recording the mobile phone or tablet screens? Is there a Morae for mobile devices? Not yet. But there are several ways to achieve the same effect and you do not have to spend that much.

A third person with a camera

Ask someone to stand behind the participant with a camera, filming over the person's shoulder. A tripod can help a lot:

Pros:

- You can record the participant's gestures and some of the context.
- The testers can use their own mobile phone. This is important because the participant feels more comfortable with their own mobile phone and without having to learn how to use a different device. Android phones vary greatly in size, format, and even in the placement of the fixed buttons.

Cons:

- The participant may feel tense because there is someone behind him and you can not see exactly what he is doing.
- You need to ask the person to leave the phone in silent mode on the desk, or it can be difficult to adjust the focus, zoom, and positioning of the camera at all times.
- From the distance and the angle, it is difficult to see exactly what is on the screen. You will have the person's hand in front, maybe a shoulder or shaggy hair. Anyway, the video will not look so good.
- You have to be careful with reflection and the brightness of the screen.
- You cannot keep up with what the person is doing.

Application that records the mobile screen

If you have a budget available, you can use a tool like UX Recorder, which records your phone's screen and syncs with the front camera. The downside is that it is only available for iPhone and works like a *lie* browser—not for testing apps.

Make sure that the application records the location where the person touched the screen. This helps a lot in analyzing the video later:

Pros:

- It is not invasive; there is no other camera pointed at the participant
- The video is good; you can see clearly what happens on the screen
- The person can move at will with the cell phone

Cons:

- You cannot see the user's finger and the gestures that the person makes with their hand (at most, the program signals the place where the person touched, but it is not the same thing)
- You need to have test devices. It is annoying to ask the person to install an application on their mobile phone
- You cannot keep up with what the person is doing
- Some recording applications may slow down the phone

Sharing the phone screen with your computer

Very similar to the previous technique, but in this case you do not need to record directly from the cell phone. The idea is to share the screen of the mobile with the computer and record the screen of the computer (with Camtasia, for example). On the iPhone, you do not even have to install anything—just use Airplay and an application installed on your Mac or PC to allow screen sharing. On Android, there are apps for this, and some models already come with native screen sharing:

Pros

- Not much invasive (especially if you do not need to use a cable, the tester will barely notice it)
- For iPhone users, you do not need to install anything on your phone.
- The video is good
- You can keep track of what the person is doing on the phone without having to peer over their shoulder

Cons

- You cannot use that person's phone if it's an Android
- You cannot see the user's fingers and the gestures that the person makes with their hand

The idea is to be able to shoot the cell phone from above and allow the person to pick up the cell phone normally, or almost normally. If you have money, there are ready and well-articulated solutions, literally, such as Mr. Tappy. If you do not have enough of a budget, you can assemble your own appliance with the help of a friend or someone else from your team or in a place that manufactures acrylic pieces.

Support coupled to the cell phone

The important thing is to mount something light, and do not disturb the movement move; use a right angle to shoot without disturbing the person's vision. And think of a way to *stick* the cell phone there. It may be with Velcro, double-sided tape, or a fixed cell phone. There are those who use a document camera, with fixed focus, but a webcam with an adjustable focus may be enough:

Pros:

- You shoot the person's finger and the interaction on the screen.
- One can pick up the cell phone and move with it, and maybe even walk away, until the camera cable runs out.
- Because the camera is attached to the computer, you can keep track of what the person is doing.
- If you have Morae, you can use it to sync the two cameras.

Cons:

- The participant's movements are very useful, but get in the way when you want to see what's on the screen.
- It can affect a person's behavior—with extra weight, they will hold the phone in a different way.
- It's kind of hard for a person to forget they're being filmed.
- Depending on how you *stick* the cell phone there, you cannot use the participant's cell phone.
- You have to be careful with reflection and the brightness of the screen.

Stand with camera resting on the table

This is a simpler method: just have a stand (again, the acrylic stores help a lot) and support it on the desk by putting the camera face down.

If you want to invest a little, there are cameras that already come with support, such as Ipevo:

Pros:

- You shoot the user's fingers and the interaction on the screen.
- The person can pick up the cell phone and move around with it, with some mobility, as long as they do not leave the camera's range of action.
- Because the camera is attached to the computer, you can keep track of what the person is doing (and adjust the camera if necessary).
- If the media is loud, you can use the person's cell phone and also see a bit of the context—sometimes you can shoot a note or use two simultaneous phones.
- If you have morae, you can use it to sync the two cameras.

Cons:

- The person's movements are very useful, but get in the way when you want to see what's on the screen
- If you move too much, the camera may lose focus or you may stop watching the screen
- You have to be careful with reflections and the luminosity of the screen; Ipevo has an accessory to prevent the reflection of light which helps a lot

You can also consider using more than one of these different methods.

Tips to run usability testing with a prototyping tool

There are several different ways to do the usability test, but they all have some basic precepts in common:

Use realistic content

Users, both during testing and in the real world, rely on content to assist in their decision-making. Generic placeholders are not intuitive to anyone. It is not necessary to have 100% content in the project if this does not make sense for your final product. Take the time to add realistic content, images, and text to your high-fidelity prototypes before the test.

Use realistic data

As described, unrealistic data at best will be a distraction and at worst an obstacle. It does not take much effort to populate generic email addresses and this will produce more accurate results.

Designing your well thought out tests

Think about time. Anything between 5 and 10 clearly defined tasks in a 60–90 minute session is typical. You should test the core product functionality—login procedures, conversion funnels, and the like, before spreading your coverage throughout the product.

The way you talk about your tasks or questions is also crucial to getting useful results. Choose carefully between the direct tasks, the scenarios (Tingting Zhao explains the difference concisely here: `https://design.canonical.com/2013/08/usability-testing-how-do-we-design-effective-tasks/`), and the tasks, closed or open. Closed tasks have only one possible positive result, while an open task can produce some results and still be defined as successful. Susan Farrell explains how and when to take advantage of these different tasks here: `https://www.nngroup.com/articles/open-ended-questions/`

Whatever type of task you do, success criteria must be clearly defined and agreed upon for each one. Confused accounts of user experience, generally positive, are unlikely to impress interested parties or potential investors. They will want to see the metrics and success rates, black or white.

Moderate or not moderate?

Prototypes, no matter how high fidelity, will never be as comprehensive as the final application or website. Users will probably have questions about what you want to do, or how they can do it. When testing a prototype, you will probably want moderators there to address these uncertainties and make sure that you are not wasting time and money.

Learn from failures as well as successes

A user who *failed*, which have a problem to complete the task, can say much more than a user who was successful in completing the task, so write it down. Document in detail which test participants had difficulties and at what times—this will help the user interacts with the interfaces faster.

Do not interfere in the middle of the test

It is a common situation—a test participant has a problem and is struggling to complete a task. The temptation on the part of developers watching is to stop the test or intervene. But watching participants struggling with their prototype can help solve existing problems. Asking the users why they fought or what they were trying to do will produce more interesting results than holding their hands through the test.

Avoid resolving ad hoc bugs

Correcting failures without first evaluating all the evidence is never a good idea; actions based on poorly formed assumptions go against good usability testing practices. A better approach is to use the testing phase of the prototype and observe and analyze as many problems as possible without interfering; then, you will be in a stronger position to start coding.

Summary

Before delivering the final wireframes and maps to the Dev and Design teams, as good practice you should test, validate, and refine what you have designed. In this chapter, you learnt about this process and how to create and test the different levels of prototypes (conceptual, lo-fi, mid-fi, hi-fi). You also saw a few options for tools to help you to prototype and run tests (online, in person, moderated, unmoderated).

In Chapter 10, *Implementing UX Solutions*, you will see how to implement the UX solutions.

10
Implementing UX Solutions

You have spent a few weeks identifying UX issues and validating options, so now it is time to have these solutions implemented. You will need to sync the UX solutions with the design, development, and product teams. To make the communication effective, it is important to create clear and digestible documentation and being able to communicate well with the teams responsible for the UI design and develop/implement the UX fixes.

Besides good documentation with clear specification, it is a good idea to present the full project, with the research finds and solutions tested to contextualize what we need to do. The ideal way is to get these other teams involved from the beginning: you might be surprised with the ideas and solutions that the teams can come up with.

Also, as we saw in Chapter 9, *Prototyping and Validating UX Solutions*, it is important to align the solutions that you validated before to what is technologically viable and consider the technology limitations. Good communication with the other teams will also give you an idea of effort needed and the product owner will be able to evaluate the timeline and capacity in order to add the development on the roadmap if needed.

In this chapter, we will see how to create good documentation that communicates well with the other teams, especially the developers. We will cover the following topics:

- Communicating the project
- Creating documentation
- Test for QA

Communicating the project

One of the main tasks of UXers is communication. It is important to keep stakeholders informed along the whole project, also it is great to create a final document where the whole project is explained and everyone involved can be on the same page. You can create either a presentation or an A4-format document. You can use a canvas model for it.

UX canvas

In order to improve the understanding of the stakeholders about the user's needs and the project's directions, as well as the team involved in the development (designers, developers, and so on), a tool was created to leave this in a totally visual and interactive way, UX canvas, inspired by the classic business model canvas.

Developed by two Brazilian students, Maria Fernanda Parisi, and Daniel Ranzi Werle, as a final project for the Postgraduate Certificate of the Instituto Faber Ludens, it is a great tool to clearly communicate the main aspects of the UX project to different stakeholders, including the design and development teams. The following canvas helps map the various aspects that influence the user experience. The canvas might be especially good for product owners:

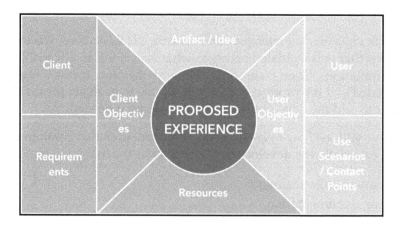

In order to help you to fill the canvas, you can answer the following questions:

- **Client**: Who are our customers?
- **Requirements**: What do they ask?
- **Client Objectives**: What they want to achieve?
- **Resources**: What do we have or need to have to do this project?

- **User**: Who is the end user?
- **User Objectives**: What they want to achieve?
- **Artifact/Idea Problem**: What is the main problem that users currently face? (I took the liberty of changing the name and purpose of this quadrant, to add more tension/movement to the dynamics).
- **Proposed Experience**: (Here we leave it open to be shown something generic or more detailed, provided that the proposal is clear to listeners).

The differential of this tool is its focus on the concept of experience of the use of the project, and it can be applied at any time of the project. It is up to the team to decide the level of detail of each block.

Lean UX Canvas

You can also use the Lean UX Canvas, created by Jeff Gothelf (`medium.com/@jboogie`):

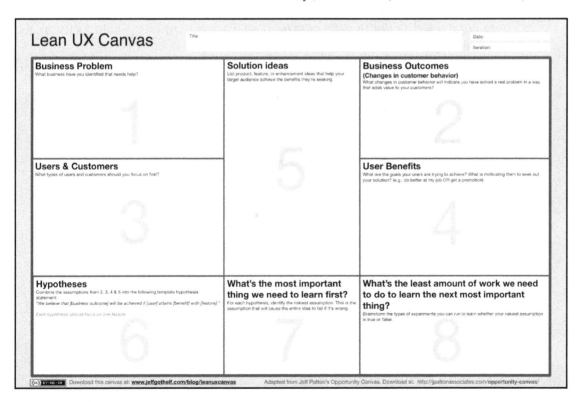

Lean UX Canvas

1. **Business Problem**: What business have you identified that needs help?

2. **Business Outcomes (changes in customer behavior)**: What changes in customer behavior will indicate that you have solved a real problem in a way that adds value to your customers?

3. **Users and Customers**: What types of users and customers should you focus on first?

4. **User Benefits**: What are the goals that your users are trying to achieve? What is motivating them to seek out your solution? (for example, do better at my job or get a promotion).

5. **Solution ideas**: List product, feature, or enhancement ideas that help your target audience achieve the benefits they're seeking.

6. **Hypotheses**: Combine the assumptions from two, three, four, and five into the following template hypothesis statement: *We believe that [business outcome] will be achieved if [user] attains [benefit] with [feature]*. Each hypothesis should focus on one feature.

7. **What's the most important thing that we need to learn first?**: For each hypothesis, identify the riskiest assumption. This is the assumption that will cause the entire idea to fail if it's wrong.

8. **What's the least amount of work we need to do to learn the next most important thing?**: Brainstorm the types of experiments you can run to learn whether your riskiest assumption is true or false.

Any of these canvases can be used in the beginning of the project to put everyone on the same page. You can update them along the project process and re-present it to the stakeholders when you have a significant iteration to the document. It is important to review it by the end of the project to remind everyone from where was the start point and link it to the results.

Creating documentation

As part of the communication job, you have to create documentation with the dev and design team that will actually implement the results. It is important to create clear documents in order to let them easily understand what has to be done. As a good practice, you may want to organize a presentation for them and let them ask questions and interact with you.

It is also important to be available for them to ask you anything while they are designing and coding the implementation. If you made sure to keep them involved along the project and managed to have a good relationship with them, probably you had a great brainstorm session in order to find together suitable solutions for the UX issues based on your research.

Make sure to keep every documentation well organized in accessible folders: you can use Google Drive, Dropbox, Sharepoint, or any other cloud drive to share them, for example.

You can also use tools such as Quip, a nice tool in research documentation and insights, which can be used to write down everything that is learned from clients and what is researched to be shared with the team.

Like Google docs, your team can work together on the same document, but what has helped us a lot are the *Mentions*. Quite easily, we mention `@membroDoTime` and the file is already shared, accessible, and with the mark of the point of attention that this member should visualize.

You can also view a timeline with your team's edits, as well as chat through chats inside and outside each document. The document is automatically versioned, and you can go back to some previous revision if necessary.

Editing lists and paragraphs is fairly easy and quick notes are very easy to create and share.

In the following sections, you will find examples of deliverables to use with the dev and design team (which you probably will also be able to use to communicate with different stakeholders if needed).

You can also consider use Trello (`https://trello.com/`) and Slack (`https://slack.com/`), really great tools and largely used by UXers and Dev teams, to communicate with stakeholders.

Annotated wireframes

You have probably already created the wireframes of the project proposing the changes and fixes for the UX issues you have found on your research and analysis. To share them with the dev and design team, you can add notes to the wireframes that will help them to better understand what you have envisioned as solutions. You can describe behavior, explain the options, show drop-down content, hover, and so on. To make it easy for you, you can think of these notes in two ways:

- **Annotations:** Are higher level descriptions of pages and content
- **Functional specifications:** Detail how everything works and are connected; makes design build-ready

In the following figure, for example, you can see notes used in a Balsamic wireframe:

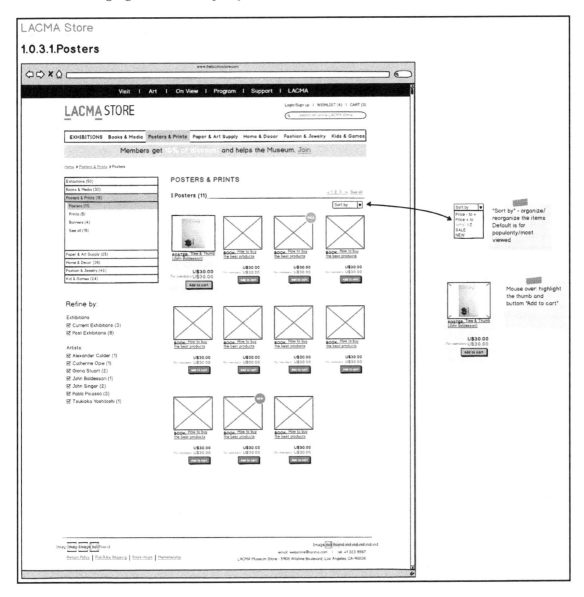

Notes(in yellow) used in a Balsamic wireframe

You can also use it to show what happens in each part of the screen when the user interacts, for example, with no need to create a screen for each of them:

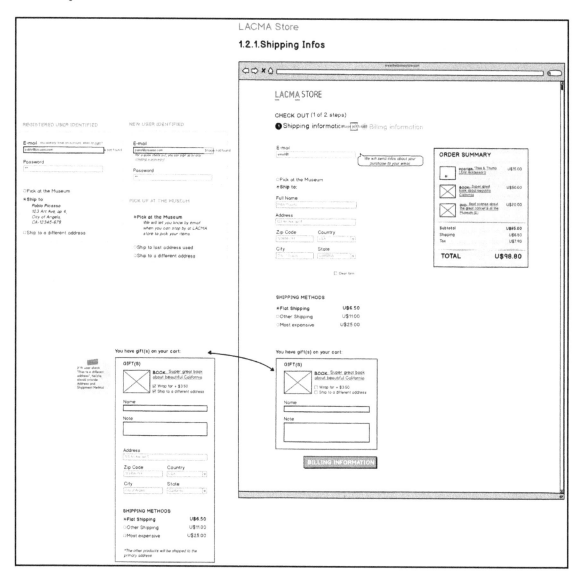

Notes (left side) used on Balsamiq

You can also explain details of colors chosen for the design:

Stages

Also, the user will be filter the list based on their stage of relationship:

 Green: the user didn't started a chat with him or her

 Orange: a chat was started but the user was not allowed by the other to see her/ his full profile

 Red: a chat was started AND the user was allowed by the other to see her/his full profile

Filter options

Besides being able to choose a list of AND/OR male/female, the user will also be able not only to filter by verified plates, but also choose the search radio.

Or you can simply add notes to each part of the screen with annotations to the dev and design teams. These are high-level page descriptions. The goal here is to describe the page in a way that highlights priorities and basic purpose and functionality:

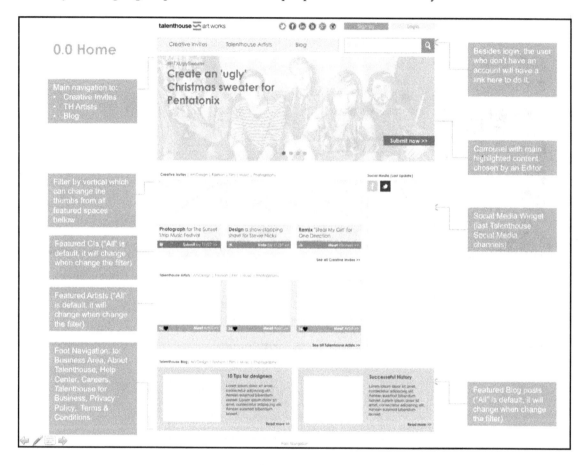

High Level page descrptions

You can also document wireframes at a modular level to clarify where everything in a module comes from. Below you see all widgets from the wireframe together:

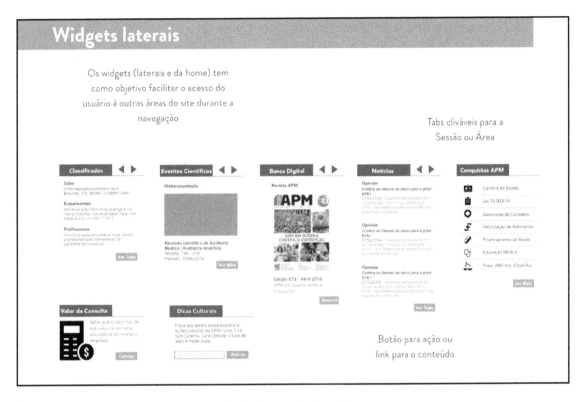

Organize elements together from wireframe

Functional specs should clearly indicate where links go (use page IDs), what actions do, and any error cases. It is important to remember the different cases for your system, each has their own design problems to solve:

- New user or first launch with no content or history
- A typical user with content and history
- An extreme user with tons of content

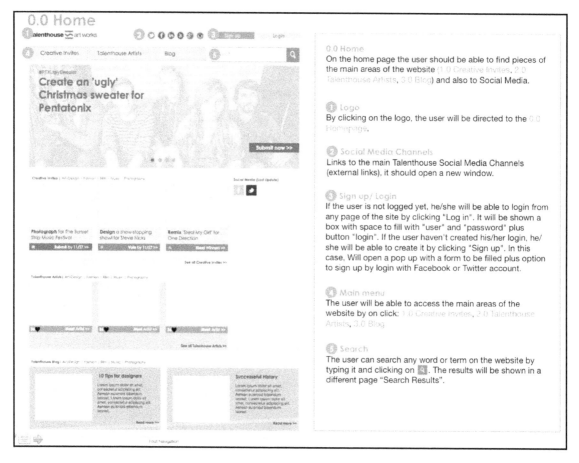

Notes for wireframe

You can also use the wireframes for technical specs, which will describe very detailed specifications.

It is rare to have to go this far, but it is useful if developers use a different language or are far away. Animations can help fill in communication gaps to make it easier to show, not tell.

Prototype

Prototypes can be great ways to communicate to the other teams what are the UX solutions. In Chapter 3, *Exploring Potential UX Solutions*, we saw how to use them for testing and iterating. Now, the idea here is to use them to demonstrate to the dev and design team flows and behavior:

Prototype Screen on Invasion

You can also record you using the prototype and make a video to which you can also add annotations if you want:

You can watch the video here: https://youtu.be/RHZltp76CaA

System state inventory

It can be pretty useful as well to add System State Inventory to your documentation. This **SSI (System state inventory)** will describe different parts of the screens:

0.0 Home

talenthouse art works

The users should have an overview of what he/she can find on our website.

Logo/claim
The current site use only the icon form the logo. The idea here is use the full logo (icon + name + claim): "Talenthouse – Art Works

Primary Navigation
This Primary Navigation should show the user an "overview" about what he is going to find on the website (Cis, Artists's Portfolios, Blog)

Editorial
Highlighted 3-5 pieces of content from the whole website chosen by an Editor.

Featured Cis
Featured Cis which can be accessed directly or also be accessed through Vertical pages.

Featured Artists/Artwork
Featured artwork from Talenthouse Artists' Portfolios

Featured Blog posts
On the Home page, the user will be able to see featured blog posts.

Login
Being logged will allow the user submit their artwork to the Cis and also create/ edit his Portfolio.

Search
The user should be able to search any content from the website/blog.

Social Media Widget
Social Media API to show the last Social Media updates.

Footer Navigation
Link to our Business Area, About Talenthouse, Help Center, Careers, Talenthouse for Business, Privacy Policy, Terms&Conditions

---

Sitemaps/app maps

A site map is a visually organized model of all the components and information contained in a digital product. It represents an organization of an application or the content of the site. Along with wireframes, they are one of the most important UX deliverables and are rarely ignored in a UX design process.

Sitemaps help define Information architecture—an art and science of organization and labeling of the components of a product—to support navigation, searchability, and ease of use; They also help define a taxonomy interface and user interface.

Sitemaps are accessible benchmarks for the feature and they adjust as the product evolves based on iterative prototyping and user tests. During the design workflow, a numbering system is often employed to keep everyone on the same page while discussing the content of the product.

Sitemaps will help the dev and design teams understand the high level of the project. Make sure to create clear and simple maps that can be easily understood. But remember that the main goal here is to clearly communicate the project with different teams that are involved. You can use, for example, different colors to show the different levels, indicate with a colorful dot which area needs login, and so on:

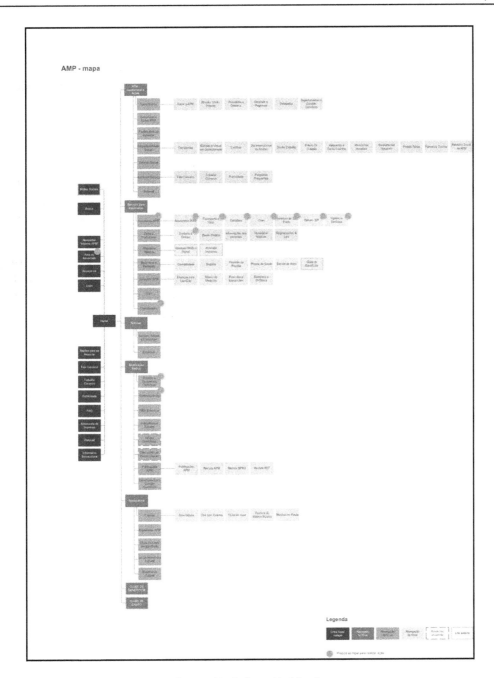

Sitemap used for visually organizing information

Flows

An experience map is a visual representation that illustrates a flow of a user within a product or service—your goals, needs, time spent, thoughts, feelings, reactions, anxieties, expectations—that is, a general experience throughout your interaction with a product. Usually, it is a linear timeline and it shows points of contact between the user and the product.

User journeys and user flows are more about a series of steps that the users take in order to interact with a product. They demonstrate behavior, functionality, and key tasks that a user can perform. By examining and understanding the *flow* of various tasks a user can perform, you can get an opinion about the type of content and functionality of a user interface and the type of user that the user needs to perform.

What is the difference between a user's journey and user flow? Think of a stream of users as the user working on a task or goal through their product or service, for example, booking a car at Uber; a user journey illustrates a larger picture. A user journey expands beyond the tasks and looks at how a specific customer interaction fits into a larger context.

User flow is the path a user follows through the product or service and it doesn't need to be linear, you can break it down into task flows that will show the path to the user to complete a specific task using your product or service. You can also deliver a wireflow, which is a specified flow in a wireframe style to represent interactions and it will show entries and exits, steps, connections, and decision points.

Documenting may require animations or flow diagrams. Flows using screenshots and page IDs often go a long way to helping developers understand how things connect and how logic works. Even a simple thing like a login screen can require a lot of documentation:

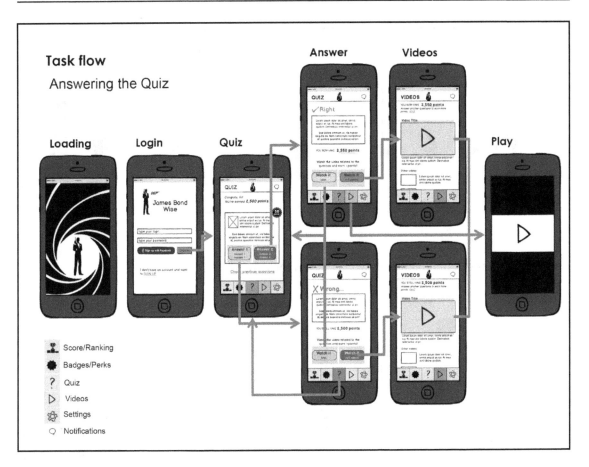

Task Flow

Storyboards

Storyboards are also a great tool to communicate with. You can either use them to show the context in which the app, for example, will be used:

Storyboard

Or to show in more details flows, clicks, behavior, and so on:

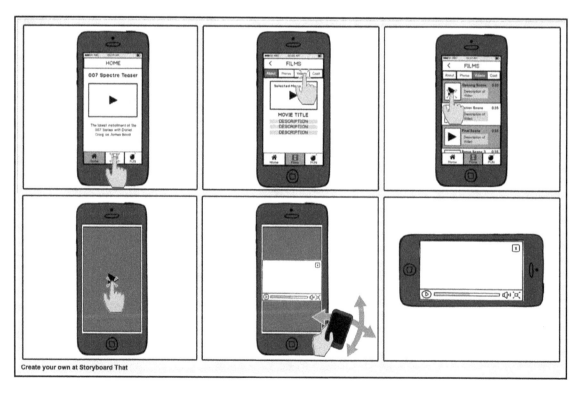

Storyboard

User stories

A breakdown of each task the user wants to accomplish while interacting with the product. It is good to remind the team of the motivations that leads the audience to use each of the features of the product, as well as the way they will go about doing it.

Usually, the tasks to be performed by the team are written in user stories format, or simply stories. These are requests for value items for the project that is being developed and it contains three pieces of important information:

- Why it is important that the system has this functionality
- What kind of user benefits more from this functionality
- Objectively, what the software does

Knowing the motivation and importance of each story, we are able to prioritize them better. The objective request of a new party makes it easier for those involved to understand what is to be produced. The type of user that will use the system makes it much easier for developers too, who will know with whom to ask questions, if they arise, and even what the focus of this functionality is.

This technique is used in the definition of the backlog. In scrum, for example, the backlog consists of a simple list, enumerated from top to bottom, of the features with the highest priority to the lowest priority. Therefore, the product backlog is a list of all desirable features in a system, with an order of priority. And this *linear* form of organization contains some problems in Jeff Patton's vision, such as the difficulty of understanding and communicating the product's *vision of the whole* to stakeholders. Already in the question of prioritization, in most cases a contemplation only from the point of view of the business and not from the utility from the point of view of the users.

Testing for QA

QA, or quality assurance, is a common practice in the final stages of the digital product building process.

At this stage, QA engineers typically test each of the features that have been implemented and verify that they are working properly and within expectations. If they encounter a bug, they usually forward it to the development team (if it is a frontend or backend implementation technical problem) or design (if it is a visual, writing, or browsing issue).

It is as if at this stage you passed a fine comb through the product, to check for problems from both a creative and technical point of view.

The problem is: QA engineers are not always trained professionals to check the quality of the user experience. Not because they are incapacitated professionals—far from it—but because this type of verification requires a broader understanding of the context in which experience takes place.

UX's work does not end in technology

It is still common, however, that UX professionals consider that their work is finished when developers begin to build the product that was designed. Perhaps by inheritance from waterfall (cascade) methodologies, where the work of one area ends when deliverables are passed to the next area (as in an industrial production line). But even when the product is already 100% implemented, the work of UX is not yet finished.

Keep in mind the meaning of UX: User experience

If the user clicks a button that does not work, this will cause a problem in the user experience.
Similarly, if the user clicks a button that does not work the way they expect it to, this will also cause a problem in the user experience.

This line is very tenuous, but one thing is clear in this story: you cannot expect a QA engineer to figure out how the user expects the button to work. After all, the QA engineer was not present in the design process, did not talk to consumers, and often fails to see the broader context of where that experience is going – let's face it, nor is that the focus of their work.

That's why the partnership between UX designers and QA engineers is so important in the final stages of the project. A UX designer can (and should) help the QA and development team always visualize the broader context where experiences are going: where the user came from, what they have in mind when they get there at that point in the flow, and what will happen next.

QA needs to take into account the context

As said before, user story is a concise description of a user need of the product (that is, a *requirement*) from that user's point of view. User story seeks to describe this need in a simple, lightweight way. Widely used as part of agile methodologies such as scrum, one of the principles behind user stories is that the product could be fully represented through the needs of its users.

The most traditional way to use user stories is in the product backlog as an input and write them on post-it notes, one per post-it. Some teams usually print cards with the skeleton of the user story in it, not to forget any of the three pieces of central information, and even with other fields such as the number of points in that task, the acceptance criteria, and so on.

Think about the user stories that QA takes into account when validating a feature:

As a user who just bought a product, I want to evaluate the quality of the product with one to five stars.

If you are a QA professional, you will probably start the test as follows: with a product page open in your browser, you will test whether by clicking on the stars the website will compute your assessment of that product, and whether it will display a message of success.

If you are a UX designer, by the very nature of the skills you have developed throughout your profession, you will think more comprehensively about how the user gets there. You will probably open the post-purchase email you receive from the virtual store inviting you to evaluate the product, click the link, drop the product page, and there at the top of the page will try to look for the button to do a review. Or you will open the homepage of the site, log in, try to find the link my *products*, and there try to find the link to do the review. Is the whole flow working (from the user experience point of view) to allow the person to leave an evaluation about the product they bought?

The test gets much wider, right?

And at that time you are much more likely to encounter problems or bugs that would not be visible if you tested the feature in isolation.

Of course, this type of testing can be done on navigable prototypes (or even paper prototypes) before implementation even begins. But it is not because the usability is good in the prototype that it will necessarily be good after the final product has been implemented.

There are several factors that occur during the implementation that will have a direct impact on the user experience: slow loading of pages, login, session, and cookie problems, URL implementation, frontend and backend integration decisions, layout in specific breakpoints for responsive design, design changes in the last minutes of the second time, and so on.

Expecting the final product to come out exactly the same as the layout you created in Photoshop or sketch is almost unforgivable innocence—unless this is the first project of your life. And blaming developers for implementation issues without doing anything during the project to improve this is a blatant irresponsibility for whoever claims to be the ruthless defender of good user experience. Never fail to test and keep this good practice as a routine. Create a sharable spreadsheet and add anything there that needs to be fixed or polished. Remember to ensure good communication and relationships with the teams.

Summary

In this chapter, you saw a few examples on how to create documentation to reach a great communication with other teams that are involved in the project and will be responsible for the implementation. To make communication effective, it is important to create clear and digestible documentation. It is important to be able to communicate well with the teams responsible for the UI design and develop/implement the UX fixes.

Besides finding time to present the UX fixes to the team, it is important to be available in case they have any questions during the implementation and also to avoid something being misinterpreted and implemented in a wrong way. It might be possible that a few changes might be needed or solutions may need adapting and the teams will have ideas to discuss. Just make sure that you are aware if everything is fine and your findings are being followed. With the solutions developed you will want to test and validate the solutions implemented.

In Chapter 11, *Measuring UX Solutions,* you will learn how to measure UX changes.

11
Measuring UX Solutions

In the last ten chapters, we've been talking about how to fix UX issues. In order to verify if all your efforts were made in the right direction, it is important to measure the impact of these changes. For this, you should define UX metrics that will show it.

In this chapter, you will understand that when measuring the impact of fixing UX issues, it is important not only to validate the success of the changes that were made, but also to show the stakeholders the importance of continuing to invest in UX.

In this chapter, we will cover:

- Measuring results of implemented solutions
- Metrics and KPIs for UX
- Reporting results to stakeholders

Measuring UX

In Chapter 1, *Understanding UX and why it is important*, we mentioned the importance of UX and the **Return of Investment** (**ROI**) of UX. In order to demonstrate it, as we mentioned before, you will need to define metrics and **KPIs** (**Key Performance Indicators**) with the stakeholders, in the beginning of the project. The measurements, or KPIs, will show the success of the UX fixes and can be derived from a variety of sources, such as user research (usability testing, surveys, structured interviews, heuristic evaluations, card sorting, heat maps, A/B tests, and so on) and/or analytics, task success rate, time on task, page views, clicks or taps, and so on.

When linked to use, or rather the user experience, KPIs should be defined in a comprehensive format, but they should be able to show the main usage problems and be able to measure whether business objectives are possible to achieve effectively.

The metrics should be chosen as soon as possible. A good time is during the process of user research, as that is when the designer learns the essentials of the client's business and transmits the possible failures that he has identified or that his users transmit to him. High-level metrics such as conversion rate or browsing time are often chosen. These types of metrics can vary for many reasons: promotions, campaigns, users who read a whole site before buying any product, and so on.

With user experience metrics, those that are easy to measure usually do not represent the UX, as is the case with the number of page views or the number of users. Some of the usual metrics in UX are: the success rate in the task, the perceived success, the time spent on a task, the use of search or navigation, the **System Usability Scale (SUS)**, the data entry, the error ratio, and the use of the back button.

All these metrics are collected during the usual usability studies, such as the *tree test* or a *think aloud* test, but there are other types of metrics that can be classified into three types: usability metrics, engagement metrics, and conversion metrics.

Keep in mind that a purely quantitative analysis can lead to blind decision-making. Forgetting emotional aspects in the development of a design and usability project can mean the failure of an advertising campaign. Quantitative data tells us *what*, *when*, and *where*. Qualitative data is about *why*.

The relationship between UX research, design, and analytics

The metrics that we extract from the monitoring of a website must serve, fundamentally, to detect the problems encountered by users and the obstacles that hinder the achievement of your objectives. Once a problem is detected, the qualitative and quantitative analysis will help us generate a creative proposal for its solution. This is, in part, user-centered design, but also data-driven design.

Applying data-driven methodologies to web design, we find the constant need to establish and measure KPIs. This forces us to have an ongoing conversation with the marketing team, account managers, and business intelligence. In conversion rate optimization projects, the iteration becomes much more relevant: finding the obstacles to conversion requires constant monitoring of the website. The qualitative and quantitative data helps us to make hypotheses of improvement and to make decisions.

Metrics tracking provides information which, when combined, helps us to get a deeper understanding of people's needs. This is essential for you to be able to establish a reactive experience that can change according to the context of your audience. This means that keeping track of how people are perceiving and using your product is critical to determine if it has been a success and plan future steps, or whether it needs change so that it is not a failure.

It's important to note that analyzing metrics is not impending or excluding knowledge: do you analyze metrics or do you think of the user experience? In fact for us, UX designers, having the maturity to work with metrics means having access to knowledge through information. This gives a clearer picture of patterns, associations, and behavioral anomalies—people with their contexts and needs.

Rochelle King, VP of user experience and design of *Spotify*, tackles this point in an incredible way in her TED Talk, *the complex relationship between data and design in UX*. In it, she explains how her team tracks metrics for UX decisions, such as how they used metrics to choose between a lighter or darker interface.

Netflix is a good example: they often test the image of programs that appear in the grid of the app in order to use the one that generates more engagement. By doing A/B tests and analyzing data, they can decide which cover works best to catch user attention.

Another point that deserves to be highlighted is the fact that in order to work with metrics effectively, it is fundamental to have established and understood the purpose of the UX project. Otherwise, the metrics will only show what you want, and this is one of the biggest dangers.

Finally, metrics do not only refer to web analytics information, but to any type of data that can be collected through the contact points of your product, such as: customer suggestions and critiques, product list best selling terms, most searched terms, most used terms in product reviews, main reasons for cancellation of purchase or a subscription, posts that generate more interactions in social networks, monitoring, and understanding of consumer moments, main navigation flow, more articles viewed on your blog, and so on.

Planning

Metrics tracking should be a topic addressed from the beginning of product design, simply because metrics are needed to understand where we are treading, where and how we are going.

So, even in the planning phase, begin by stating the purpose of the product: what are we trying to solve? What do I want to give to people? And contrary to what you may imagine, this answer does not magically appear to you. It is only determined after understanding a whole chain involving questions (many), people, and an initial load of information and alignment with business expectations. We can call this the stage of *unpacking* or *immersion*, following the Google design sprint model: `http://www.gv.com/sprint/`

After determining the points that will indicate the success or failure of your product, disseminate them so that they become part of the teams' understanding. It is necessary to know the follow-up models and establish a collection strategy.

Approaches

To get answers, we need to ask questions—there are basically two different approaches: quantitative (big data) and qualitative (small data). When we speak of quantitative analysis, we mean *what is happening?* And for qualitative *why is this happening?*

So, user experience KPIs can be measured in two different ways:

- **Quantitative**: In this approach, it is possible to evaluate how many users were actually able to complete a workflow, what navigation errors were made, and what the most urgent and least urgent corrections are that should enter the team queue involved in the project. Data is usually collected from a large sample of users and there is no user interaction, just monitoring through tools such as Google Analytics.
- **Qualitative**: This is the best way to evaluate the performance of the product. Data is collected with a small number of users because it is necessary to interact with it through a usability test or an interview. This type of data guarantees real feedback and allows you to accurately identify whether the product meets the needs of the user and is able to direct the team's next steps.

It is important to understand that one mode does not replace the other and that, for assertive analysis, it is important to cross-reference both data to make a decision that actually has a positive impact on the product.

The vast majority of metrics are marketable, and they are easier to define, but they are not experience-oriented and thus do not reveal much about user satisfaction. See this comparison:

MARKETING METRICS	UX METRICS
Conversion rate (site, campaign, social)	Task success rate
Cost per conversion (CPC)	Perceived success
Visits to purchase	Time on task
Share of search	Use of search or navigation
Net Promoter Score (NPS)	Ease of use rating or SUS
Pageviews	Data entry
Bounce rate	Error rate
Clicks	Back-button usage

According to the UX Matters website, the most commonly used metrics are measures of performance, such as:

a) **Completion rate**: The proportion of participants who were able to complete each task. This rate will show the degree of difficulty of the task and point observations to facilitate the accomplishment of the task. Although we should aim for a completion rate of 100%, according to a study by Jeff Sauro, the average task completion rate is 78%, which also highly depends on the context of the tasks that are being evaluated. To calculate effectiveness, we could use this equation:

$$Effectiveness = \frac{Number\ of\ tasks\ completed\ successfully}{Total\ number\ of\ tasks\ undertaken} \times 100\%$$

b) **Average completion time**: All completion times for the task divided by the number of participants who completed it. This metric is important because the more difficult and time-consuming it is to perform a task, the more chances the user will have to abandon the system. To measure efficiency here, you will take account of task time, which means how long the participant takes to successfully complete a task in seconds and/or minutes. To calculate the time taken to complete a task, you can simply subtract the start time from the end time:

$$Task\ Time = End\ Time - Start\ Time$$

c) **Steps to completion**: How many and what steps the participant takes to perform a task. Are there repeated steps among the participants? Here, the important thing is to detect if the participant follows the flow that the team developed, or if they succeed through another way, being able to identify new forms of use of the product. You can use the number of clicks the participant takes to complete the task.

d) **Error rate and severity**: How many times a given error has appeared and how serious it is. Has the error occurred with only one participant or several? Did the error make a bad impression, making it impossible to complete the task? Categorize the errors presented and prioritize the most severe ones. Studies by Jeff Sauro showed that the average number of errors per task is 0.7, with two out of every three users making an error. Only 10% of the performed tasks didn't have any error, which means that it is perfectly normal to have users making errors when performing tasks.

e) **Satisfaction rates**: Are you satisfied with the system, would you recommend the product?

These are objective measures that record what people actually do, but there are also subjective measures, such as ease of use, that are able to gauge how people perceive an experience after use.

It's nice to merge them because the user experience is not just about ease, but it's also about motivations, attitudes, expectations, and so on, and in order to do this analysis, a set of information is needed. That is, the goal of UX metrics should be to bring users into the post-implementation analysis to *fill in* the answers that will be missing within the marketing, and marketing metrics across:

- **Context**: Helps fill in the *how* and *why* by observing interactions and the different goals and behaviors associated with users
- **Connections**: Helps fill in, in addition to what happened and *why* happened, the gap between the insights that emerged during the development process and what was tracked after the product launch.

UX KPIs

It is essential to define KPIs for your UX project. You have to agree with a stakeholder about them and make sure they are clear to everyone involved. You can consider three important metrics to measure in any product:

Usability

Usability metrics focus on how easy it is for users to accomplish tasks on your site or application. These metrics include the time in the task, the success rate in this task, and the ease of accomplishing it. You can also include more specific metrics, such as icon recognition, menu navigation, search performance, and so on.

With a qualitative usability test, it is possible to analyze flows and interactions and the feelings involved, such as satisfaction, frustration, and hesitation.

Usability testing is the most commonly used technique for verifying how easy an interface is to use. In general, it is a qualitative methodology, where a specialist observes between 5 and 12 users performing tasks on the site or application. To obtain metrics, it is necessary to perform the usability tests with larger samples—at least 20 users.

Quantitative data can also be obtained with usability tests. For this, non-moderated remote tests are performed through online tools to obtain specific metrics. In this case, studies are usually done with 100 or more users.

Engagement

Engagement is one of the most commonly used metrics on many sites. Understanding it can make a real contribution to how much people interact with a site or app: how much attention they put into it, how much time they spend on a particular flow, how happy they feel about it, the number of page hits, or even sharing on social networks.

Time is an essential factor in engagement metrics, but it can be combined with other metrics, such as page views, scrolling for certain page ranges, or a flow of action. Engagement is not easy to understand and it produces better results when combined with qualitative perceptions.

Conversion

Conversion is the most used metric and the one that worries companies the most, because it shows if the site is performing as expected or not. The conversion can refer to the number of sales made, in the case of an e-commerce, or to other indicators, such as the number of people who registered to receive a newsletter, or the number of people who clicked on an advertisement.

The math is simple: the number of sales (or another indicator) has been divided by the number of visitors who entered the site and the conversion rate is obtained. Of course, it may be more complicated than that, but that's the general concept. If the site received 1,000 visits and 10 products were sold, the conversion rate was 10/1,000 = 1%.

Metrics in this category help identify trends and, most importantly, design new solutions so that the product is more attentive to the needs of its users. It is usually the primary metric of a business, but it represents a small number of users and its analysis must be done in conjunction with other metrics so that the *why* can be identified.

To find out why your conversion rate is low or why it has started to drop suddenly, it is advisable to perform usability tests with real users, typical of the target audience, and observe how they use the site or application—where they have doubts, where they do not know what do, and why they give up.

It's no use asking the users why they gave up the purchase. It is necessary to observe what they do. Only then will you only know exactly why your site does not convert, where the problems are occurring, and what should be done to resolve them.

The three types of metrics are important for different aspects of the user experience. The three should be balanced if we want to launch a digital product with the highest possible quality and guarantees. We should not obsess only with one type of metric, since all three are important and it is difficult for a digital product to succeed if it only is succeeding by the standards of one of the three types of metrics.

You can also consider other kinds of metrics, such as:

Performance: These are metrics related to the success of the business behind the product, such as purchases, accesses, capture, registrations, and churn. This type of information will vary according to the context of your business. Performance metrics are also determinant for validating hypotheses via the A/B test. Version A had a higher performance (according to established goals) than version B.

Behavior: This refers to the perception of how people are using your product—the way you navigate, interact, handle your product, which streams you use, and the most clicked components. Here I have quantitative and qualitative data—for example: I can have a macro view of the most used components through a screen-recording and complement this with a *tagging* by segment of my audience, which quantifies the clicks on these components, linking the clicks to conversion data at the end of the funnel. Here's another example: imagine you're experiencing a low click-through rate on the main **CTA** (**Call To Action**) of a page. I can use heatmaps to try to identify which elements may be causing a distraction and affecting my core activity.

Base: These are metrics that can be collected on any type of session, page, or part of the product. They help me in comparing data from prior periods and give me visibility if something escapes the pattern of previous behaviors (for products that do not have benchmark metrics)—for example: visits, engagement, length of stay, and bounce-rate. An important point is always to compare or analyze ranges of data per period, taking into account external actions that may have impacted access flows or the use of the product itself.

Two other interesting ways to measure your UX fixes are SUS for Usability performance and **NPS** for customer loyalty for a company's brand, products, or services:

SUS (System Usability Scale)

Usability is hard to measure—or at least quantitatively. A usability test with actual users of the product can quickly point you to tasks where people are having more difficulty in your product, but it still cannot indicate *how big* the usability problem is, on a numerical scale.

This is where numerical scales of usability come in, such as the SUS, the **SUMI** (**Software Usability Measurement Inventory**), the **SUIZ-Q** (*Standardized User Experience Percentile Rank Questionnaire*), and **QUIS** (**Questionnaire for User Interaction Satisfaction**)—among others.

But let's focus on the system usability scale: one of the best known and simplest methods of ascertaining the usability level of a system. The popularity of the method is due, among other reasons, to the fact that it presents an interesting balance between being scientifically accurate and at the same time not being extremely long for the user or the researcher.

The method was created by John Brooke in 1986, and it can be used to evaluate products, services, hardware, software, websites, applications, and any other type of interface. The criteria that the SUS helps to evaluate are:

- Effectiveness (can users complete their goals?)
- Efficiency (how much effort and resources are needed for this?)
- Satisfaction (was the experience satisfactory?)

The questionnaire consists of 10 questions, and for each one, the user can respond on a scale of **1** to **5**, where **1** means **Strongly Disagree** and 5 means **Strongly Agree**:

Strongly Disagree				Strongly Agree
1	**2**	**3**	**4**	**5**
○	○	○	○	○

Ideally, the SUS (quantitative) test should be applied at the end of a more qualitative usability test, after the user has attempted to perform a certain set of tasks using the site or app.

Here are the 10 basic statements that can be adapted to fit the context of your product:

- I think I would use this system often
- I find the system unnecessarily complex
- I found the system easy to use
- I think I would need help from a person with technical skills to use the system
- I think the various functions of the system are very well integrated
- I think the system shows a lot of inconsistency
- I imagine people will learn how to use this system quickly
- I found the system clumsy to use
- I felt confident using the system
- I need to learn several new things before I could use the system

Here's an example form:

		Strongly Disagree				Strongly Agree	Scale Position	Calcula tion	Score Contibuition
1	I think that I would like to use this mobile app frequently	☐	☐	☐	☐	☐	4	4-1	3
2	I found this mobile app unnecessarily complex	☐	☐	☐	☐	☐	2	5-2	3
3	I think this mobile app was easy to use	☐	☐	☐	☐	☐	5	5-1	4
4	I think that I would need assistance to be able to use this mobile app	☐	☐	☐	☐	☐	1	5-1	4
5	I found the various functions in this mobile app were well integrated	☐	☐	☐	☐	☐	4	4-1	3
6	I thought there was too much inconsistency in this mobile app	☐	☐	☐	☐	☐	2	5-2	3
7	I imagine that most people would learn to use this app very quickly	☐	☐	☐	☐	☐	5	5-1	4
8	I found this mobile app very cumbersome / akward to use	☐	☐	☐	☐	☐	1	5-1	4
9	I felt very confident using this mobile app	☐	☐	☐	☐	☐	4	4-1	3
10	I need to learn a lot of things before going with this app	☐	☐	☐	☐	☐	1	5-1	4
							TOTAL		**35**
							x2.5		**87.5**

Once you get the results, you need to do some accounts to get to the final score:

- For odd answers (**1**, **3**, **5**), subtract **1** from the score that the user responded to.
- For even answers (**2** and **4**), subtract the answer from **5**. That is, if the user answered **2**, count **3**. If the user answered **4**, count **1**.
- Now add all the values of the 10 questions, and multiply by 2.5.
- This is your final score, which can range from 0 to 100.

The system usability score average is 68 points. If you scored less than that, you're probably facing serious usability issues with your product.

It is not 100% scientific, and SUS is only meant to help designers and researchers understand how serious the problem is. If a site has results below 50, it's a sign that investments in design and usability need to be prioritized within your business plan—before bad usability drives your product to failure.

NPS (Net Promoter Score)

The **Net Promoter Score**, or **NPS**, is a methodology created by Fred Reichheld in the USA, with the objective of measuring the satisfaction and loyalty of consumers of any type of company. Its wide use is due to the simplicity, flexibility, and reliability of the methodology. Bad NPS ratings in most cases are related to bad UX and bugs.

The NPS, as it is commonly called, was presented in an article in the Harvard Business Review in 2003 (Harvard University Review - USA). After the article was published, the author published two issues of the book *The Definitive Question*, which today is considered indispensable material for managers of methodology.

Companies of all sizes and corporations around the world that reference product quality and service use the Net Promoter Score research model and methodology to measure how much their consumers/customers are loyal to their brand.

Fred Reichheld and Bain Fellow's team launched a research project to determine if a different approach would prove more fruitful. Working with data provided by Satmetrix, they tested a series of questions to see how responses correlate with customer behavior.

As it turned out, one question worked best for the more mature competitive industries:

On a scale of 0 to 10, how much would you recommend company X to a friend or colleague?

High scores on this issue are strongly correlated with repurchases, indications, and other actions that contribute to the growth of a company. In 11 of the 14 case studies, no other issue was so powerful in predicting behavior. In two of the remaining three cases, other issues won, but the *likely to recommend* question was so assertive that it could serve as an example for leaders.

The final question developed, of course, is the ultimate question of the title of the book launched by the researcher. Responses to it are the basis for a company's Net Promoter Score calculation.

To test the link between Net Promoter score and growth, research teams have compiled dozens of leading companies in a wide range of industries. What they found was convincing. Although the scores varied widely in each line of business, Net Promoter Score leaders, on average, grew at more than twice the rate of their competitors.

The NPS is ranked by a simple question: *On a scale of 0 to 10, how much would you indicate our company to a friend?* The formula is simple:

> *Net Promoter Score =% PROMOTING CLIENTS -% CLIENTS DETERRANTS =% NPS*

But what are the types of customers? Based on the grades 0 through 10, customers will be ranked in three ways:

- **Notes from 0 to 06—Detracting clients**: Those customers who indicate that their lives have worsened after the purchase of the product or service of the company mentioned. They criticize the company in public and would never do business with the company again, except in extreme situations.
- **Notes 07 and 08—Neutral customers**: Those customers who buy only the products and services that are really necessary. They are not loyal and they are not company enthusiasts.
- **Notes from 09 to 10—Promoter clients**: They started to have a better life after the beginning of the relationship with the company/product/service/brand. They are loyal, offer feedback, and are enthusiastic:

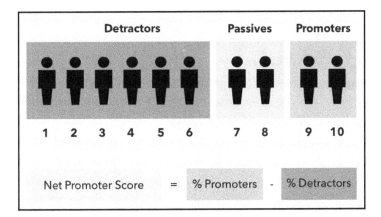

In a simple example, let's say that you received 60% of Promoters and 20% of Detractors: doing the accounts, you will get 40% NPS, and in this case 40% will not be a good NPS—although you have a larger number of promoters than detractors, you'll still be on a bad note on the Net Promoter Score. You can use online tools to measure this, such as `Delighted`, `Promoter.io`, and `Starred`.

It is very important that, in addition to the form with the notes received, you propose a field where people can submit observations of why they had the reaction they did, so you can collect feedback that can improve your product and make life even easier for your users.

Keep in mind that the use of NPS can have its drawbacks. The methodology is so streamlined that it does not help us understand why a customer is a detractor or promoter. The key question (*How likely is it that you will recommend [company name] to a friend or family member?*) encompasses all of your client's points of interaction with your company, making it difficult to understand which aspect left your client more dissatisfied.

To solve the disadvantage of the methodology, companies usually associate the NPS score with complementary questions according to the score in the key question. If you have an online store and your customer, for example, is a detractor, complete the search asking them to point out which aspects should be improved and provide a list.

Another disadvantage of measuring NPS is the difficulty of isolating the individual events that generate dissatisfaction to the customers. If you have improved your primary reason for detraction as previous research has indicated, but it has worsened other aspects of your system, your NPS index is likely to remain low. This disadvantage is also linked to the breadth of the general perception that the index captures.

Framework H.E.A.R.T.

Developed in partnership between Digital Telepathy and Google Ventures, the framework can help product owners or UX professionals define which numbers will indicate whether the product is achieving its expected success or not.

Defining UX metrics is a bit more difficult and subjective than defining business metrics (number of products sold, number of leads generated, and so on), but the framework can help.

The framework, called **H.E.A.R.T.** (**happiness, engagement, adoption, retention, task success**), is nothing more than a series of metrics that you can apply to the entire product or to a specific functionality that you plan to release.

We can call each category letter, and their meanings are:

- **Happiness**: Measures the user's attitudes and level of satisfaction, usually collected through a survey. For example, satisfaction, perceived ease of use, and net-promoter score.
- **Engagement**: Measures the level of user involvement with your product, which can be the number of times they interact with your product in a seven-day period. Typically measured via behavioral proxies such as frequency, intensity, or depth of interaction over some time period. Examples might include the number of visits per user per week or the number of photos uploaded per user per day.
- **Adoption**: Measures the number of new users arriving to the product through some functionality. For example, the number of accounts created in the last seven days or the percentage of Gmail users who use labels.
- **Retention**: Measures the frequency with which users return to the product. For example: how many of the active users from a given time period are still present in some later time period? You may be more interested in failure to retain, commonly known as *churn*.
- **Task success**: Measures the effectiveness, efficiency, and rate of errors committed when attempting a task. This category is most applicable to areas of your product that are very task-focused, such as search or upload flow.

The categories can be used in different analyses and it is not necessary to use all of them at once, as it is also possible to create others. What is important is to use the items that make sense when the product is experienced and that are appropriate for its business objectives.

Within each category it is necessary to analyze three important points:

- **Goals**: In a comprehensive way, each metric meets a goal within the product
- **Signals**: At various times during product use, the user will issue high and low signals that will help to understand the failure or success of some goals
- **Metrics**: Must be very specific and always remembered at any point in the project

Now that you know all the categories and evaluation points, let's see how HEART is represented graphically:

THE **H.E.A.R.T.** FRAMEWORK

	Goals	Signals	Metrics
Happiness	The app helps the users to get the rhythm/beats when they are performing music	- High ratings on the app store - Positive reviews - High downloading rate	- Ratings - Downloading rates - Shares / likes on social networks
Engagement	The app acts as a companion whenever users are performing/ practicing music	- Users are spending a lot of time on the app	- Click rates - Time spent on the app
Adoption	Users have developed the habit to use the app when they are playing music	- Users start to use the app more frequently - Increase in the number of new users	- Number of new users each day / week / month - Number of users each day / week / month
Retention	Users continue to use the app	- Number of returning users	- Renewal rate - Repeat purchases - Number of active users
Task Success	Users completed their performance / practice with the app	- Users used the app for more than 3 mins	- # of users who use the app for more than 3 mins - # of users who use the app for more than 5 mins

Within each blank rectangle must be described the metrics to be measured. For example, on YouTube the main goal is engagement: *we want our users to enjoy the videos they watch, and to continue to discover more videos and channels.* For YouTube search, the success metric could be: *when the user searches, we want him to quickly find the most relevant videos or channels.*

The creators of the framework advise that the UX team decide which of these metrics should be used or combined for the product in question. They also advise that, as with metrics in general, you need to repeat the surveys with each product change to understand and relate the variations of it.

Defining UX metrics

One important thing that you need to keep in mind when defining UX metrics is that if you want to define metrics that really impact the product, they should not only think about improvements in the user experience, but they should also be linked to other product objectives. So, it's nice to think of three *dimensions*:

- Descriptive metrics, to help describe what happened
- Perception metrics, to focus on how customers perceive the product
- Result metrics, to help describe what customers have done or expect to do based on their perceptions

It is also important to redeem design principles, personas, and everything the product has from user information, and that can help define UX metrics.

In other words, defining metrics is a big job; if you are measuring the right thing, you will be able to change the *world* of the product in a positive way, because it will have a solution that is much more people-oriented than the inner will of the company that develops it.

Quantifying the user experience is the first step to making measured improvements. One of the first questions with any metric is, *what's a good score?* Keep in mind that a good score depends on the metric and context.

Tools and methodologies

There are several ways and tools to accompany an experiment, which we already mentioned before. For example:

- **Metrics analysis**: Consists of collecting and analyzing metrics extracted from tools such as Google Analytics or Adobe Analytics. They are data related to hits, clicks, times of permanence, conversion funnel, and the performance of marketing campaigns.
- **Churn analysis**: Churn is a metric that measures the number of customers who are no longer part of the base of your business on a monthly basis.
- **Questionnaires**: Well known to us UX designers, is the collection of responses related to a particular context of your customer base or target audience. Questionnaires are developed according to the needs of your product. For example: do you want to identify your customers' feelings about your product or understand if they would be inclined to a new product type?

- **Heatmaps**: This is a tool well tied to digital products and it maps the areas with the highest index of an interaction of the mouse, such as clicks and scroll.
- **Screen-recording:** Following the same heatmap principle, mapping user interactions to your digital product; the difference is that it records sessions and shows how people navigate through it.
- **Service ticket analysis:** If your company has a relationship service or customer service, it certainly has a record of the services rendered. It pays to select some of these records for analysis.
- **Customer Interviews**: If your company knows your customers well and has a good relationship with them, it makes it easier for you to conduct interviews to understand how they perceive your product and in what context they enjoy it. It is an opportunity for you to start collecting real information about the people behind your audience.
- **Stakeholder Interviews**: If you do not have the money or access to your audience (two very common barriers), you can always talk to people in your own organization, gather some assumptions, and get their views. Stakeholders who deal directly with customers are a rich source of insights.
- **Ethnographic research**: This is the study of human behavior from an anthropological perspective, coming from human sciences. Approaching within our context of UX, unlike the customer interview, in which you bring people together and ask a series of questions, you go to them and observe how they perform their activities in the context of their culture.
- **Analysis of interactions in social channels**: If your product has social channels, it's worth taking a look at media reports and taking advantage of diving a bit more into the profile of people who relate to your product through these channels. It is possible to identify patterns in language, subjects of interest, and even recurring or salient points of attention.

Each of them allows you to have visibility through different perspectives, but they all provide information that relates to and helps in understanding how people are perceiving and using your project.

Google Analytics

In `Chapter 4`, *Increasing Conversion with UX*, we learned about quantitative and data analysis, and you should definitely consider those tools to help you to analyze the UX metrics. In the following sections, you will find nine quantitative-specific metrics that we can extract from Google Analytics to facilitate the decision making of the UX/UI team. It does not have to be KPIs directly, but signals (signals) as identified in the HEART framework of Google.

Conversion rate (CR)

Conversion rate is one of the best known and most important metrics. However, it is a dangerous piece of information because it is the first one that the sales team will look to, but it is not always the main indicator of the operation of a website (either e-commerce or a lead generation landing page). This can be explained in several ways (as this article in Smart Insights does: `http://www.smartinsights.com/goal-setting-evaluation/goals-kpis/` `why-conversion-rate-is-a-horrible-metric-to-focus-on/`), but we should consider the fact that not all conversions have the same value and a high conversion rate may not mean high performance of a website, for example.

That said, the conversion rate is the metric that, in general, will help us determine the performance of a website: of all our users, what percentage become customers?

A conversion is the unique achievement of an objective that will generally be something such as sale, registration, or contact. So, the conversion rate is the conversion rate by users of our site:

$$Conversion\ rate = Conversions\ /\ visits$$

It is very important that we define what is a conversion on our site. In this way, our conversion rate can be translated, for example, into the following objectives:

- Registered users
- Unique sales
- Leads: contacts made

In Google Analytics, we will have to define and configure the objectives that we will measure as conversions. It is not a default metric, since each website has its own objectives. Google explains it well here: `https://support.google.com/analytics/answer/1012040?hl`.

Bounce rate/Bounce rate

The bounce rate measures the ratio of users who left the website having visited only the page we are tracking. In other words, the bounce rate of our contact page measures the percentage of users who arrived directly here and, without having visited any other section of our site, they left.

It is used to measure the level of engagement of a landing page (landing page). For websites with only one page (not even a *thank you* page), the bounce rate will always be 100% and, in that case, we will not be able to use this metric in our decision making.

Exit rate/Exit rate

This metric measures the percentage of users who left the website from the page we are tracking—the ratio of sessions in which the last page was the one we are measuring.

It's easy; the exit page of a site and a session is the last one that was seen in that session. It can help us determine which pages are causing the abandonment of our users. It could be a page where the navigation is confusing or where the content does not correspond to what the title promises, or simply is not of quality.

Average session time/Session duration

This is the average time of the session. That is, the average time users spend on our website.

For a site where the content is massive and dynamic, this metric is fundamental. For an e-commerce, the average session time can help to understand the decision process of a purchase by the users, the ease of use and understanding of our site. Very high session times with very low conversion rates may indicate that the purchase process is a hindrance to usability. If, in addition, we check very high departure rates on our cart page, we can start thinking about reviewing the experience of using our checkout process.

Page views per session/Page per session

Little to explain, right? It is closely related to the average session time, but it still speaks to us more about the level of user interaction. In blogs and content sites, the average number of pages/sessions can speak directly of the success of the website: how many more pages per session—more attraction—is caused in the readers/consumers/users. If it is high, it is more likely they will become recurring users.

In online stores, the number of pages per session can help us to know how quickly and easily users find the product they are looking for. It can also help us explain the average ticket for our sales, as well as elaborate cross-selling strategies.

Sessions/Sessions

This is not the most important metric for the design and usability team. However, knowing the statistical sample from which we try to draw conclusions may be relevant to understanding the statistical significance of the data. Knowing the behavior pattern of a user on a website with little traffic is much more complicated. We can use the Page Analytics extension for Google Chrome, for example.

New visitors versus recurring

The experience of using as a new visitor should not be the same as that of a recurring visitor. Right now it is the workhorse of many websites: the customization of the offer. For the returning user, we already know many more things than the new user: we know what they expect from us and what they like. This useful metric of Google Analytics will help us to measure, in addition, the level of loyalty that we are achieving with the design, the usability and the experience of using our website.

Clicks/Click Through Rate (CTR)

The CTR is fundamental, especially in the design of online graphic advertising. The Clicks ratio measures the percentage of users who click on an ad or banner with respect to the total number of users who view it:

$$Clicks\ ratio\ (CTR) = clicks\ /\ impressions$$

Average ticket/Average order value

There is no turning of the page: the higher the average ticket, the better. The **average order value (AOV)** is the average value of our unique sales, the average value of the carts processed.

What direct relationship can there be between a UX decision and the average ticket? The company must determine an average ticket according to its volume of traffic to guarantee the viability of the business. And in this case, it is not about increasing the conversion rate, but rather that the conversions return more value; the users should be buying more products and the most expensive ones. This metric is used to track the performance of promotions and other value changes, such as offering a bundle of a product or service. The experience of use and design of the site should favor the user that is willing to add more products to the cart or add those of greater value.

Crossing qualitative with quantitative

The numbers are just data; you are the one who will carefully investigate and interpret what they mean—but there are no easy conclusions. Any single piece of data, be it either qualitative or quantitative, will clarify or nourish you with enough information to make decisions. You can follow the formula K.Y.U., which is basically:

> Collect quantitative data (the facts) + qualitative data (the reason for the facts)
> =
> K.Y.U.: Know your user.

This is about knowing the user better, revealing certain behaviors that help identify the need for new functionalities for the product, or identifying patterns that contribute to the evolution of your products. A case that exemplifies this study well is Netflix, which identified, through the metrics, in which episode a series became addictive. Series such as *Breaking Bad* and *The Walking Dead* leave their spectators addicted from the second episode, while others from only the eighth episode forward. From this, Netflix sought the formula to produce its own series that are not to be missed.

Crossing information and understanding what they represent in your ecosystem is extremely important for turning hypotheses into claims and still identifying opportunities. Do not believe in isolated data; try to confront information by crossing the methods and see if they make sense. Search for comparison between periods and establish sample ranges.

And, finally, involve the right professionals. You, as a UX specialist, need to have people who understand metric analysis and **BI (Business Intelligence)** so that your insights and assumptions do not contaminate the data, so you can get the most transparent and pure input possible for smart decision making. Also, get this kind of information to reach other teams and other levels of your organization. Develop reports, collect analysis, and prepare follow-up dashboards.

Preparing reports for the stakeholders

Metrics can be used in favor of the project because they are a language understood by everyone, from more technical to business. Once metrics are identified across all industries, design initiatives will gain respect and investment more easily.

In addition, data is also allied to align the internal team members. The results of an investigation allow the company to develop and internalize a shared vision of its users. This shared vision provides the impetus to establish a common, user-centered philosophy across the organization.

But remember, not everything is a design problem. The user is only one of the variables of the digital product, which can also be impacted by technology, business purpose, operations, and marketing.

The importance of metrics is obvious as a valuable UX tool. However, numbers alone will not give you answers—there is no absolute truth in the data. They are a designer's best friend, but we must know how to use them not to make rash decisions. With them, we can learn about our users by investigating each hypothesis raised.

It is crucial to share all this knowledge with all the stakeholders. The best way to do it is to prepare reports.

Creating reports

Writing the report may seem like crashing headlong into a brick wall. Where to start? How to format? What to include? We'd like to offer some suggestions on how to improve the way you write reports by focusing on format flexibility (customizing your report to your audience) and the ease and speed of reading (do not force your audience to work for the information you're trying to convey).

Begin by thinking of the executive summary as a brief report that can be read in isolation. Make it engaging by beginning with good quotes and including positive discoveries. Talk about what you learned, not your methodology. For broader reports, turn your survey questions into headings for discussion sections, so that readers can see your results in the form of clear answers to their needs. Keep everything terse and clean by removing extraneous data, tables, and descriptive paragraphs. Instead, use graphics and screen captures with captions. This chapter describes these and other techniques to make your reports easier to read and, as a result, have a greater impact.

Executives have become numb to copious amounts of data. What actually provides meaning and drives change is the ability to share a story. Using metrics supports a story and provides credibility. Thoughtful visualizations maximize the impact of the data. So, at the early stages of any measurement efforts, it's also wise to consider how this information will be visually represented. It's a key part of how the story will be told.

In Chapter 3, *Exploring Potential UX Solutions*, you will find more ideas for creating visual ways to demonstrate UX reports.

For a usability test report, you can use this structure:

- Audience tested (for example, women, 30-45, single, and so on), tasks performed, and questions asked
- Graphs with key task conversion metrics, task execution time, closed-ended question results (for example, how many have recommended the product), and success metrics (for example, success if the participant took less than five minutes to complete the test)
- Video clips or screenshots of the main problems encountered
- More relevant comments and suggestions from participants, especially those that are repeated
- Different paths traced by users
- Positive and negative points of the system observed by the participants
- Possible solutions and recommendations

Alternatively, you can start with a rainbow sheet by simply cataloging the observations you have made and quantifying the number of participants who went through each observation. Each column represents one participant.

Summary

In this chapter, we had a chance to go deeper into UX metrics, KPIs, and ROI. By understanding what you are measuring in order to validate the changes you made to fix UX issues, you can demonstrate to the stakeholders the value of investing in UX. Besides deciding which metrics and KPIs really matter for your project, we also saw different methodologies for qualitative and quantitative approaches.

All these methodologies and analyses should end in a clear and well-structured report that will help the stakeholder understand the results of the projects and the need for making decisions or taking different directions. At this point, you might need to decide if the product, service, website, or app needs more improvement and ideation.

It is important to keep in mind that fixing UX issues is not a closed project with a single end. Think of this process as a continuing one, where you must keep checking, evaluating, changing, measuring, and so on. Remember that user behavior can change, and so can their needs. Keep listening to them and have them as the center of your project to keep meeting their expectations.

Keeping Up to Date

Working with UX requires you to keep yourselves constantly updated, find and try new tools, discuss with other professionals, and so on. In this appendix, you will find a few links to great references, sources, and discussion groups to help you in this mission.

Usability.gov

Usability.gov is the leading resource for **user experience** (**UX**) best practices and guidelines, serving practitioners and students in the government and private sectors. The site provides overviews of the user-centered design process (`https://www.usability.gov/how-to-and-tools/resources/ucd-map.html`) and various UX disciplines (`https://www.usability.gov/what-and-why/user-experience.html`). It also covers the related information on methodology and tools (`https://www.usability.gov/how-to-and-tools/index.html`) for making digital content more usable and useful at: `https://www.usability.gov/`.

Nielsen Norman Group

Since 1998, Nielsen Norman Group has been a leading voice in the user experience field (`https://www.nngroup.com/articles/definition-user-experience/`), conducting groundbreaking research, evaluating interfaces of all shapes and sizes, and guiding critical design decisions to improve the bottom line. Learn more at `https://www.nngroup.com/`.

UX Magazine

UX Magazine is a free community resource that explores all facets of experience design. They work closely with practitioners and industry leaders versed in all areas of UX to provide a steady stream of engaging and useful content. See more at `http://uxmag.com/`.

UXBooth

The UX Booth is a publication by, and for, the user experience community. Our readership consists mostly of beginning-to-intermediate user experience and interaction designers, but anyone interested in making the Web a better place to be is welcome. If you're interested, join us and discuss best practices and trending topics, or share your experiences at `http://www.uxbooth.com/`.

UXMatters

Founded by Pabini Gabriel-Petit in 2005, *UXmatters* provides insights and inspiration to experienced professionals working in every aspect of user experience and also those who are just beginning their journey in the field. Find more at `https://www.uxmatters.com/`

Smashing Magazine

Founded in September 2006 in Germany, Smashing Magazine delivers reliable, useful, but most importantly practical articles to web designers and developers. They don't care about trends; they care about things that work or fail in actual projects. They are, and always have been, independent—11 years, and still ongoing. Read more at `https://www.smashingmagazine.com/`

UX Blog

The UX Blog was founded by Nicholas Tenhue in 2015 as a resource for user experience design, user research, and UX strategy. The blog collaborates with UX Practitioners and thought leaders from a broad array of disciplines to give their audience insightful and actionable advice that has practical application in the work place. Check it out: `https://theuxblog.com/`

UXaday

Created by @sovesove , the idea of this site is to create a directory of useful and innovative user experience stuff from around the world. It's all about knowledge sharing, a daily inspiration, and directory of useful resources and tools for user experience designers. You will find great stuff here: http://www.uxaday.com/

Designmodo

Founded in 2010 by Andrian Valeanu, Designmodo delivers (https://designmodo.com/) useful information about the web design and development industry. In 2011, Designmodo began to create and sell premium UI kits that evolved into creating advanced website builders made exclusively for web developers, making Designmodo a pioneer in UI kits and static website builders. Find more at https://designmodo.com/.

UX Collective

UX Design Collective curates some of content and gives it back to the community in a more structured and digestible way. The polar bear is a reference to *Information Architecture for the World Wide Web,* one of the most famous books on UX. You can also write for them, take a look: https://uxdesign.cc/.

UXMyths

UX Myths collects the most frequent user experience misconceptions and explains why they don't hold true. You don't have to take our word for it, UX Myths will show you a lot of research findings and articles by design and usability gurus at http://uxmyths.com/.

UX Checklists

A few specialist have put together a checklist for UX projects, which you definitely should bookmark; they can be found at the following site:

```
https://github.com/uxchecklist
```

```
http://fabricio.work/checklist/
```

```
http://uxrecipe.github.io/
```

UX Forums

You can make and answer questions from the community. The following are a few *question and answer* platforms used by user experience researchers and UX experts:

```
https://ux.stackexchange.com/
```

```
https://www.reddit.com/r/userexperience/
```

```
https://community.uxmastery.com/
```

```
https://www.webdesignerforum.co.uk/
```

```
https://www.designernews.co/
```

```
https://theuxlist.com/
```

Designer Hangout

Designer Hangout is a dedicated, invite-only network of UX designers and researchers who discuss trends, give advice, share stories, uncover insights, surface opportunities, and connect in-person. As a UX practitioner, Designer Hangout is your *secret weapon* to progressing your career and accomplishing your life goals. Together, we will create the World's most reliable brain trust for UX designers in a fast-paced age. Join the group at `https://www.designerhangout.co/`

UX Design Community

UX Design Community is a platform for designers and researchers to share inspirations, resources, and knowledge to help each other to grow; it can be found at `http://uxdesigncommunity.com/`.

UXPA

Founded in 1991, the original 50-member group has grown to serve a community that includes nearly 2,400 members worldwide by promoting UX concepts and techniques through their annual international conference, publishing new UX findings through both the **Journal of Usability Studies (JUS)** and User Experience Magazine around the world; it can be found at `https://uxpa.org/`.

Other Books You May Enjoy

If you enjoyed this book, you may be interested in these other books by Packt:

User Experience Mapping
Peter W. Szabo

ISBN: 978-1-78712-350-2

- Create and understand all common user experience map types.
- Use lab or remote user research to create maps and understand users better.
- Design behavioral change and represent it visually.
- Create 4D user experience maps, the "ultimate UX deliverable".
- Capture many levels of interaction in a holistic view.
- Use experience mapping in an agile team, and learn how maps help in communicating within the team and with stakeholders.
- Become more user focused and help your organisation become user-centric.

UX for the Web

Marli Ritter, Cara Winterbottom

ISBN: 978-1-78712-847-7

- Discover the fundamentals of UX and the User-Centered Design (UCD) Process.
- Learn how UX can enhance your brand and increase user retention
- Learn how to create the golden thread between your product and the user
- Use reliable UX methodologies to research and analyze data to create an effective UX strategy
- Bring your UX strategy to life with wireframes and prototypes
- Set measurable metrics and conduct user tests to improve digital products
- Incorporate the Web Content Accessibility Guidelines (WCAG) to create accessible digital products

Leave a review - let other readers know what you think

Please share your thoughts on this book with others by leaving a review on the site that you bought it from. If you purchased the book from Amazon, please leave us an honest review on this book's Amazon page. This is vital so that other potential readers can see and use your unbiased opinion to make purchasing decisions, we can understand what our customers think about our products, and our authors can see your feedback on the title that they have worked with Packt to create. It will only take a few minutes of your time, but is valuable to other potential customers, our authors, and Packt. Thank you!

Index